MW01067530

"Entering the Monastery renders the moment-by-moment, undisguised experience of Zen practice in America with unsurpassable immediacy, sincerity, the warmth of full human presence, and down to the ground detail.

It should become a classic."

-- Jane Hirshfield, Poet

Entering *the* Monastery

Renshin Bunce

*A Memoir of
12 years in and around
San Francisco Zen Center*

Second edition, lightly revised February 2017
Copyright 2014 by the Author. Self-published on www.createspace.com
ISBN # 9781496188977

This book is dedicated
to the memory of my teacher, Myogen Steve Stücky

Forward

When I began meditating, being a monk was far from my mind. I just wanted relief from the endless monkey mind that kept me veering back and forth between anxiety and depression. By the time I began meditating, I'd been through hundreds of hours of therapy, had put down booze and drugs and done a lot of 12 step work, and been active in a Christian church. I was divorced and beginning to support myself moderately well by selling real estate. But something was missing.

Although I'd gone to San Francisco Zen Center to hear the Saturday morning talk off and on through the years, hoping to hear some words that would put my mind at ease, meditation didn't seem to be in my skill set. Any time I tried to sit still without any distractions, the monkey mind just got worse.

But meditation was the last shot I had left to shoot. So at 45, I went to the Vipassana teachers in the Bay Area, and they taught me how to sit still. Meditating alone at home was nearly impossible, but when I meditated with a group I had no choice but to stay on my cushion, so I found a weekly sitting group. And that was where I began to hear the Buddha's teachings, and those felt like the words I'd been looking for.

Finally I found my teacher. His name was Steve Stücky, and he was a Zen priest. Of all of the flavors of Buddhism I'd experienced, Zen was my last choice. It seemed too rigid, too formal, too foreign. But because it's what had produced Steve, I gradually began to meditate in the Zen style, and finally decided to sew a rakusu – the sacred garment that represents the Buddha's robe – and take my vows with him.

During this time, I'd also begun to explore this thing called the internet. Eventually, I signed up for The Well. Based out of Sausalito, The Well was one of the earliest experiments in social media. This was before there was a point and click interface, and I had to take classes to learn how to navigate my way around its system. In 1993 I went to a party and learned the commands, rushed home and logged on, and I've been on The Well ever since. So that was where I began to document my Zen life, first talking about sewing my rakusu in 1995, then undertaking my first non-residential practice period at City Center in 1999, and eventually moving to Tassajara, the Zen monastery in the Ventana Wilderness, in the fall of 2000. I took a laptop to Tassajara with me, wrote when I could, and put my writing on floppy discs that I mailed out to a friend, Elaine Sweeney, who put them online for me.

This book is a record of those online postings. I've edited out others' responses and, though I've been temped to edit out some of my own words, 99% of what I wrote is still here. My beloved teacher died six months ago, and it's the grief I feel over his loss that gives me the energy and the courage to move these most intimate thoughts from the enclosure of The Well and out into the wider world.

The question those of us living monastically most often hear is "What's it like?" I offer this book as an answer to that question.

The photographs are mine.
Cover design by the talented and patient people at Ingalls Design.

Gratitude

I'd like to thank the people on The Well who encouraged me to keep writing. I'd particularly like to thank Rev. Kathy Whilden and Elaine Sweeney, two dharma pals who are also on The Well, and whose support made it possible for me to live at Tassajara.

Thanks is not a strong enough word for Zenkei Blanche Hartman, former Abbess of San Francisco Zen Center, who gave me the gift of ordination and showed me how to be a sewing teacher. Nine bows to you, Blanche, and then nine again.

Thanks to Shunryu Suzuki Roshi who came from Japan to bring Zen to America, and did it in such a way that his teachings continue to sing through time; and to the institution he created, San Francisco Zen Center, still going strong and offering the dharma to anyone who walks through the door at City Center in San Francisco, Green Gulch Farm in Muir Beach, and Tassajara Zen Mountain Center in the Ventana Wilderness. Long may it wave.

And of course the whole thing wouldn't be possible without my late teacher, Myogen Steve Stücky. Words are not adequate to express my gratitude to him for his teaching and his unconditional love. His memory is a blessing.

Blanche's Hands

Topic 187:
Sewing My Rakusu

Sunday, February 18, 1996

I don't know why going to Green Gulch still intimidates me. I have driven that curvy one lane road down into the Zen Center farm more times than I can count. And still it can happen, as it did today, that I drive it with an anxious feeling. All I've ever been able to figure is that I'm afraid that the people at the other end of that road will declare me "not spiritual enough" and send me packing. They haven't yet.

Today I began sewing my rakusu. This is the bib-like garment which Zen students wear to indicate that they are "Disciples of the Buddha." It's about 18" x 24", dark navy blue cotton, with lots of little panels. It's all sewn by hand. It's sewn by the student, presented to the teacher, and then given back to the student by the teacher in the jukai (lay ordination) ceremony. The student takes her vows in the ceremony: taking the three refuges (in Buddha, Dharma, and Sangha) and taking the precepts (not to kill, steal, lie, etc.).

I began meditating eight years ago. I came to Buddhism with my usual zeal and began sitting long retreats with Vipassana teachers right from the start. Last summer I sat a one-month retreat with a Tibetan teacher. But Zen has always scared me. It's so austere. It's so focused on form. There's so much ritual. There's so much room for error! In Vipassana, the students walk into the meditation hall wearing any old thing, plop down in their place, close their eyes, and have at it. In Zen, the students wear black, everyone bows like mad, and ideally everyone sits in the same posture and moves in the same way. So why I am taking my vows in the Zen tradition?

It's mostly because of my teacher, Myogen Steve Stücky. He's a Zen guy, always has been a Zen guy, probably always will be a Zen guy. Through him, I've come to understand that these ancient rituals are designed to help me, not just to confuse and test me. I've been sitting with Steve for two years, and in the last year have been active in creating a Zen Center with him: we've written articles and bylaws which have been filed with the State of California, and we've made a meditation hall (zendo) out of a carport in his back yard. I'm President of the Board. When we had our first 3 ½ day retreat (sesshin) last January, it was clear to me that it was time for me to make an outward sign of the inner commitment I've made to this practice. When I asked Steve whether I could sew my rakusu and take my vows, he agreed.

I called Green Gulch and was told to just drop in on a Sunday afternoon to begin sewing my rakusu with Meiya, the longtime resident who's the sewing teacher there. When I got there, about a month ago, Meiya asked me to come back later. I tried to go over last Sunday and just couldn't. Couldn't! Got as far as Mill Valley and turned around and drove back home! And then, at home, I saw in the current Green Gulch announcements that today, Saturday, there would be a full day of sewing with Meiya for anyone who was sewing a rakusu or priest's robes. So this morning I began.

I rolled into Green Gulch at about 10 a.m. The sewing session started at 9, but the announcement said that we were welcome to participate in all or part of it, and so I let myself move slowly this morning. There were about seven people sewing in silence in the library when I entered. The library has a wall of glass windows, which look out on the deck toward a meeting room. The roof above the meeting room is tiled, and grass seed has caught hold among the tiles. The bright green grass was beautiful against the wet gray day.

Measuring and making the rough cuts (taking a piece of fabric from a bolt and cutting it into seven main pieces) with Meiya reminded me of other sewing I've done. When I was young I loved clothes and had little money, so I learned how to make my own. And then I learned how to sew fast. I could whip up a little dress, from raw fabric to finished product, in one caffeine- and nicotine- ridden afternoon.

Now, at Green Gulch with Meiya, in a room where the only noise was the sound of our shears slicing through the fabric, I had to pull back from "knowing." I forced myself to pause, breathe, and approach this piece of fabric. In this sewing practice, as in my zazen (meditation) practice, there was a right way, and the right way wasn't necessarily my way. So I cut slowly and carefully.

Meiya got two of us started marking our material. The rakusu is made of a fine pima cotton, very soft to the hand. She showed us how to sharpen our silver pencils and how to make accurate measures on our cloth with metal rulers and plastic right angles. Necessary conversation took place in soft voices. I told my first lie within about half an hour of arriving. Meiya asked me whether I'd been practicing my stitch. "I feel ready to start sewing" I answered. I hadn't practiced at all, but how could I tell her that?! I hate practicing! I like doing!

Another woman sitting near me was sewing on a new brown okesa (the large toga-like garment worn by priests) for Norman Fischer, the co-Abbot of Zen Center. This robe was an ongoing group project. A thin quiet young man, about 30 years old, was sewing his own black okesa for his ordination. The black robe is for regular priests, and the brown robe is worn by priests after they've received Dharma Transmission. Three of us were just beginning our rakusus. There was another woman sewing, but she was on the other side of the room and I don't know what she was working on.

Sandy and I were drawing our lines at the same time, on a board set over a coffee table. The bright shop lights that had been brought in for the day helped a great deal. I couldn't help noticing that I was getting done much more quickly than she, while her lines were more precise than mine. I tried to keep my eyes on my own project and remember to breathe. When I was finished drawing lines, Meiya showed me where to cut the panel into ten pieces that would then be stitched back together in a way that's intended to be reminiscent of a rice paddy.

I began to stitch. I began to rip out stitches. Meiya explained that consistency was of primary importance, and that the size and spacing of my stitches (within very narrow parameters) would be a kind of signature on my work. I ripped out more stitches. We are to recite, "I take refuge in the Buddha" with each stitch. Sometimes I remembered. Sometimes I was lost in thought. Sometimes I was singing a song in my mind. Someone plugged in the iron and it blew the fuse, and I was able to sit back and watch a bird hop around on the roof across the way while it was being fixed.

Physical comfort was an issue. There are two couches in the library, and the one couch seat that had good light was already taken. I ended up next to that seat, directly under the bright shop light, on a meditation bench. I put my left foot under the bench, and put my right foot flat on the ground so that I could use my right knee as a little table for my sewing. This worked quite well, and I sat in this position for about three hours.

My partner, the woman who was marking her fabric at the same time as I, went back to practicing her stitch. I began whipping through my work. I noticed that when I fantasized around the idea of this journal, my stitches became erratic and had to be ripped out. I was glad when Meiya said that it was time for lunch.

I sat next to Meiya in the dining room. I asked her how many rakusus she thought she had helped with. Meiya is thin and pale. The most prominent feature on her face is her nose. She wears large glasses. Her head is shaved. She appears to be wonderfully at ease in her body. Meiya rolled her eyes and made a puffing noise. Oh so many rakusus. Certainly more than 50, she guessed. But less than 100. Oh, probably closer to 100. I noticed my need to quantify, and also noticed that Meiya, the sewing goddess who walks among us, appeared to have already given this question some thought. Thank you, Meiya.

Sandy remained silent across the table from me. Don, the fellow who's sewing his priest's robes, spotted a friend and moved over to catch up on gossip with her. He's a student of Maizumi Roshi and apparently lives in Colorado. The dining room was full and noisy, and I saw many familiar faces from the time I've spent at Green Gulch and Tassajara. I wondered whether I could live here with these people.

Meiya gave us an hour and a half for lunch, so I decided to walk to my car and get my camera since the light was so lovely. I walked up with Sandy and learned that she lives in Sacramento and will be driving (nearly 2 hours each way) to and from Green Gulch on Saturday (for rakusu sewing), Sunday (for Sunday morning zazen and lecture) and Monday (for a class with Reb) this week. She lived at Green Gulch ten years ago. She works as a secretary. I got my camera, made sure my new car was okay, and took a lovely walk through the gardens. There was a wonderful cold wind blowing, just enough to be refreshing, and I felt relaxed and quiet and cheerful.

After lunch, I moved on to the next phase in my sewing. I had stitched together two pieces (ranging in size from 4"x 5" to 3"x 3.5") five times. Now Meiya opened these pieces up, turned the cut edge under on one of them, and showed me how to stitch that edge down. The stitches are teeny, not even as large as a grain of rice, and are about 3 centimeters apart. It was only when I commented on how large and clumsy these stitches seemed, that we noticed that I hadn't listened closely and was doing the work wrong.

During a lull, I asked whether there would be a break for tea. What a great response I got: we all trooped downstairs and had tea and brownies. I felt a surge of power. We had the dining room to ourselves, and Meiya answered our questions. It was mentioned that many Japanese priests these days get their okesas (the large toga-like garment) from the okesa store rather than sewing them themselves—Meiya's not a real emotional gal, but I could tell that she took a dim view of this! There was a story about someone who had been sewing a rakusu for one of the abbots out of a print fabric with pictures of a cow jumping over the moon. Meiya clearly disapproved. She talked about how we have to learn the traditions before we can break them. The phrase "you have to learn the scales before you can play jazz" came to mind.

In the afternoon, a woman joined us who I'd met and liked during my first try at sewing. She'd finished her rakusu and had her jukai ceremony. Now she was learning an advanced technique. Meiya became relatively loquacious. Sewing is a practice in Zen, just as much as zazen or cooking or gardening are practices, and Meiya is deeply into it. She went to Europe and worked with other Zen sewing people in France and Italy. She worked with one of the great Japanese teachers there, and showed us the books that he'd written and had given her copies of. She showed us photos of okesas made by masters. She showed us the page in his book where there's a picture of a rice paddy on one page and a picture of a rakusu on the page facing it. She was quite transported. It was lovely to see.

We sewed again in silence for a short time, and then Meiya noticed that it was 4:00 and time to clean up. We bowed to the altar and then to each other when we were through.

All of this repeating "I take refuge in the Buddha" with each plunge of the needle brought up my old resentment toward Shakyamuni Buddha. I went back to Steve to talk to him about this for the second time

This started on the Tibetan Buddhist retreat I did last summer. Tibetan Buddhism uses "Guru worship"—meaning the altar and walls were covered with pictures of guys who we were supposed to venerate and bow to. Also, all three of the teachers on the retreat were guys. I've had many wonderful women teachers in Vipassana and Zen, and so I wasn't so sure about this. One night I raised my hand during the question period and asked the retreat leader, "Where are the women in this tradition?" I don't remember what he said, but I do remember the book that another retreatant slipped me later that evening. It was called *Early Buddhist Women,* and I was shocked at what I read.

The Buddha's mother died when he was a baby, and he was raised by his aunt. When he reached enlightenment and began teaching, people rushed to him. His aunt was among them: she brought a gang of her lady friends, and asked Shakyamuni to help them awaken. He refused and sent her away. She went to his favorite student, Ananda, and asked him to plead their case. Because it was Ananda, the Buddha agreed, and then allowed women to receive the teachings. This made me so mad! My anger is partly around basic feminism, but it's also involved with my disappointment. I'd thought that the Buddha was perfect, that in fact achieving perfection was what enlightenment looked like. This didn't sound at all perfect to me.

My usual (non-Tibetan) practice doesn't involve worship, so I was okay on that score; but it does involve trying to do what he did. The Buddha said, "I point the way. Try doing what I did, and see for yourself." Now I wasn't so sure that I was interested in what he was pointing to, if it meant being so blind as to indulge in sexism. This remained quite troubling to me for the rest of the retreat.

When I got back home, I took my problem to Steve. It turned out that my feelings were so hurt by the Buddha's actions that I cried when I told him about them. Steve told me that the Buddha was subject to the cultural conditioning of his time, and that that's why he acted that way. Steve told me that even after his enlightenment, the Buddha was still working on his "stuff". This was amazing to me. It also felt like bad news.

As I continued to talk with Steve about it, I saw that I'd hoped that if I sat long enough and well enough, I'd become perfect and not ever again have to deal with "stuff." All of my teachers without exception have talked about Buddhist practice not having any goals—and every time I've heard this a little voice in my head has said "yeah sure." I had a big goal: enlightenment and the end of all pain forever! And now I was seeing that enlightenment might really not look the way I expected it to.

When I felt the negative reaction to taking refuge in the Buddha when I first was learning the stitch from Meiya, I went back to Steve for help. He told me that "taking refuge in the Buddha" wasn't referring to the historical figure of Shakyamuni Buddha. He said that the Buddha we take refuge in is the Buddha within. He touched his hand to his heart. We talked about the Buddha within me, within him, within all living beings. This is so hard for me to get. I keep running from myself, trying to perfect myself, looking for something outside of myself for help: and all roads keep leading back here to the place where enlightenment already exists.

And so, because of the gentle help of my teacher, who gives me such a feeling of safety that I can even express such a sacrilegious feeling as being mad at the Buddha himself, I was able to take refuge while I sewed (when I wasn't chattering away mentally) in this Buddha right here, yes this one, who's in my heart and in yours too, over and over and over again.

Friday, March 1, 1996

My teacher called me on the phone last night. I don't know what he was calling about, because as soon as I heard his voice I began babbling about the hard time I've been having. I've been quite sick for nearly two weeks, stuck home alone with the contents of my head for company. I told him that I was unable to practice. I told him that I felt that I'd been cast out of the garden, and that living in these awful negative mind habits was made worse by my knowing that there was another way of being.

Then he talked. He told me that even Suzuki Roshi had troubles sometimes, and that Suzuki Roshi wrote about those troubles being the practice. He said that if I couldn't sit, I could meditate lying down, and that if I couldn't sit for 45 minutes I could sit for ten minutes and that if I couldn't sit for ten minutes I could practice following one breath, just get myself into any stable posture and follow one breath and then the next and then the next.

He said that I was still in the garden, and that this was just what the garden currently looked like. My tears of frustration changed to tears of relief at this news. I think I'll try some sewing today.

Thursday, April 25, 1996

My Sundays recently have been full of work, and every weekend passing by has held regrets that my unfinished rakusu is sitting gathering dust. A friend told me that he had begun sewing on Tuesday nights at City Center with Vicky Austin and he was liking it quite a bit, so I called Vicky and asked if I could join in with her. She said that Blanche (the Abbess) was now leading the group, but that she knew I'd be welcome any time. So tonight I went to City Center to sew for the first time.

The sewing room at City Center is quite different from the one at Green Gulch. It's a small room, and sewing is done at tables with high stools. At Green Gulch we sewed on the floor on zafus (meditation cushions) in a room about five times the size of this one. And, of course, when I sewed at Green Gulch it was daytime and this was night. But the difference between the two experiences was mostly about the people. When Blanche entered the room I got a big smile and a hug from her. There was more conversation here, and more of a feeling of a warm community of (mostly) women working together than I'd experienced before. We went back into silence as soon as someone reminded us, and I think that I caused a lot of the chatter.

After we'd been sewing for quite a while a woman named Shelly came in and once again we broke silence as everyone greeted her and she looked for the scissors she'd lost. I put down my sewing and smiled in anticipation as I waited for the noise to die down. "Hey Shelly" I said and she turned around, saw me, and nearly screamed. It was so great. I met Shelly in the Vipassana community when I first began sitting eight years ago, and went to my first three day retreat with her in 1988. The last time I saw her she was Volunteer Coordinator at Spirit Rock, the Vipassana center in Woodacre. I never expected to see Shelly in a Zen context any more than she expected to see me, and to encounter each other in the sewing room over our rakusus was an amazing experience. After the fun of it, the smiling and hugging and exchanging phone numbers, she left the room and I returned to my place and then just stood still and felt a great wave of affirmation pass over me. After you've shot every other angle you can shoot, there's nothing else left to do but sit down at Zen Center and get ready to take your vows, I guess.

May 9, 1996

I sewed again tonight.

Blanche was the only teacher we had, and she was perturbed about it to the point of asking us to speak to some of the other sewing teachers and see if they could come and help.

It's very hard to get Blanche's attention, particularly since you can't say yoo hoo or anything and she's helping about ten of us simultaneously. Once I'd finished two 6" seams, the front of my rakusu was done. I stood and waited for Blanche for about 15 minutes. She told me to iron it. I did. I stood and waited about another 15 minutes. She measured the piece of interfacing that will back the rakusu and I cut it. Another wait. She told me to get the rakusu aligned evenly from all four edges of the interfacing. I did and waited some more until it was 9:00 and time to bow out. I left with every cell in my body expressing an impatience that I couldn't wouldn't and didn't show.

Sunday, June 2, 1996

I didn't sew this week. I felt that I was going out too much, and needed Thursday to stay home and be quiet. But something that happened the week before has really stuck with me.

There was a quiet joking conversation taking place around the sewing table about men/women. Blanche was digging it and chatting right along. Then, when there was a pause, she suddenly said, "But we don't really need to work on creating more dualism" and so we all dropped the topic.

But, you know, in the ten days since this took place I've seen it constantly in my own approach to things: my mind is just busy as a beaver creating more dualism at every opportunity, digging in further on the illusion of differences instead of leaning back and relaxing into the unity that's really at work. Stressing the differences between men and women (and hey, vive la difference, don't get me wrong!) is just one symptom of this old habit.

Friday, September 6, 1996

I went to Tassajara this week, and took my rakusu with me. I was glad I did. On Tuesday morning I sewed for several hours with Eva and Ed Brown while they worked on Ed's new brown okesa which he's sewing because he's receiving Dharma Transmission from Mel Weitsman later this month. Ed's an old friend, and passing time with him in this way was a great pleasure. Eva's about my favorite of all of the teachers who've helped me sew: she gave me the printed instructions and answered my questions when I couldn't figure out what to do.

With Eva's help, I finished the frame around the body of the rakusu. It's sewn with tiny stitches on the edge both front and back, and then the same tiny stitches (the "refuge" stitch) are done through the middle of the frame and on the outer edge of the frame. I'll finish these by Sunday and then go back to Green Gulch for the next step with Gaelyn.

For a while there I was feeling like a flake, as if I should have started and finished at the same place with the same teacher in a nice tidy amount of consecutive weeks. Now I feel as if it's appropriate for who I am that my rakusu has been sewn at all three of San Francisco Zen Center's locations, and with all of its sewing teachers. I've never done anything in a "nice tidy" linear fashion, and why should I start now? This is who I am, and this is what works for me.

When I talked to my teacher today, I told him that I'd be ready for lay ordination in plenty of time. And I will.

Saturday, September 14, 1996

I finished the body of my rakusu on Thursday night. The last part was the squares, also known as "the little devils." They are 1" square pieces that overlap the frame by 5 cms and their stitches go through to the white silk backing. Since the thread is navy, the stitches are quite visible. Several people have said that this was the hardest part of their sewing.

Last Sunday at Green Gulch, when Gaelyn first showed me how to do them, I said that it was a good thing I'd had so much practice on the stitch before we got to this point. An hour later, after laboriously applying one square and then seeing that it had gone on crooked and would have to be redone, I was singing a different tune.

They're sewn with the refuge stitch. I found myself repeating, instead of "I take refuge in Buddha," "Little Devil, Little Devil, Little Devil" with gritted teeth. I ironed them and basted their corners under so they wouldn't stick out and then, after the first one went on crooked, basted the squares onto the rakusu. I pulled the needle in one side and out the other, instead of sweeping it through, to control the size of the stitch on the reverse side. They still came out wrong.

By Thursday, I approached them differently: I undid the pins and basting and held them along the chalk line with my thumb. I moved my needle through the fabric in the usual way, trusting it to form even stitches on the reverse side. I did the last two this way, and they're perfect. I thought of the calligraphers who practice for years so that they can spontaneously draw a circle. Then I took a piece of white fabric and rubbed the chalk lines off.

Finally, I just sat and looked at the rakusu and smiled. It's beautiful.

I also did the long running stitches on the straps this week. All that remains is to turn the straps inside out, attach them to the body of the rakusu, attach the flap in the back with the pine stitch, and sew the little case which the rakusu lives in. I'll at least get all that started at Green Gulch tomorrow.

My jukai ceremony is in three weeks. The awareness of it is always in my heart, and these weeks feel like a sacred time in my life.

Monday, September 16, 1996

I thought that I'd finish my rakusu yesterday. I was wrong. I had to sew the interfacing into the straps and get them turned, and somehow that's all I had time for. I think I was too busy showing everyone the finished "face" (I was incorrect when I called it the "body") to get much sewing done. When our time was nearly up, I asked Gaelyn whether it was realistic to think that I could finish my rakusu next Sunday and get the instructions for sewing the case it travels in and do that at home in the following week and she said yes. She gave me the written instructions for what I need to do this week, which will be to stitch the flap that goes on the back of the neck.

Another woman who's hoping to take her vows at Dharma Eye on October 6th was at sewing class yesterday. Andrea has cancer and is going through a rough course of chemo so she doesn't have much strength, and she hasn't gotten very far in her sewing. I called Sandy, the third person set for the jukai ceremony, (whose rakusu has been finished for over a year) and we're going to get together with Andrea and sew her rakusu with her. Then, after sewing together, the three of us can be ordained together.

Wednesday, September 18, 1996

On Sunday, one of the students asked why we couldn't just send away for a rakusu (there's a center in Salt Lake which sews them by hand) instead of sewing it ourselves, and Gaelyn explained that this was part of our lineage. She talked about the two teachers who had brought this method of sewing to San Francisco Zen Center, and pointed out the picture of one of them – Joshin-san -- on the altar in the library. She said that she was a "ferocious" sewer and I asked what that meant— she explained that it meant that when students began rakusus and their work languished, the teacher took over the rakusus and finished them. She just could not stand to think of unfinished rakusus lying around. Then she mentioned that this was the teacher who cut off one joint of her little finger when she changed teachers. "What???" "Yes, she cut it off to prove that her changing teachers was not a decision she arrived at lightly." I held up the back of my hand with all of my fingers curled toward the palm, a little forest of stumps celebrating the large number of teachers I've been privileged to claim for my own.

Monday, September 2, 1996

As I drove into Green Gulch yesterday I was anxious—extremely anxious—but only because I absolutely had to finish the rakusu and get it to my teacher.

I remembered my feelings on the first day of sewing, and noticed how different this was from the fear of being unacceptable at Green Gulch. I'm quite at home there now. Meiya was teaching this class, and I thought it poetically appropriate that the teacher who I started with would be the teacher who I finished with. During the afternoon, my practice was in staying with my body as I waited for Meiya's instructions, feeling myself strain forward toward the end of the class, nearly panicked about not getting everything done by then.

First I had to iron the straps, and then I sewed the back square into place and turned it inside out. It came out a little crooked, but Meiya yanked it into place. Then I sewed the straps onto the front of the rakusu and did the pine stitch on the square. The pine stitch, which I'd heard other students complain about, was fun for me. I drew a grid with the silver pencil and then stitched the design with doubled thread, both pieces lying perfectly next to each other and not twisting up. I'm sorry that I can't draw a picture of the pine stitch here.

When it was done and I looked at my rakusu, I couldn't stop the tears from coming. Meiya doesn't react to such shows of emotion, so I tried to stop them. Two of the other sewers quietly congratulated me. I finished in plenty of time.

When I left Green Gulch I felt wrung out and let down. It's been a hard week anyway. I dealt with my feelings by eating junk food and buying shoes. Tonight when I gave the finished rakusu to my teacher (he'll now write his name and my new Buddhist name on the white silk panel and return the finished product to me at my ordination) I was able to say, "If you do the work, eventually you finish."

Wednesday, October 9, 1996

Andrea and Sandy and I were lay-ordained Sunday at Dharma Eye Zen Center.

The ordination was at the end of our quarterly 1 ½ day sesshin. We meditated from 8 a.m. to 9 p.m. on Saturday, and then from 6 a.m. to 10:30 a.m. on Sunday.

We had a rehearsal of the ceremony on Saturday afternoon in Steve's living room. The four of us went over sheets of paper which had everything printed out: when we were to stand, kneel, and bow, and what we were to stay, including the Robe Chant which was I was supposed to memorize in Japanese and still felt about half-confident of.

During rehearsal, Steve showed us our lineage papers, the "Blood Vein." This is a sheet about two feet long which he had lettered with the names of all of the teachers, tracing the 92 steps from the Buddha through Steve to me. The papers are very beautiful, and generally they're kept folded and placed on the altar. Since they're so great to look at and took so much work on his part, it seems a shame not to display them, but he says that that's considered showing off, and I suppose I'll do as he says.

Our zendo is very small, and we all had family and friends coming to watch the ceremony. So we removed one screen from the back of the zendo so that chairs could be set in what's usually the entryway, and we also undid the screws from one set of doors which run the length of the building (this is/was a garage) so the doors could be opened to spectators.

After the last sitting period, which was the only one of the whole session in which I seemed to be practicing zazen rather than gnawing on my exhaustion, we opened the doors and rearranged the mats. Our friends arrived and settled down, and Steve gave a Dharma talk about the meaning of the vows. He explained that a Boddhisatva was "a wisdom being" and that the ceremony celebrates people entering the sangha, and we make a big deal out of it because it's such a wonderful thing. He said, "The world in its suffering and in each life's moments of joy and aggravation needs all the Boddhisattvas that we can muster, develop or conjure up," and he spoke of what a pleasure it was for him as a teacher to find people who want to make this commitment.

After the talk, Sandy, Andrea and I went into the living room. The first thing I learned was that we wouldn't have the printed sheets that we'd used the day before. If I'd known, I'd have paid much closer attention during the rehearsal; once again, the way I do my practice reflects the way I do my life.

Linda Ruth Cutts had come from Green Gulch to help us, and she started us chanting "Om Shakyamuni Buddha" (if memory serves) slowly and quietly. Sandy and I stood and Andrea, conserving her energy, sat on the couch. After about ten minutes some impatience began to set in—continuing to chant, we even began to look at our watches and make faces at each other. Finally, Linda Ruth came to get us. The three of us followed her and presented incense at three altars, continuing to chant, and then entered the zendo. It was packed full, and felt very ceremonial and serious.

Steve was sitting with his back to the altar, a low table in front of him. There was a bowing mat directly in front of the table, and three zabutons with zafus behind it. Sandy and Andrea and I did three full bows (from a standing position to our knees with our foreheads on the ground and back up again) and then sat on our zafus. I looked up nervously and there was: Steve. Not some scary guy who was going to judge me, not someone who was waiting for me to screw up, but Steve. It was a wonderful moment. I immediately relaxed and began to enjoy myself.

The ceremony was great. We took our vows entering the Boddhisatva path, and agreed to keep the precepts. Then, one at a time, we knelt in front of Steve as he gave us our rakusus and lineage papers, and he called us by our new names. We were teasing him during rehearsal, trying to find out what our names were, wondering whether we'd be called "Dirty Socks" or "Stubborn as a Mule." When I heard my name in Japanese, Ren Shin Ji Ko, and the translation, "Lotus Heart Boundless Compassion," I felt a rush of joy at my teacher's confidence in me. I do believe that, in this regard at least, he knows more about me than I know about myself. That's why he's my teacher.

After receiving our rakusus, we returned to our places and, standing, did a little chant where we promised to "wear this robe of Buddha with the mind and body of its sacred meaning." Then we sat down, removed our rakusus from their envelopes, placed them on our heads, and did the Robe Chant. Fortunately, Steve asked everyone to join in, and so my hesitation and fumbling were lost in the crowd. Then, finally, we were wearing our rakusus, and we had been ordained.

In the garden after the ceremony, after the hugging and picture taking, I looked at the back of my rakusu. On its white silk panel, Steve had written my Dharma name with its translation, and also a passage from Dogen that I particularly love:

> "The whole moon and
> entire sky are
> reflected in dewdrops
> on the grass, or even
> in one drop of water.
> You cannot hinder
> enlightenment,

just as a drop of
water does not
hinder the moon
in the sky."

I felt overwhelmed by his generosity in putting this great passage from this great teacher on my rakusu.

Yesterday, in our regular Monday evening sitting group, as we chanted the dedication at the end of zazen

"May our intentions equally permeate every being and place with the true
nature of Buddha's way.
Beings are numberless; I vow to awaken with them.
Delusions are inexhaustible; I vow to end them.
Dharma gates are boundless; I vow to enter them.
Buddha's way is unsurpassable; I vow to become it,"

I thought of when I was first sitting with Steve and had to have the dedication and vows on a slip of paper in front of me so that I could chant them with the group, and I thought of how it seems like that was just yesterday, and yet somehow here I am, knowing the words not just by heart but in my heart and wanting them to be true, wanting to live them, so badly that I'm now chanting them with my rakusu hanging around my neck, and I'm filled with wonderment. And it is as the Buddha says, that life is like bubbles in the stream, like a candle flickering in the wind. That flick of the eye was nearly three years of my life, and so my time to use this body and mind to move closer to enlightenment is three years shorter than it was when this story really started.

Trying to find the quote about the bubbles and the candle, I came across this quote from Huang Po. It seems like a good way to end this topic, and so I leave it for you:

Our original Buddha-Nature is, in highest truth, devoid of any atom
of objectivity. It is void, omnipresent, silent, pure; it is glorious and
mysterious peaceful joy—and that is all. Enter deeply into it by
awakening to it yourself. That which is before you is it, in all its fullness,
utterly complete. There is naught beside. Even if you go through all the

stages of a Bodhisattva's progress toward Buddhahood, one by one; when at last, in a single flash, you attain to full realization, you will only be realizing the Buddha-Nature which has been with you all the time; and by all the foregoing stages you will have added to it nothing at all. You will come to look upon those eons of work and achievement as no better than unreal actions performed in a dream.

The Buddha Hall at City Center

Topic 246:
Winter 1999 Practice Period
City Center

January 15, 1999

Tomorrow I start the practice period at City Center.

It lasts for two months and I'll do it as a non-resident. The commitment is to sit daily, preferably at City Center; have regular interviews with a practice leader; sit two one day sesshins and a final seven day sesshin; attend one class (mine will be the teachings of Suzuki Roshi on Monday nights); attend Wednesday night lecture; and attend Thursday morning for a student talk. Abbess Blanche Hartman will lead the practice period. We had our first organizational meeting last Wednesday night, and it looked like there were about 30 of us who'd signed up. This comes at a good time in my life, since I'm in love with sitting and my business is relatively slow. Still, at this point, it seems to be quite a large undertaking.

I'm feeling pretty nervous now. It's 8:30 and I was working until 7:30 and I have to be in bed at 9:30 to get up at 4:30. My God what have I done. Just as I was pulling in the driveway at the end of my work day, I realized I had to zoom up to Toys R Us. We need to bring an object to place on the altar that reflects our intention for the practice period. Since I want to make my practice less rigid, I thought a Slinky would work. I got a nice junior sized plain metal one. I have a little pile of stuff by the front door, placed there tonight so I can just grab it on my way out tomorrow: zafu, oriyoki (bowls we use for eating in the zendo), rakasu, and Slinky. Yup. That works.

January 17, 1999

The Slinky is in place. At dinner after the one day sitting, Blanche said that she hoped everyone would keep their explanations short, as the opening ceremony otherwise runs way too long. "But I've been practicing a great speech all day!" I whined in my mind. Still, I narrowed it down to one sentence.

Those one-day sittings are rough. The first day of sesshin is the hardest physically and mentally. Even if I get to bed early the night before, my body's unhappy about getting up at 4:30. So I was plenty groggy for the first two sitting periods. After that, though, there's so much activity — service, temple cleaning, breakfast, lecture, practice interview, service, lunch, work period — that there's no time for sleepiness. There was finally a good chunk of zafu time in the afternoon, and Blanche's lecture and Mary's advice – Mary Mocine, the Director of City Center, will be my practice leader -- in our interview helped me to focus a little.

The opening ceremony was so pleasant, and the people seemed so lovely, that I left with the feeling that we were embarking on something that would be a lot of fun.

January 19, 1999

I called Steve yesterday to tell him that I'd be at Dharma Eye's regular Monday night sitting, but that I wouldn't be able to stay for tea and discussion since I had to get up at 4:30 today. As five of us sat together in that little back yard zendo, I felt overwhelmed with emotion. As I told him as I was leaving, "I feel as if I'm embarking on a great journey. Because I am." He gave me a big hug, and we thanked each other for our practice.

So I was home by 9:20, and puttered around putting the house in order. I was in bed before 10, with my alarm set for 4:30. I took some Kava Kava to help me sleep, and felt it relaxing me during the puttering phase. But the sleeping phase didn't come. And it didn't come. I tried every sleeping trick I know. And it still didn't come.

The last time I looked at the clock, it was after 11:00. I woke many times during the night. The best image I had of my state of mind was of a kid who was all excited about the first day of school. And when the alarm rang at 4:30, I woke cheerful and eager.

Finding parking was easier than I expected, and so I sat in my car for a few minutes finishing my coffee and nibbling at the oatmeal I'd brought in a plastic container. I was one of the first people in the zendo. It gradually filled. The bells rang, and we sat. Sitting was sitting. Kinhin (ten minutes of meditative walking in the zendo) was kinhin. The second period of sitting was sitting again. I could hear the trickle of cars on Oak Street turn into a steady stream. Still, we sat without movement, going nowhere while the world around us woke and rushed to work. After the bell rang, I followed the crowd upstairs for service and a short cleaning period.

I'd carried my zafu upstairs to use during service, and tucked it by the stairs for safekeeping while I did my job. When I came back, it was gone. I finally found it on the last zabuton on the hall leading to the zendo. Whew! I'd thought we could leave our personal stuff in one place for the duration of the practice period, but there was no one to ask so I took the zafu out with me. Maybe I'll chain it to my foot.

The world looked very beautiful when I came out of the Laguna Street door. It's been raining and is still overcast. These days always remind me of Paris, and I get a moment of being a tourist in my own city. Fell Street was jammed full of cars, too many to cross even though the light is green, each with its one person dressed and ready to face the day. I walked to my car with my zafu in my hand and a goofy smile on my face.

January 20, 1999

Today we have our first practice period tea. We arrive at 5:40 in the evening, Blanche proposes a topic for discussion, and we break into small groups and talk. Today's suggestion was dealing with the apparent paradox of Suzuki Roshi's saying that we should make our best effort forever, and also warning us against working with a gaining mind. There are six of us in each group, and I found it inhibiting to be sitting in a small circle talking about our understanding. When the dinner bell sounded, we finished and trooped downstairs for pasta and salad. I ate with Blanche and she assured me that by the end of the practice period I'd just be chatting away with my tea group.

Finally, Wednesday means that someone gives a talk and tonight it was Gil Fronsdahl presenting his PhD dissertation on the origins of the Bodhisattva idea. The lecture was quite interesting, and I'm fond of Gil, but I must say that it was amusing to look around and see the number of people who were taking little snoozes. 8:45 is *late* at City Center.

January 21, 1999

The schedule was different this morning. Instead of zazen-kinhin-zazen and then service upstairs, we had zazen with an interval, a short service in the zendo, and went upstairs to hear a Way Seeking Mind Talk. The idea is that we students give a little talk telling the other students how we ended up here. The talk we heard this morning was so sweet that it made me cry several times. When it was over I'd had enough and zoomed out and home, even though Mary has encouraged me to stay for breakfast on the mornings when I sit.

After dinner last night, a friend said that he thought I was doing it the hard way, getting up at 4:30 one morning and 7:30 the next. I think he might be right. It might be easier just to get up at 4:30 every morning and sit at City Center every morning and have it be settled. We'll see. My mind is still busily working it, trying to find out how I can do the minimum and/or trying to find out how I can do something that honors both Zen and me.

January 22, 1999

I woke up at about 5:00 this morning, looked at the clock, thought briefly of going to City Center for the 6:05 sitting — and rolled over and slept for three more hours. Yet I was more tired today than I was yesterday, when I got up at 4:30. I think it might be right, that I'd be better off just gearing my life to getting up at 4:30 every day.

I had a great practice interview with Mary before the evening sitting. I talked a lot about the fear that I've been seeing in myself manifesting as feeling that if I don't do everything perfectly I'll be tossed out of the zendo for forever. She asked how the critical voice in my head had been this week, and I told her it had been fine because I hadn't given it anything to yap at me about. I mean, there I was, sitting in my car for ten minutes before I went inside and still being one of the first people on the cushion. I told her that I thought I needed to be late — to have the experience of arriving after the bells, and survive it.

Mary came up with something better: I'm instructed to ask the ino (zendo head) to put me on the schedule as doan (bell ringer). That way I can make my mistakes in the biggest possible way — and, hopefully, survive them.

The funny thing is how much I want to sit. While Mary and I were talking, I heard the first hit on the han downstairs and felt all my yearning turn in that direction. Or was it that I wanted to get away before she peered more closely into my heart and/or cooked up any more assignments for me.

January 25, 1999

I did, indeed, get up early and go sit. My mind began bargaining hard as soon as I sat down, telling me I could skip service and soji and leave after the second period of zazen. I finally convinced myself that I hadn't noticed the signs on the block where I'd parked, and that I was in danger of getting a street sweeping ticket. I knew I was weaseling, but since I was in extra credit territory anyway (I only signed up for early mornings on Tuesday, Thursday and Saturday) I let myself get away with it.

Then I was really glad I was in the zendo, because there was a "monk leaving the temple" ceremony for my good old friend Dick C. Dick and I first met years ago when he was looking for tenants for his Pacific Heights apartment, and I became his rental agent. "Where will you be going?" I had asked in my professional capacity, and he said that he'd be moving into a place called Zen Center. We've been friends ever since. In the time that he's lived at Zen Center, he's gone through some serious health problems. In his leave-taking this morning, he alluded to them as he voiced his gratitude to the community. It was quite touching. In fact, it's a good thing that I don't put on any make-up when I go to sit in the morning, because I seem to be moved to tears more often than not.

January 25, 1999

It was the first meeting of Blanche and Michael Wenger's class on the teachings of Suzuki Roshi.

The class was fun. I just love Blanche, and love having an excuse to sit and look at her. We saw a part of a movie shot at Tassajara with a quickie teaching by Suzuki Roshi in the middle. The guy just radiated energy and joy. In our discussion afterward, someone asked whether he had any "blind spots." Blanche mentioned that he was quite absent-minded. Her husband Lou called out from the back row, "tell them about the glasses." Blanche told us that once Suzuki had been giving a dharma talk and went upstairs to get his glasses — and forgot that he was giving a talk and didn't return. Lou yelled, "When we went to get him, he was reading a book."

Blanche talked a lot about Suzuki's ability to make a dharma talk out of anything, that there were talks that he prepared and worked hard on, but there were also profound teachings given on whatever was happening in the moment.

January 26, 1999

Jeffrey the ino called this afternoon to ask if I could be doan on Saturday mornings. I said sure. He was doing this laughing thing. Then I went and sat a double header at 4:45 and 5:40 and had dinner with Jeffrey and Mary and they were both doing that laughing thing.

Mary had asked if she could train me, and I soon found out what the merriment was about. I thought the bell ringing was in the zendo going bong bong bong for the start of zazen, but it turned out it was upstairs in the Buddha Hall for the whole service that on Saturday mornings is quite long and involved. I was thrilled at the prospect of ringing that gigantic beautiful bell, and even more terrified by it since while I was binging and bonging the room would be full of people who actually knew what they were doing and would know every time I screwed up. Whew.

Mary and I went through the whole service together, she chanting and bowing and doing incense and me binging and bonging. There are many many opportunities for public humiliation here which, if you recall, is why she wanted me to be a doan in the first place. But she kept laughing and said "I thought maybe Thursday afternoon or something, but not Saturday morning" Whoo boy.

I often feel that I'm getting some special treatment around Zen Center. Well, when I don't feel like everybody hates me and is about to tell me to leave. But this is in the special treatment category. For Mary to take 90 minutes from her harried life to do the training is very generous. For Mary and Jeffrey to trust me to do this stuff is huge. I feel that I'm being moved right into the heart of it very quickly.

January 28, 1999

The bells in the zendo are always a signal to do something — start meditating, stop meditating, start walking, stop walking, bow, bow again, bow some more, leave the zendo. The bells during service are similarly signaling the time to bow, the time to stop bowing, and the times to start and stop the chant. When a chant is repeated more than once, there's a bell to say, "This is the last time for this chant." There are also internal bells within chants which are directed only at the doshi (priest who's leading the service).

Zen is so much about the rituals, and understanding and applying them is a lifetime undertaking. That's some of the point. There's stumbling through a form, then there's mastering it, then maybe there's understanding it, and possibly even becoming it. It took me several years to know that the forms are there to help me; before, I'd seen them merely as ancient rites, tests, and tickets to ride. Now I see them, or some of them, as places to rest my weary heart and mind.

After breakfast this morning, I went back to the Buddha Hall alone and practiced my bell ringing.

January 29, 1999

Much anxiety this morning about tomorrow's bell ringing escapade. Jeffrey the ino couldn't be found this morning and I have a couple of burning questions for him. I hope I can find him by phone today. What I'm watching is that thing that says "Life will be so great when this is over with," which is one of the main things that keeps me from experiencing any life at all.

We did something in service this morning that I've never heard before. We each had a copy of the *Diamond Sutra* which we read out loud at the same time but not in unison. I sat in stunned silence for a minute or two, and then began whispering along, and finally read out loud. I've never heard a chant that was so free form. It seemed that the finish was arbitrary, since I'm sure there wasn't enough time for people to have read the whole sutra. Maybe they pick up one Friday where they left off the week before. It is said that reading this sutra — or heck, just reading a few lines of this sutra — is a guaranteed ticket to enlightenment, so it's a wonder that we don't read it more often!

January 30, 1999

So today was my doan debut. I felt very cool about it going in, very ready and confident, but in the event I felt overwhelmed, fearful and out of control. Between closing down the zendo and getting upstairs and getting to my seat to start service in the Buddha Hall, there was no time to catch my breath and collect myself. Just like life.

I was frantically opening the doan's book to Saturday and boom the doshi was there and I'd already missed my first cue. Several times there was a room full of people with their foreheads to the floor, me sitting at the bell, and the doshi standing at the end of the bowing mat pointing to himself and mouthing "follow me" to me. Once I actually mouthed back "I'm trying!" It seemed as if he was moving very slowly — so slowly that in some way I couldn't believe my eyes, and so I went on hitting the bell at what I took to be the usual speed. Only he, the person whose cue I was supposed to follow, didn't drop to the ground as the bell rang. Once I saw something like anger on the doshi's face, and once I saw something like irritation. I also saw that his hands were shaking, I believe from nervousness. I really felt bad.

Once during one of the chants in Japanese I realized that I didn't know where we were in the chant, and that I needed to know and pronto because there were cues coming up. I found my place, with time to spare, but the feeling of terror that swept through me was quite powerful. The whole experience was wild. The ino praised the tone I'd brought from the bells and actually stuck a little gold star onto my rakasu.

I ran to the doshi at the first opportunity to apologize to him. He said "What an interesting dance we did." I told him that I hoped we'd have a chance to do service together again so that I could do it with more honor to him. It's not the ino's praise that's echoed in my head through the rest of the day, but the look of irritation on the doshi's face. I keep remembering that the point to the exercise was to give me a chance to make my mistakes on a more public level, and in that sense it was successful. And, I'm leaving the gold star on my rakasu.

Thing is, I'm sure the guy who was the doshi has long since forgotten it, and I'm still chewing on it.

February 4, 1999

Yesterday afternoon, I remembered that I was giving the Way Seeking Mind Talk this morning. I was driving down Oak Street, on my way to meet some buyers for a $2 million house. I felt a cold chill of fear run through me. My teeth began to clench. I was fine when I was with the clients, but as soon as we separated the fear set in again. I rushed home, changed my clothes, and went to sit. I wanted to investigate this feeling. But when I sat, it was gone! I was happy and comfortable on my zafu, for a short sit before the bell rang.

I was talking to Jeffrey about Saturday bell ringing, then Mary said she wouldn't be around on Friday and invited me to have a practice interview after dinner, so it was back to Jeffrey to cancel our arrangement to go over Saturday's schedule, then it was time for our group tea talk with Blanche - all the time I carried the knowledge that I was giving the Thursday morning talk like a stone in my heart.

My interview with Mary was remarkable. We enter the room together, she presents incense to the altar, we do a full bow to the altar together, and then turn to each other and bow - and practically before we're seated on our zafus, the tears are pouring from my eyes. "I can't do it!" I tell her. "I can't do Zen, and I can't do life without Zen." She asks me to look at the fear, to find it in my body. I can't, not while I'm talking to her. It's only a concept, but still a concept that has a strong hold on me. I tell Mary about the image that's formed in my mind. I'm holding onto the edge of the raft, slowly kicking my legs in the water, peering over the edge at the people who are in the center of the raft. This goes on for years. I lift my hand to wave Hi to Mary -- and she grabs my hand and whisks me right into the center of the raft. And it's too much! I want to go back to being invisible, this responsibility and accountability is too hard. "But" Mary says, "The way it felt to me is that you reached out to me, not that I grabbed you." She says that I've made a big commitment to my practice in the last few months. I realize she's right. The story about being yanked into the center is just another way of stepping back from accountability. I did ask her to pull me in. Gradually, I see that it's not the fear of being judged that I'm feeling, but the fear of being known.

We only sat one period before the talk this morning, but it's a long period with an interval. Long enough for my ego to try to literally choke me to death. I felt my throat closing, felt my heart pounding, tried to count breaths and got lost. I was too distressed to even practice my story one more time. There was nothing to do but watch my physical manifestations of fear. It was also the morning of the Suzuki Roshi memorial, and while we stood at the temple's founder's statue, everyone chanting something I don't know, I thought of Pogo. "We have met the enemy, and he is us."

I met Jeffrey by the kitchen altar. He lit incense and walked me into the Buddha Hall. I paused at the door to look at the group, sitting quietly on their zafus, waiting to hear me. Jeffrey handed me the incense in front of the statue of the Buddha and I placed it in the clean incense holder, and let myself look at the statue's face for a moment after my bow. "Help Me," I thought. And then I was bowing to my zafu and bowing to the group, and like magic 30 or 40 people returned my bow. Then I was seated and arranging my legs and my robes and getting wired with a device for one of the women who's hard of hearing.

And then I was talking. Except I couldn't. My throat was still so tight that I could hardly get any sound to come out. One of the women sitting in the chairs in the back row was leaning forward and cupping her hand behind her ear to let me know that they couldn't hear a thing. I pushed. The vocal chords relaxed enough that I could begin.

I was talking about my fear, starting with the story of driving to Jack Kornfield's sitting group every Monday night for a year before I noticed that at a certain curve in the road my heart would begin to pound and my throat would go dry, and when I noticed it I looked at it and realized that I was afraid that I'd arrive at Jack's sitting group and someone would say, "We're sorry, but you have to leave. You're not spiritual enough." As I told the story, I felt so sorry for that girl that I choked on tears but they didn't spill from my eyes. I talked about my understanding of that morning's period of zazen. I looked around the room and asked, "Who's going to throw me out? Blanche? Mary? Lisa?" And then I invoked "The great ancestor Pogo" and finally we all laughed and I really relaxed and told the story of my life.

Naturally I ran out of time. In fact, I was just getting going when it was time to stop. This is something I'm familiar with from speaking at AA meetings. The part that I remembered to put in was the part about being an Episcopalian when I was a couple of years sober, and hearing that priest exhort us to "Love one another" and my untrained horse of a mind responding "How?" I guess I didn't have to tell them that the relief of Buddhism was that by handing me a zafu they'd showed me how.

I said, "I love the Dharma and I have to be here." I'm pretty sure I said it more than once. Then I was finished and Jeffrey and I left the hall and he gave me a bow and a hug, and Blanche followed and did the same, and I followed Blanche and her jisha to the kitchen altar as she presented the incense and then I looked behind me and the whole group was in a standing bow about 30 feet behind us so apparently I was supposed to be back there with them and I'd done something wrong, but this was not a morning on which the word "wrong" applied, so I just stood and waited and sure enough soon enough we were all in the kitchen and then eating and the morning was over.

February 5, 1999

I went and sat tonight since I slept in this morning. Zen Center is so different at 4:30 in the afternoon than at 5:30 in the morning. Lots of people are bustling about. And talking! Everywhere I went (going to the bathroom, putting my shoes away, putting my zafu away, leaving the building) there was someone who had something to say about my talk. It's really pulled me into the community much more thoroughly. It's great to be exchanging words with so many of these gods and goddesses.

Yesterday afternoon I left a message about the talk on Steve's (my teacher's) answering machine. Today he left a message back on mine saying that he'd already heard about my talk from someone else before he heard about it from me! Whew! Call the self-clinging ambulance! But I guess what he heard was okay, and I guess I can live without knowing what it was.

When I'm not on the zafu or chatting my way around Zen Center, I'm having a very pleasant life. All of this sitting, and the hard work that goes with it, does seem to be softening me. I'm not as rushed and have more time to be pleasant with the people who I interact with; they, of course, are usually willing to return that pleasantness. I don't seem to have as much desire to change the nature of the situations I meet. And that is Zen.

I just started reading David Chadwick's book about Suzuki Roshi. He starts with a story wherein he raises his hand during a Q&A period and asks Suzuki Roshi to please just explain in simple terms what the heck it is he's talking about. Everyone laughs, but Suzuki considers the question and then answers, "Everything changes."

February 6, 1999

During my talk, I mentioned a friend who died last year. Then I noticed that a woman was crying, and remembered that she was a friend of Shelly's too. Yesterday morning, during the break, I had a chance to talk with her.

She wasn't crying about Shelly, as I'd assumed. She was crying because she'd realized that she, too, didn't think she deserved a seat in the zendo. It took her a long time to say this. I'd been sitting on a bench in the hall with a resident who I don't really know yet, and the third woman stood by us, crying some more, while this conversation took place. We invited her to sit with us, and the resident ran and got her a cup of tea. Then the three of us sat close-hipped on the bench, giggling about being three birds on a wire. I was summoned for tea with the shusho (head student), but checked and saw that it was five minutes before that event really started so I stayed with my new friends for a few minutes more, just being happy to be in bodies together.

February 7, 1999

Okay, here's something else from yesterday. Kokai Roberts (that might be close to the way her name is spelled) gave the talk. She was Head Student during the fall practice period at Tassajara this year, and told us what that was like. I went to the Q&A, and the discussion centered on whether doing a practice period at Tassajara was necessary to be a good

Buddhist. Kokai, who has a wonderful dry delivery, finally pulled back in her chair and said, "Okay guys, I'm going to tell you something." Long pause. "The Dalai Lama never did a practice period at Tassajara." Case closed!

February 8, 1999

I've been sitting in an area on the floor, just around the first corner into the zendo. Both the shusho (head student) and doshi (top dog in the zendo at that time, usually the abbess) do a jundo in the mornings. This means that they walk rapidly around the zendo and sort of review the troops. We, the troops, greet them as they pass by raising our hands in gassho. This morning I arrived a little late and had to stand in the entry hall while the jundo took place. After the doan rang the three bells, I was able to enter and sit down. I can't tell you how happy my heart was to see that there was still a place available in my usual area. When life is whittled down to practically nothing, we become attached to the little shred that's left quite quickly.

In the morning, there's still some stuff that happens after everyone in the zendo is settled in. First, the person out in the hall gives us what I've come to think of as a little concert on the big drum. I think there's some bell ringing, too. It goes on for quite some time. And there are usually some people moving around the zendo. I think it's about people being called for dokusan (an interview with the teacher). There's someone who sits on the tan (the raised platform that the zabutons and zafus sit on) behind me who frequently appears after zazen has begun who moves so quietly that they're a bare flicker in the corner of my eye. There's a place in the floor that squeaks right near where I think they're sitting, but it never squeaks for them. It's like a wraith moving by, they're so slow and quiet. This is a very senior person. The one who's been out in the hall giving us the little drum concert enters after they're finished banging and bonging, and I can usually hear them across the room.

In our tea on Saturday, Jack, the shusho (head student), told us that Blanche had said to him, "Can't you tell the shuso to learn to walk silently in the zendo? Can't you tell him to learn to watch his teacher and learn to walk the way she walks?" He presented it as an example of the endless subtleties that are available to us in the forms. I wonder how he walked today.

Sitting on my zafu this morning, turning my attention to the varied sounds of walking behind me, it occurred to me that I haven't the faintest idea how I walk. I mean, I perfected that zendo walk several sesshins ago, the one where I slide the foot forward and put the ball of the foot down before the heel so I won't thud. But how do I really walk.

My soji cleaning job this morning was to sweep the third floor women's bathroom. I'm really getting pretty whiny about this. Why do I always have to sweep the bathroom??? But I go ahead and do it. On my way up the stairs, I stop to watch the priests bowing at Suzuki Roshi's memorial, which is a nearly life-size statue of the great man inside an alcove on the second floor. I'm never sure whether I should bow and go to my job, or wait until they're through, but I think it's wise to err on the size of reverence around Zen Center so I usually stand and watch. Today Hoitsu Suzuki Roshi, Suzuki Roshi's son, was leading the bows. He's in town for Saturday's benefit.

And today the bathroom floor really did need sweeping. I also enjoyed seeing that someone had left a copy of People magazine propped up by one of the toilets. I guess we can't read Dogen Zenji all the time.

February 9, 1999

Having class on Monday night gets me out of 300 Page at 9 p.m., I'm home at 9:15, I putter around for a while and get to sleep around 10:15 — and I'm always grumpy on Tuesday mornings with less than seven hours sleep. This morning I was nonetheless up and out the door by 5, with a funny *deja vu* experience as my foot stepped into the hall, and on my cushion by 5:20. But I wasn't happy to be there, no not one bit. I sat with sullenness and rebellion, and skipped service and soji.

February 11, 1999

Although I got plenty of sleep Tuesday night, I bagged sitting Wednesday morning. It only took me three weeks to settled into a rut of "no sitting Wednesday or Sunday mornings" and by God I'm sticking to it. Which gave me more time to get ready for Andrea's funeral.

Three of us took our vows together at Dharma Eye in October of 1996: Sandy, Andrea and I. Andrea was very up front about being there for the healing, since she'd already been fighting breast cancer for some time. If meditating and vowing would help, she was there for it. Andrea had two little girls, 5 and 8 years old, and wanted at least five more years for the sake of the younger one. She did indeed experience remission, but when the cancer came back it came back like a train going off a cliff, and she died last week.

I haven't been to a Jewish funeral before. I was shocked to see that the body was there in a coffin, repelled by the sight of people struggling to carry it to the gravesite and wrestle it into the ground, and horrified at the sound of the first shovel full of dirt hitting the wood.

I had a practice interview with Mary last night, and she asked me whether Andrea and I were close. I told her about Andrea saying that my sewing her rakasu case for her was her first experience of accepting kindness from others, but that didn't really answer the question. What is "close"? I know that I'm sorry she's dead, and that I also seem to be pretty pissed off.

When I got home from the funeral, I laid down on the bed for a minute before doing some work, and zonked right out. I came to suddenly, just in time to hustle over to Zen Center for the 4:45 sitting. Except that I didn't. I thought of skipping the tea and talk, too. I dragged myself around the house and forced myself over to Page Street in time for tea.

Hoitsu Roshi, Suzuki Roshi's son and the current Abbot of Rinso-in, the Suzuki family's temple, is in town, and so we had a group Q&A with him rather than breaking up into small groups. The first question from a student began, "Dogen says" and at the mention of the great man, Hoitsu rocked back in his chair, kicking his little tabi-ed feet up in the air and rolling his eyes. He's very humorous and self-deprecating. His English is hesitant. And yet there were several times when he was talking that it occurred to me that I was listening to a great Zen master from Japan, and that this was a great privilege. No more of a privilege than listening to one of the American Zen masters, certainly, just a more obvious one.

During dinner, I sat next to the woman who's giving the Way Seeking Mind Talk this morning. I asked her whether she was nervous. Her answer: "No." Oh. Okay.

In my interview with Mary, I said that the aftermath of my talk last week was that I felt "folded in" to City Center, the way we used to fold ingredients in when we baked stuff.

Naturally we talked about death and, as I repeated "What a mystery," she recommended that I read Case 55 in the *Blue Cliff Record*. So I survived dinner and the talk and coming back home and going to bed. I tried to read Case 55 but was too tired.

Again I got plenty of sleep, and again I woke up angry and rebellious. But it would be too disrespectful to not show up for the talk, and so I pulled myself out of bed and got to the zendo on time. My sitting was restless and irritable, just showing up and doing my time. I day-dreamed about what to wear today and pondered whether or not I'd stay for breakfast.

Anna had written her talk out, and she read it to us and then took questions. I briefly grappled with guilt that I hadn't left time for questions when I spoke, since they seemed so meaty, so "Zen." But that guilt passed quickly. I did what I did, and that talk of a week ago seems like it was a lifetime ago by now. But here's the funny part. By the end of the talk I could see how beautiful the light was on the wall, and I could feel my rebelliousness and anger fade. Not disappear, but fade. And when I put on my coat and left the building, giving myself permission to not eat with other people in the morning, the street outside looked beautiful again.

February 14, 1999

Today I sat a half-day at Dharma Eye. Steve talked a lot about Andrea, our friend who we buried last Wednesday, in the Dharma talk. It just destroyed me. Tears were running down my cheeks for most of the hour that he talked.

He told this story. The night before the funeral, Blanche went to the funeral parlor and helped several other women wash the body. Then, by pre-arrangement, she called Steve and the two of them sat zazen by the coffin. While they were sitting, Steve saw a green light and realized that it was Andrea in a green dress. She was standing by one of her paintings and said to him, "You and I have talked a lot about states of mind. Well what do you think of this state of mind." Then she touched the painting with her paintbrush and the whole thing turned into luminescence. He said that Andrea had been a great teacher for him, as the two of them had had many talks about death and life and fairness. He said she initially wanted to know "Why?"

I sit directly across from Steve in our small zendo, and when he said that, I opened my eyes and looked at him and asked "Why?" soundlessly, but he didn't answer me. I can accept conceptually that everything rises and passes away, and that there's no birth or death, but Andrea's death still saddens me greatly.

February 21, 1999

We had our second one-day sitting yesterday. I came down with a killer cold on Friday. I've always been worried about sitting while sick, and it crossed my mind to skip the sitting entirely. But then I remembered a woman telling me that it was interesting to watch a giant cold move through her body during sesshin. And I realized it would be pretty wimpy to cancel because of a cold. I mean, what if enlightenment came, and I wasn't on the cushion because of a runny nose?

When I asked the ino whether my doan duties would extend to the one-day sitting, he said that someone had volunteered and that I was better off since being doan means watching the clock all day. I agreed, although a little twinge of regret passed through my mind. I still want to ring those bells on the big Saturday service and do it better this time.

I'd checked the chart on Friday night and left my zafu, rakasu and glasses at my place, which was up on Blanche's tan, just inside the door and at a 45-degree angle from Jeffrey the ino. When I first sat down, he was seated facing out, and my heart sank. The sesshin at Green Gulch which I call "seven days of hell" was the one where I sat right under Norman's outward-seated gaze. I can crucify myself on the altar of looking good. What relief when Jeffrey turned to face the wall after everyone was settled in the zendo.

Occasionally the teacher leading the sesshin will give us some guidance while we're sitting. During the first period yesterday, Blanche invited us to pay attention to the energy in our lower abdomen, which she called our place of strength. For years I've been hearing Zen teachers tell me to "breathe from the hara" but I've never been able to. First I followed my breath at my nostrils and then, a few years ago, following some instructions of Steve's, I began watching my rib cage expand and contract; that has provided me with countless hours of pleasure. But somewhere in the last few weeks, without my planning or manipulating it, my attention's moved down to my hands in their mudra as they rest on my belly which is softly rising and falling. I pause at my keyboard and look out the window and can feel it now, the miracle of the lungs pumping away whether I'm paying attention or not, the fact of the whole body breathing.

I was a breakfast server. Mary was the head server, the one who stands inside the zendo door and directs the servers, and Terry, another friend, was the one who directs operations at the tables set in the hallways. There are, of course, fancy Japanese names for these jobs, but I don't remember them at the moment. I was the only one on the crew who hadn't served in this zendo before. Mary gave us instructions while the rest of the sesshin was at service, and then we had time for a merciful cup of tea and slice of bread before serving. By that time I'd been up for three or four hours without anything to eat.

By this time, I was already pretty quiet and settled. Serving's always made me nervous in the past, but I didn't feel nervous at all. I attribute that to the change that's happened in my relationship to the City Center community over the last few weeks. I felt like a cog in a wheel, the one cog that happens to have my name on it. And I stood, sleeves down, trusting those who were in charge to steer me in the right direction, trusting myself to remember how to bow and spoon and walk. And as I waited, I thought about the forms and my relationship to them. I noticed how different this feeling was from other times of waiting to serve.

I tried out some words, maybe getting ready to write this to you. I wondered if it was about "using the forms instead of being used by them" and tried out variations on that theme, including "being used by them instead of using them," but none of them seemed right. Too much I, too much effort.

Then I thought it was about wearing the forms from the inside out rather than the outside in. When I first really started trying to be a Zen student, I started trying to sit up straight. In Vipassana, it didn't matter. In Zen it did. And so, for the pleasure of my teacher, I began yanking at my spine to straighten it. This was sufficient unto the time.

Although it caused great tension and ultimately great pain, the spine gradually became straighter. Then there was the sesshin where I learned to expand my chest rather than yank at the back of my neck, and that's probably when I began to sit straight. I had stopped wearing a shell of "straightness" and learned to straighten my posture from the inside rather than the outside.

40

My understanding about wearing the form of serving was the same as my understanding about wearing the form of straight spine. Serving became no longer about looking good to the seated forms in the zendo. Serving became about -- serving. I've always been so tense that I've held my breath while I served, and emerged from the zendo gasping for air. Yesterday I just breathed and just served. There was, I have to tell you, a series of three stops where I poured water into peoples' bowls and it was the Buddha pouring water for the Buddha. It was Patacara watching the water run over her feet and waking up. It was water pouring from the pot into the bowl, nothing more and nothing less.

With this head cold, I was very focused on emptying my sinuses at the start of zazen so I wouldn't need to move and blow my nose during the sitting period. And when the bell rang, I lunged for the Kleenex that I had tucked up my sleeve.

This meant that for once I was focused on my sinuses instead of being focused on my bladder. Zen is so regimented that you really have to keep an eye on the schedule and make sure to pee while you have a chance. Once many sesshins ago I had to run out of the zendo and go to the bathroom while 60 people sat and waited for me to return before lunch could be served, and I have gone to some extreme lengths to avoid that happening again. For several sesshins after that one, I'm sure I took a bathroom break during every period of kinhin, whether I needed to or not. And I'm very careful about my liquid intake, probably to the detriment of my system.

Yesterday I was keeping an eye on my cold medicine intake and nose blowing and cough drop consumption and realized that I'd relaxed about bathroom breaks. At this moment, this appears to me as a fundamental lack of trust of my own body; as if I see it as something I'm engaged in a wrestling match with, fighting for control of my attention and energy. Maybe, if I can learn to trust the forms in the zendo, I can also learn to trust my flesh and blood to take care of me. Just maybe.

I just got some new tapes of talks by Suzuki Roshi, and have been listening to them while I drive around. I've also just finished David Chadwick's book about Suzuki's life. And so I just heard the talk, "Sun Faced Buddha, Moon Faced Buddha" the talk that he gave in this building to tell his students that he was dying and that they shouldn't be upset because the Sun Faced Buddha lives for 1800 somethings but the Moon faced Buddha lives for one night and there's no distinction because they're both Buddha.

That phrase, "Sun Faced Buddha, Moon Faced Buddha" ran through my mind all day, and I believe it gave me the final release on my friend's Andrea's death. At 46, she was just a moon faced Buddha.

But the thing is, we're all moon faced Buddhas.

Toward the end of the day, when I was tired and cranky and wanting to go home and put my feet up and do something besides pay attention, I thought, "You know, you'll be dead soon enough, and wishing you had this opportunity, wishing you had this body that's able to sit zazen with you, so enjoy it while you've got it." Yeah. Brought me right back to my breath, it did.

February 25, 1999

I had dinner with someone I've been intimately acquainted with (we were both attendant on a mutual friend who died last summer) who's also in the practice period. He laughed merrily when I told him that I'd been attending all of the scheduled events. He's been doing very few of them, and has done many practice periods. I'm now learning that those of us who show up for everything are the exception rather than the rule.

I'm thinking about when I quit smoking. I was one of the first people to quit with Nicorette gum. I watched a friend, a hard core smoker, quit with it, so I got some too, read the instructions, followed them, and was freed from nicotine. It worked. I know people who've used it since then who've done it their own way, and not stopped successfully. I've always been glad that I didn't know there was any option but to do it the way the Nicorette people said to. And I feel the same way about the practice period. Doing the whole thing is working.

I had a practice interview with Mary last night between dinner and the talk. At its conclusion, I noted there had been "Three big questions and three big answers" and I thanked her.

Blanche gave the talk and Mary and I sat on either side of Brian. Several times during Blanche's talk I had to resist the urge to lean across Brian and give Mary a significant look. As we were leaving the Buddha Hall I whispered to her, "Was Blanche listening in on our interview?" Mary had that little smile on her face and whispered back,

"Yes." It was downright weird the way Blanche talked about the same things Mary and I had just talked about.

One thing Blanche didn't talk about was my growing interest in moving into City Center. I've been spending more and more thinking time on this — and at the same time, I know I shouldn't be making any major decisions right now. Mary and I talked about the several different ways one can live in the building (I could continue to work outside, I could quit my job and work for Zen Center, I could move in for a limited time only, etc.) and also the idea of doing a practice period at Tassajara next winter. She told me to let it be right now and see how the idea develops. But at least it's out in the open. The smell of smoke coming from the burning building of my life is quite compelling, as is my happiness when I'm in Zen Center.

February 27, 1999

I was Saturday morning doan again today, for only the second time. I went into Zen Center early yesterday and read through the service and practiced my bell ringing. When the nerves began to arise, last night and during zazen before service this morning, I recalled the lesson of last week and told myself "Let the form arise from the inside, don't grasp at it from the outside." That was actually very helpful. When I refreshed my memory yesterday, there was one part of the service that baffled me (the incense offering after the nine bows). I asked Jeffrey to explain it to me while we were waiting in the hall for him to give me the signal to begin the show, and he did — but during the event, I went back to being baffled and screwed up totally. But that was the only part I screwed up and I remained reasonably comfortable with the rest of it.

During our break between breakfast and the second period of zazen, Jeffrey asked me to fill in as doan during the lecture. I was hurrying back to the zendo for the second period of zazen, and listened impatiently as he explained the format. I knew it wouldn't be a problem, since all bell ringing is outlined in the doan's book, which is kept by the bells. Well, it wasn't. So there I was, with the Buddha Hall stuffed full of people, trying to remember how the bells went. The first part was easy enough, but I couldn't remember what I was supposed to do after the lecture. So I listened to the talk with half an ear and cast my memory back to the myriad other ends-of-lectures I've heard in my Zen life.

Lou Hartman was sitting right next to me, and I was tempted to lean over and ask him for help. As it turned out, I didn't need to. When I moved the striker to the bell prematurely, his hand shot out from his robe and made a "halt" gesture. I did. And when it was time, Kosho, the head student, leaned forward from Lou's other side and nodded "Now." Whew.

When it was all over, I thanked Lou. He said "Yes, the tendency is, when you first start, to ring the bell any time anyone does anything." I agreed. Such a sweet face on that man.

March 3, 1999

I sewed with Blanche last night. I decided to make a rakasu case for my teacher, who never completed that part of his sewing when he got dharma transmission and is carrying his brown rakasu in a beat up file folder. It was so sweet to be sewing again. The sewing room has the feel of being the last little bit of space left when City Center was getting portioned out. You walk out the door of the main building, across the courtyard, up some wooden stairs, and into a space with an ironing board, a room with two waist-high tables, and a space beyond that room with a table about 2' off the ground and a ceiling so low that I can't stand upright in it. That's the table where I sat across from Blanche and another gray-hair who was sewing her okesa (the priest's outer robe) with Blanche's help.

First Blanche and I pawed through hunks of fabric until we found something that we thought would work for my project, and then I spent the rest of the evening cutting two perfect squares, one for the outside and one for the lining. I was pleased that Blanche gave me the fabric and a piece of paper with the dimensions and left me alone — or flattered might be a better word than pleased.

There were lots of people sewing rakasus, waiting for either Blanche or the other sewing teacher to tell them what to do next. When Blanche wasn't talking to a student, she and her old dharma sister talked in low voices of this and that, and it gave me a great deep pleasure to sit working with them, in the circle of their comradeship.

March 8, 1999

I used the word "rebellious" about my practice last week. But that didn't really hit it. I was surprised when I looked back at my week and saw that I'd cut Monday night class, cut Wednesday night lecture, cut Thursday morning talk, and only sat in the morning on Monday. The other days I sat in the evening (which I'm sorry but I judge to be wimpier) and on Thursday I sat at home for a very short time. I had good reasons for each missed event, or anyway reasons that were adequate for me, but the whole picture told a story beyond reasons. Something was obviously up. By Friday, as I mentally prepared for my practice discussion with Mary, "rebellion" felt too energetic. Though I felt anger, it was more passive in nature than the energy of rebellion.

Finally I came up with "disillusionment." As I thought of it, and thought of disillusionment, I liked it a lot. This is certainly a pattern in my life, to start a project with great enthusiasm, great illusions, and then lose interest, become disillusioned, usually when I discover that the others involved, even the leaders, are just people.

So I presented all of this to Mary in our meeting. After I'd been talking for ten minutes or so, she said that it all felt as if it were coming from the head, and asked me what it felt like. I had no answer for her. She suggested that when I began zazen I try to find the feeling that lay beneath the "disillusionment." And she asked me to be careful not to think about it, just to set my intention and then return to the breath. And she asked me to pay particular attention to the physical sensations that arose when stuff came up around this. I was grateful to be given an assignment that I thought I could deal with.

What came into my mind was that during that previous practice interview, I'd said out loud that I was thinking of moving into Zen Center. And Mary hadn't contradicted me or indicated in any way that the idea was a surprising one. In fact, she seemed to already know that this was coming.

And so my bluff is being called, and that just scares the hell out of me. This life I have, with a job and friends, with service in AA and a cat and a new couch and a Nordstrom's credit card, may not be wholly satisfying, but it's my life. Moving into Zen Center is too big a change, it's too weird, and I'm not through suffering out here yet. And so I decide that the people in Zen Center, not to mention the activity they're engaged in, are stupid, and I get sulky and withdraw. I abandon them before they can abandon me. Bingo.

Blanche was doshi on Saturday morning. While I was ringing the bells in the Buddha Hall, I realized that places where I was bonging when the signal appeared in the text were actually places where the doshi was doing something, and the bonging was supposed to respond to that activity. Sure enough, during tea Blanche approached me and said "I don't mean this in any way to be critical, but do you know that the bells during the sutra are intended to coincide with the doshi's activity?" Well yeah. But you don't say well yeah to the Abbess.

We ended up sitting on one of the benches in the hall and having a little practice interview, while friends and strangers swirled around us talking and laughing. There were two friends who I know particularly wanted to talk to me, and I watched them walk by us several times and held my energy toward Blanche and this great opportunity. I told her about my understanding of wearing the forms from the inside out rather than wearing them over myself like a hard shell, and our conversation segued into doing what you're doing for yourself rather than doing it to impress others. She told me about the time she entered a room and her teacher, who was in the room waiting for her, said, "Do nothing for the eye of the beholder." And of the time she found herself walking down a hall — "This very hall, in fact" — and realizing that she was conscious of "looking good" even though she was the only one there, and what a revelation that was for her.

My problem was, of course, that I knew that during this entire conversation about learning to be oneself instead of trying to impress others, I was trying to impress her. I just didn't know how to stop.

A lovely thing happened while I was talking to Blanche. We both had been drinking tea, and were both holding empty teacups. I was sitting on her right, and her cup was in her left hand, which was resting on the cushion at her side. While we were talking, her husband Lou came up behind her with the teapot and began to fill her cup. "Watch out" I said and we both greeted Lou, who also poured me a cup of tea. She asked him what was up, and he said that he'd noticed her cup was empty. We all smiled and bowed. That man really adores that woman.

Sesshin begins next week, and so I've asked myself to return to sitting in the mornings to get my internal clock set and skip the jet lagged feeling that I often experience on the first couple days of sesshin. This will be easier now that my cold is finally gone. This morning it was not just easy but a pleasure to get up and drive over to Page Street and go through the schedule with my friends.

March 9, 1999

Last night was the last class. We heard another Suzuki Roshi tape and read the transcribed text for clarity, and then watched a video. The audiotape was more of the same, frankly, but the video was a big treat. It was a documentary made in the '60s for KQED about Tassajara. It showed Suzuki Roshi and Richard Baker and Katagiri (then Sensei, later Roshi) at Sokoji on Bush Street, all bustling around and packing things into Baker's great big white American car, and then they, with Baker's little girl, drive down to Tassajara. They stop at a diner along the way, both Suzuki Roshi and Baker in robes.

When they get to Tassajara it's really amazing. It's still being built. It's the old zendo, which burned many many years ago, and someone's chipping away at what will become the cornerstone for the kitchen. Lots of rock action, and lots of very young people. The zendo rituals, insofar as they were shown, looked even more formal than the way we do it now, but darned if the women weren't sitting in the zendo in these skimpy little '60s cotton sundresses. What a shocker.

I commented on that to Lou Hartman when the video was over, and he said that once he was carrying incense for Suzuki and it happened that when they went out the door and turned onto the path there were two girls in bikinis walking by, so the two girls led the procession and Roshi and Lou followed them in full robes. He said it was unfortunate that there wasn't someone with a camera around. I guess that's why the Tassajara brochure for the guest season asks people not to walk through the property in bathing suits.

In another part of the video, Baker delivers some long involved explication of Buddhism and asks Suzuki if he agrees, and Suzuki doesn't disagree but instead offers a completely different thought, and Baker quickly responds "That's what I always say too" and Blanche, who was sitting cross legged on the floor in front of the TV, literally doubled over laughing. It was great.

The class finished with no fanfare at all, no summary and no questions, no "What did you learn." We chanted the four vows together and bowed out and went home.

March 27, 1999

Sesshin finished a week ago, and with it the practice period ended. There was a great sense of sliding right into sesshin that I haven't had before. Instead of sitting for a couple of hours and then leaving, we just sat down and stayed there. Sort of.

I loved the schedule, which clumped together the periods of sitting and got all of the other stuff, the physical necessities, taken care of so that sitting was interrupted only minimally. There were only a few dharma talks. They put maximum effort into keeping us awake: the sitting periods were short, only 30 minutes each; one or two periods a day someone wielded the famous Zen stick; we had fast kinhin once a day; and there was even an exercise period. It wasn't sesshin lite, but it was sesshin designed with maximum regard for the western practitioners.

Blanche talked about pain a lot. In one of her three Dharma talks, toward the end of the seven days, she even talked about pain being our friend in sesshin since it keeps us awake and gives us something to focus on.

I went into sesshin with "trust" and "do nothing for the eye of the beholder" on the top of my brain. I continued with my attempt to wear the forms from the inside out. After the first couple of days the body settled in and the mind gave up on its attempt to create some excitement, and there was nothing left to do but sit. Nothing but, as Mary said in our one interview, the breath and the wall. The experience of that last one-day came into my mind, of telling myself to stop fussing about my physical discomfort because the time would be here soon enough when I'd want nothing more than a body that could sit zazen. I began asking myself, "If this were the last period of zazen you could ever sit, what quality would you want it to have?" And that extended to kinhin, working in the kitchen, and interacting with my roommates.

I requested an interview with Teah after I had a panic attack. She was an odd choice since I'm so scared of her, but her job is Head of Practice and that's what my questions were about. I thought. Whatever those questions were, there was a two day lag between requesting the interview and being called for it, so the questions were long gone.

Teah started our discussion by saying "Wow, that's an old rakusu! We haven't been making them like that for years!" I showed her the back of it, to show her the date of my jukai. We looked at my Zen name and at the quote from Dogen which Steve wrote on the back, the quote which again I'd been peeking at and reciting in my mind:

"The whole moon and even the entire sky are reflected in dewdrops on the grass or even a single drop of water. You cannot hinder enlightenment, even as a single drop of water cannot hinder the moon in the sky."

Taking to her now, she was the opposite of scary. Looking into her eyes was to look into emptiness.

At the end of the interview, Teah told me that I had a lot of courage. I felt several reactions whoosh through my mind. And told her so. I continued to be proud of her comment for the rest of the day. But one of my reactions remains true: that anyone who's willing to sit on a zafu for even one minute has courage. This is, as I said out loud to her, not an undertaking for wimps. At the end of the interview I felt I'd established a connection with this woman which will serve me well in the future.

On the next to last day, Blanche gave a short talk about the shuso ceremony. Kosho Jack McCall was head student (shuso) of this practice period, and his graduation from that position is celebrated by a very high-church ritual in which, after much ceremony, he is asked a question by each person present which he must answer. Since I'd known this was coming, ideas for my question had been flitting through my head since the beginning of sesshin. Blanche said that to do the ceremony honor we should ask our question from the heart, that in fact it should deal with the very core of our practice. So since I'd been sitting with "What if this were the last moment of your life."

The last couple days of sesshin are really cashing in on all the hard work that's come before, and that's what these days felt like. I was really cruising. I had an interview with Mary scheduled, but when I saw her in the kitchen I whispered to her that I'd rather sit than talk. That's a new one for me.

On the morning of the last day of sesshin, I can usually feel my energy beginning to lean toward the world and its comforts. I deliberately held myself in this sesshin, one moment at a time. And in that silence and concentration, I saw what my real question is. All I had to do was to take the time before asking it to remember what quality to bring to it if it were the last question I could ever ask.

The final oryoki meal was served by the senior teachers. I've never seen this before. We're all seated at our places, but the heavies who sit at the corners of the zendo are notably missing. Then the first server to come in is Blanche, and she's carrying the meal board wiping cloth. This humility brings tears to my eyes, which come and go through the meal. There's a time after serving before cleanup during an oryoki meal when all the fuss and ceremony is over and the door which the servers use is closed, and you just eat. And so while we were finally chomping away, it occurred to me that all the senior teachers had gone and left us, the next generation, alone in the zendo without them. It brought my attention back to trust, and gratitude for their trust in us to carry the teachings on which have been given so generously to us.

The Shuso Ceremony took place upstairs in the Buddha Hall after the last sitting period in the zendo. The questions really varied in their seriousness, and so did Kosho's answers. One student asked about "grace," and Kosho's "Grace is 'things as it is'," a famous phrase from Suzuki Roshi, took my breath away.

I was in the far corner and so was among the last of the students to ask my question. The others had remained seated, but my view of Kosho was blocked and I wanted to see him so I raised up on my knees, gathered my heart, and called out "Shuso, I'm afraid of dying. Can you help me to understand what death is, so I won't be so scared when my time comes?" He said that no he couldn't, he was sorry but he didn't know — but suggested that sitting in meditation and watching each breath die in the moment might be a good place to start. I felt that I'd exposed myself fully, and felt safe with that exposure.

After the ceremony, in the hallway, Lou Hartman approached me and said "There's one person in that hall who really needs zazen. That one person is you. It's zazen that will answer your question."

On the Monday morning following sesshin I leaped out of bed and raced down to the zendo to sit. I sat every day, either at City Center or at home on my own, and was there at 6:15 this morning to act as doan and ring the bells for the big show. This arbitrary mark of "end of practice period" has gone by, and practice, the breath and the wall and the silence, continues.

On the Monday night after sesshin, Wendy Johnson gave a talk at Dharma Eye. I knew it was important to Steve, and so I made a point of showing up. Both of Wendy's parents died last fall. She talked about death and hopelessness and suffering after a lifetime of practice in the most raw terms imaginable. She talked about not giving a damn about which foot someone uses to enter the zendo - just get in here and sit down.

It was only while listening to her that I realized (as those of you who've been reading along might have already figured out) that my practice period and sesshin were all about death. It was triggered by

Andrea's death back in February, but under that particular death was the fear and fascination about it that are always with me, that are probably what brought me to practice in the first place.

I light-heartedly put my slinky on the altar last January and declared my intention during practice period of becoming more flexible, and this is what I got.

I believe that writing these reports gives me an additional reason to focus while I'm doing the tough work of showing up on the zafu. Just as I'd rather sit with people than sit alone, apparently I'd rather keep a journal with others watching than scribble away in solitude. And so nine bows, and then nine bows again, to those of you who have been willing to read through this journey with me.

Tassajara

Tangaryo (First) Practice Period
Tassajara

December 27, 2000

Zen is experiential.

All the words in the world are of little consequence compared to the power of sitting still and silent for hours on end staring at a wall. But I still want to try to convey something of my first practice period at Tassajara before the memories are too faded and tattered by the attempt to tell them to my friends as I reenter the world.

Tassajara is in the Ventana Wilderness south of Carmel Valley, reached by driving for an hour over a one-lane dirt road that goes up a mountain and then descends into a deep valley.

The whole place is about one mile long. At the mid-point, where the road comes in, there are the three main buildings: the zendo, the dining room, and the kitchen. To the east, across a 20 foot long wooden bridge, is a clump of small cabins, the large lower garden, and a swimming pool. To the west, there are some stone buildings including the office, some posher guest rooms, and, further down, the communal baths. Tassajara Creek runs through it, constantly making its presence felt through the noise of rushing water. Tassajara is completely off the grid, and is lit primarily by kerosene lamps although a few of the buildings now have electricity.

Long before Zen Center bought the property, it was a rustic resort. We now are open to paying guests from May to September and become a full-blown monastery for two three-month practice periods a year.

Zen is all about the forms, and Tassajara is a high temple of Zen in America. I've been practicing intensively at Zen Center's temple in San Francisco for a couple of years, and probably thought I was pretty slick, but at Tassajara I was a beginner again. I rebelled against the Japanese-ness of it early on, and was soothed by Blanche's reminder that the forms are there to help us wake up in each moment, and not just a bunch of meaningless rules. So I stopped fighting and began to pay close attention to the way I walked, sat, held my hands, and ate for 90 days.

The things that we take for granted — sleep, privacy, and heat, for instance -- were withdrawn. Zen itself is designed to throw us off balance, and the practice period schedule is designed to keep us ragged. It sure worked.

In an average day we meditated for two hours and then bowed and chanted for another 30 minutes before we even saw a tiny speck of food. We did 27 full bows (from standing with our hands in prayer position to going down on the knees with the forehead touching the floor) in an average day and sat six periods of zazen ranging in length from 40 minutes to an hour. Meals were served in the zendo as we sat cross-legged on our zafus, the portions were small and the time in which to eat them was rushed. We were in silence from wakeup until after lunch, and even then the chances to talk were limited. The schedule was on a five-day cycle, with three days of monastic practice, one day of work, and one day with free time between breakfast and dinner.

It seemed that the bells ringing to tell me I had to be some-where never ended.

We were in robes from the start of the day until after lunch. Sometimes I'd use a ten-minute break to lie down on my bed. The robes are so complex to get in and out of that I'd leave them on while I lied down straight on my back with my arms at my sides, just like a corpse, trying to satisfy both my need for rest and my need for a tidy appearance.

My hair was a couple of inches long when I arrived, and not long after that I buzzed it down to one inch; there was no time to attend to even two inches of hair.

Laundry was done by hand in an outdoor shed and hung on lines to dry. The laundry room was one of the great gathering places on days off.

The diet was vegetarian and also wheat-free and dairy-free. Each meal had either tofu or beans for protein. There's a "back door" area of the kitchen where there's always a big bowl of fruit and, after lunch, bread and peanut butter and various jams and jellies. I ate at least one peanut butter sandwich every day. During sesshin (more intensive periods of meditation) the bread was withdrawn, and I saw students smearing peanut butter directly on bananas and woofing it down. The food was good but monotonous. It began to feel that there were five basic menus that we kept rotating through.

Of the 45 people in this practice period, 22 were there for the first time — tangaryo students, we were called. We remained in a special category and rotated through several jobs — lighting and extinguishing the 30-some kerosene lamps that lit the paths, ringing some bells, and serving meals. We were pretty evenly divided between men and women, and probably also pretty evenly divided between people below 30 and those above 50.

We became the student body in a very deep and profound way. We worked for two hours a day during a regular monastic schedule — we cooked, dug ditches, harvested persimmons, cleaned rooms for guests, and cleaned the zendo. I generally cooked. In the kitchen, we always worked in silence on assignments like rough chopping three gallons of onions or pressing and slicing 15 blocks of tofu. We had four sesshins (periods of more intense meditation) during our time there, and I spent one of those working in the kitchen.

After the initial shock to my system, both physical and emotional, I settled in happily at Tassajara. My 57-year-old body became leaner and stronger, and my resistance to the relentless nature of the schedule subsided. I found space and time to explore the teachings, and moved into the opportunity that presented itself to experience them directly. I formed some very precious one-on-one relationships. Gratitude arose. There was freedom in surrendering to the restrictions imposed on us at Tassajara, and an incredible luxury in having all of my basic needs met.

It may be months and it may be years, but I'll return to Tassajara as soon as I possibly can.

*Statue of Suzuki Roshi
in the Kaisando (Founders Hall) at City Center*

Life 134:
Entering the Monastery

July 11, 2001

I quit my job yesterday. I've been selling real estate in San Francisco for 16 years six months and 15 days, and I quit. I did it because I'm preparing to fully enter San Francisco Zen Center. I did it because I can't ask someone "what kind of property are you looking for?" one more damn time.

I did what's called a practice period at Tassajara last fall — which means that I lived at a monastery in the Ventana Wilderness for three months with 45 other monks. Tassajara's yearly schedule consists of two formal practice periods, a four month summer guest season, and two one month work periods in between the start and end of the guest season. The guests who come to Tassajara are also known as our benefactors, since the money they pay to hang out in the wilderness and eat great vegetarian food is a major source of income for Zen Center.

When I left, it was with the idea that I would return as soon as possible. At first I thought I'd straighten out my worldly affairs and be back in April in time to work there over the summer and "earn" the tuition for my next two practice periods, but my stepmother seemed to need my help and so I thought I'd work at real estate over the summer (and make enough money to get out of debt) while I gave her the help she needed, and return for the fall practice period at the end of September. As it turned out, she didn't need my help, and I was unable to find that money tree in real estate this year. And so: I quit. And am now making the rounds of the directors of Zen Center's three locations (300 Page Street in San Francisco, known as City Center; Tassajara; and Green Gulch, our farm by Muir Beach) looking for a bed and a job. So far I've been unsuccessful — but at least I don't have to do real estate any more, and I still have a roof over my head.

Today I've been recovering from the boldness of my action, finishing up real estate stuff, and looking around my apartment trying to figure out where to start in compressing 58 years of living into a monk's cell.

I first heard about Zen in 1964. I was living at Bush and Octavia, across the street from the original Zen Center where Suzuki Roshi taught.

I heard about it, and chose not to cross the street to meet the guy. But that decision was understandable: my informant told me that Zen was about "ending desires." It's not. I'd say today that Zen is about learning to live with desires. I do regret never having met Suzuki Roshi.

My next chance was in 1978. I was coming to the end of 20 years of hard drinking; in my desperation, I started going to the Saturday morning talk at City Center, and was taken to Green Gulch on a Sunday morning to hear Richard Baker give the talk there. There, I picked up a copy of *Zen Mind Beginners Mind*, the collection of talks by Suzuki Roshi. When I got home, I flipped through it. What a disappointment. All he talked about was zazen (meditation). I wanted the answer, and I wanted it immediately. I put the book down for about ten years.

In the meantime, I sobered up. The 12 Steps specifically mention meditation, and on my 9th sobriety birthday, I sought out someone who could teach me that skill. I ended up with James Baraz, who teaches another form of Buddhism called Vipassana, and Jack Kornfield led my first sitting group. I occasionally sat down at Green Gulch with Ed Brown, but I found Zen much too intimidating to embrace easily. Naturally, Zen is where I ended up.

I have been freaking out about the one-wayness of this decision. It feels as if I'm going down the rabbit's hole and there will be no way out. This is mostly economic, but I suppose there's an emotional element too.

It's really hard for people to leave Zen Center, and I'm already so old that I'm less likely to be able to make that change in the five or so years that I imagine my training will take. I have several close friends who are either Zen Center residents or priests, and I'm relying on them heavily.

Last Saturday I was helping prepare for a ceremony at Page Street, and was working with a woman who's been living there for about a year. While we were working together, she said that she was always glad when I was around the building. I said I was trying to move in and she literally clapped her hands with glee. So we talked about being a resident. I said something to her about my feeling that moving in was moving down a one way street, and she answered "Oh no, moving in is moving in to - everything." That helped.

My friend Chodron is a Tibetan nun. When we first met, she was just coming out of living at Tassajara for a few years. Then she worked at Kaiser as an accountant while she explored practice nights and weekends. She finally ordained about a year ago, shaved her head, wears red robes, lives in a nunnery, and works "small" undemanding jobs. We spoke on the phone last week, and she reminded me that I was going to something, not from something.

Renunciation frees us up for concentrating on things other than getting and spending, and it's only when I'm on the outside looking in that it feels like nothing but an opportunity for a new kind of suffering.

The kind of renunciation I know about is living simply. My little cell last fall at Tassajara was about 7 feet square, and the closet had enough room for my robes and about four shirts and sweaters. There was plenty of anxiety around which shirts and sweaters they should be — one of the first things I did after I arrived was get on the phone and mail order some stuff — but once that was settled, it was very restful to not have to face a wall of clothes and pull something together every morning.

More important was the renunciation of silence and following the schedule completely. A lot of energy gets lost in picking and choosing; having a whole bunch of decisions already made freed up my energy to explore "the great matter." Which is, after all, the point.

July 12, 2001

I'll take my computer to Tassajara this time, with an idea of sending news home on floppies. I got in on a class action suit at Toshiba, and as a result am getting a free battery and more memory on the computer. It's nice of corporate America to support my monk-hood.

Another thing I want to say. Last year, just before entering Tassajara, I became extremely nervous. I could hardly sit still, and survived by making lists and carrying them around with me. It was just the opposite of "being in the moment."

One story around that was talking with Blanche (the Abbess, my teacher) and saying "I'm afraid I'm going to be ruined!" and her saying, "Oh honey, you're already ruined."

The other story, the one that I'm holding to these days, is of a friend giving me a tape of a talk by Vicky Austin, who's currently Director of Zen Center, on which Vicky said "We practice because we want to be free." That's why I'm doing this. Because I want to be free.

And, I'm already ruined.

July 14, 2001

Today I sat a one-day at Dharma Eye, my original zen center in San Rafael. It was a warm day, and after lunch, while my body was still digesting the chili and cornbread that we were fed and the sun was beating down on the little two car garage that we converted into a zendo about five years ago, I was all groggy and spaced out — and all I could think is, What am I doing going to Tassajara, I hate zazen! I can't even stay awake for ten minutes of sitting and I'm going back to a place where we sit six hours a day!

Then I was called for dokusan (one-on-one interview) with my teacher, Myogen Steve Stücky, and things changed. Steve has always been the most demanding of my teachers, and we've had some hard times. I reminded him today of the time I ripped my rakusu off and threw it on his zafu, for instance. But there's always been a lot of love between us, too, and I believe he's been so demanding because he wants to help me, not because he's mean for its own sake. In this conversation he was so happy about my move, and so encouraging of the possibilities of my continuing to practice. I left dokusan smiling, and felt wide awake and energized in zazen for the rest of the afternoon.

The woman who's taking my cat Blue is coming to get him tomorrow. I thought about this today — had feelings about it — and talked with Steve about it too. There is no greater sign of the seriousness of my intention than my willingness to part with this cat. He was a rescue kitty, and when I got him he had real problems. He's calmed down and turned into a beautiful animal. He spent the fall practice period last year in Monterey with a good friend, and a friend of hers fell in love with him and volunteered to take him when I decided to move back to Tassajara permanently.

That's who's coming over tomorrow. We just spoke on the phone to confirm our date. She promised to spoil him. It's so wonderful that he's going to someone he already knows. After he leaves, I'll start packing. I'm already mentally sorting through books and clothes — this for Tassajara, this for storage, this to sell, this to dump. It's kind of fun. Steve said that renunciation is the path to freedom. Well all right then!

July 5, 2001

Blue is gone.

Noreen kindly agreed to take his big kitty scratching tree, and she and I had quite a time wrangling it into her Honda. We finally settled on sticking the base out of the trunk with the top of the tree extending into the back seat. Arranged around it were the sisal scratching post, the I. Magnin's bag full of kitty toys, the two litter pans, and the half-full container of kitty litter. Oh, and her clothes and stuff. She let me come back up alone and say goodbye to him, and bring him down to her in his carrier. I didn't do a long goodbye. He knew it all already anyway. But I sure did cry carrying him down the stairs and putting him in the car. Walking back into the building, I had that unreal feeling, the thoughts racing through my head that this was all some kind of mistake, that they'd never accept me at Tassajara, that I'd just given away my big beautiful Blue boy for nothing.

When I came inside I could keep busy for a few minutes, tidying up, sweeping the bits of kitty litter from the bathroom floor and the pieces of kibble from the kitchen. Removing all the evidence of his having been here, as if that would make me forget about him. Lying on the bed with my cheeks solid with tears, the thought raced through my mind "This is what renunciation feels like." But it was followed by, "No, this is one of the ways renunciation feels."

Zen is: showing up for the feelings. I'd like to have it both ways, have the monastery and the comforts of home, but I won't be able to. And the monastery is what I've chosen. I think I'll skip the Well picnic. I don't feel like seeing a lot of people today

July 16, 2001

It's interesting to watch the habit mind this morning as I move through the house without Blue. Every time I step from the sink to the garbage can, my feet sidestep to avoid his bowls on the floor. Even though there's nothing there any more.

July 17, 2001

Yesterday I fell and hurt my foot badly (damn those clogs, they are going right down the garbage chute, two falls is enough!) and also lost my cell phone. It was pointed out to me that this is what it's like to be stressed and grieving. The phone was never found, and since I was getting ready to cancel it anyway, I had service stopped today. Goodbye to good old 415 793 5811, hello to a kind of freedom. I am now down to three phone numbers, three voicemails, and three e-mail accounts. The path narrows.

While I'm waiting to hear from the Director of City Center about a job and a bed, I begin to sort my books. I have three main stacks: Tassajara; sell; and store. So far there's one Tassajara stack, about five sell and five store stacks, and about seven shelves of books yet to be sorted.

Flipping through books, I've found old notes, photographs, and inscriptions. And I found a bunch of little note pads that I used to carry on meditation retreats to be sure I remembered the good stuff. I flip through the little books randomly and find

"Life is so difficult, how can we be anything but kind." I remember Sylvia Boorstein saying that.

"Remember, even a 'bad' sit is a good sit."

"Jack on no self: if I can't control my thoughts, and I can't control my feelings, and I can't control my body, where's the 'I'?"

"My joy is as profound and valid as my sorrow."

Those are all from a little book that ends in January of 1996 with Myogen's diagram from the first time I conducted the shosan ceremony at Dharma Eye's first three day sesshin.

This one looks very old

"Day 6 - No visions, no pain, no ecstasy, no best yogi, no worst yogi, no romance, no vendettas, no fidgeting. Returning to the step ten thousand times, to the breath ten thousand and one. Writing a perfect poem. Doing nothing special."

"It occurred to me that the only self I have to be enlightened with is this one, with its obsessions, anger, and laziness, and its joy and diligence. And the only moment I have to be enlightened in is now."

No more from that book, which just hit the recycling bin.

All the other entries are very heady, from my brief flirtation with Dzogchen.

"We create a sense of self, and out of the sense of self comes the sense of separation." Oh I like that one.

"Wisdom comes from a direct experience of impermanence."

Here I'm quoting Joseph Goldstein and it's dated 7/98 *"The foundation of it all is that our actions have consequences - and all of our activity hinges on motivation."* Joseph was such a great teacher.

Here's Reb from a class at Tassajara on 6/98 *"Study karma, see dharma."*

Old-timers on the Well will remember about my friend Robert who died in Zen Hospice in I think 1998. Here's what I wrote right after his death

"6/2 - Driving to Tassajara, the tears start at the sound of my own voice on my voicemail. The Manager has group forwarded the message I left him last night telling him of Robert's death. I stop to eat and, re-entering the freeway, slow to look at the sign held by two hitchhikers at the side of the road. 'We love you' it says. I've been thinking about the feeling I had as I sat by Robert's corpse last night, a feeling of 'Who do you think you are? Who invited you to be in on this anyway? Are you sure you're welcome here?' The answer was in the sign held by the kids at the side of the road. And it was in Linda's hand as we reached to touch on the road to Tassajara, she leaving and me entering. There is a place for me here. I do belong."

Seeing these little books reminds me of the difficulty of sitting those first long retreats. What is amazing is that I continued to try. After my first seven day retreat, which must have been in about 1989, I made my famous promise to God. As I sat on my cushion for the first meditation period of the last morning, I thought *"God, if you get me out of this alive, I promise you I'll never meditate again."* That's how hard it was for me. More and more I believe that this particular kind of life, this particular spiritual path, is my karma. What else could explain this perseverance.

Maybe throwing those notebooks out is going too far. Now they're lying at my feet on the top of the recycling pile. Jeez, where does renunciation end and asceticism begin!

I went and sat at City Center this evening, and then had dinner in the dining room with Cathleen, the Director. She assures me that there's a job there for me (dismissing that whole question with a wave of her hand) but a bed's a little trickier. I finally got her to agree to meet with me at 9 tomorrow morning so we could figure something out. I am sure breathing easier tonight.

July 18, 2001

When I was starting the practice period at Tassajara last fall my mind kept telling me "This is the hardest thing I've ever done! This is the hardest thing I've ever done!" and then I remembered, "No, I sobered up!" so my tune changed to "This is the second hardest thing I've ever done!" which didn't pack nearly the punch and finally faded away.

And now for the real news: I met with Cathleen this morning, and I have a job and a bed at City Center whenever I'm ready! I set August 1st as a start date. I'll be sleeping in the dorm, which is a largish room with three beds on the third floor, and I'll be working two jobs: director's assistant in the morning and kitchen help in the afternoon. This is such wonderful news. I can finally start making firm plans.

July 19, 2001

Zen talks about "nothing special" and that's a good place for me to put my head right now. I had dokusan with Blanche last night and asked for her blessing. She said Sure, and again reminded me that this was my undertaking and that I was the one who had to do it for myself.

The first teaching she gave me, long before we were in a formal student/teacher relationship, was "Do nothing for the eye of the beholder" and that is still the top card on the deck.

I asked her what to do about the fear that constitutes about 49% of my makeup these days and she asked me to pay attention to it, feel where it's located, and be gentle with it. The other 51% is faith.

I stayed for zazen and then had dinner in the building, and am glad to tell you that there was much merriment among the residents over the news that I was going to be moving in. Huh. Maybe they want to come over here and help me carry these six big boxes of books to Green Apple today, which I'm selling because I'm just a normal person doing the everyday thing of getting rid of all of my worldly goods and moving into a Zen monastery, and doing it for myself, because I'm driven to and absolutely have no other choice, not to impress either the Abbess or you. Okay. Got it.

July 22, 2001

The knot in the pit of my stomach hasn't returned.

I spent several hours on Saturday morning with Ben, one of my closest friends from Tassajara, who was in town for a couple of days. We walked and talked through the neighborhood, from City Center to the Market Street Bank of America, back to the corner cafe for bagels and coffee, then back to the building for the dharma talk. Spending time with him reminded me of what it is I'm returning to in a very strong way, and that reminder helped my state of mind.

Then I went to the Zen show at the Asian museum with a non-Zen friend. What a great show. The surprise was that it wasn't crowded, even on a Saturday. There's a 50-minute film about life at Eiheiji, the large monastery in Japan founded by Dogen Zenji, the founder of our lineage. My friend asked "Are they in detention?" "Why?" "Because they're facing the wall like they're being punished." "No, that's just how we do it. It's so borrrrring."

And yet Ben said the last thing I said at the end of the fall practice period was "More zazen!"

July 22, 2001

Last week was so hard, moving forward just because I'd said this was what I was doing, rather than feeling that I was moving toward the life I've dreamed of. Something changed so radically on Friday, and I now have a sense of lightness and pleasure in the process. It's great.

July 23, 2001

We had a funeral for Maylie Scott at Green Gulch yesterday afternoon. She was a priest — a brown robe — out of Berkeley Zen Center, a political activist, and a wonderful woman, who died 45 days ago. There were about 150 people in the zendo, and the ceremony had lots of tears and also some laughs.

Because of the funeral, several of my friends from Tassajara were in town, and yesterday I visited with one of them before the service started. She and I have spoken about ordaining in the past, wondering what it means, wondering if/when our teachers will say we're ready and can start sewing our okesas, wondering if we might not ordain together.

This time she told me that her teacher had just given her permission, and she was now making the rounds of the other senior teachers to talk with them about it. She reported that when she talked with Norman Fischer, the ex-Abbot, he told her that two things are required of a priest. Later, as we sat next to each other in the zendo, waiting for Maylie's memorial to begin, I was thinking about our conversation and realized I'd forgotten the two things. I put my hand on her knee and then leaned over and whispered in her ear "Determination and sacrifice?" She smiled and whispered back "Commitment and surrender." Close.

July 25, 2001

I went in and did the paperwork for my new Zen Center job this afternoon. This is for my job and room that I'll take refuge in from now until the time I go to Tassajara on September 24th.

Cathleen, the Director, is someone I know very well. Her previous job was ino, the person who runs the zendo, and she frequently assigned me the job of doan which meant that I sat next to her. When you sit next to someone for several sesshins you really get to know them. So we laughed about that, we should be up and running quickly in my assignment as her assistant in the office.

Then she got very still and said "I'm going to tell you something and you can come back and we'll talk about it again in five years." She paused, groping for the words, and then stopped and said "Never mind, I'll let you find out for yourself." I naturally protested and demanded that she finish the thought.

I can't quote her exactly, but I can paraphrase. Cathleen told me that it's not that we only practice when we're in Zen Center or down at Tassajara, it's that practice is everywhere and it's happening all the time. I told her that I'd heard that, and that I was sorry that I was too weak to practice thoroughly while I was suited up and doing real estate, and that I was moving in because I needed all the help I could get. It was a sweet conversation.

July 26, 2001

Today there are not words to express how much I wish I knew what I'm going to do. I could stay at Tassajara for three months or three years. When I come back, I could come back to City Center or my own home. It all depends on me and what I want.

All I want is to be happy. How do I know what that might look like, other than staggering through this process and seeing what my heart has to say about it when I emerge at the other end.

These few days, packing for several destinations and still trying to find someone to sublet my apartment, are very difficult. I don't remember why I'm doing this, only that I am and that it seemed like what I needed to do back when I put the whole process into motion. Much attachment. Kornfield used to talk about his teacher walking up to people on retreat and saying "How are you doing?" and they'd say "Oh teacher I'm suffering so much" and he'd giggle and say "Much suffering, much attachment." Yup.

July 26, 2001

I gave my next to last sewing class tonight.

Since May, I've been going up to Dharma Eye in San Rafael and helping people sew their rakusus. On the first night, there were five people. Next week, which will be the final night, there will be one. Oh - and me, so there will be two. I rushed Carolyn along tonight to get her straps pinned to her face, so she can sew them on during the week and we can put the pine stitch on next week. John came into the city on Monday night and we did the same. Sarah sewed with us tonight; she started her rakusu six years ago and thanked me for getting her kick started again. She'll continue her sewing at Green Gulch on Sunday afternoons.

When Myogen asked if I could teach sewing at Dharma Eye, and Blanche gave her permission, I thought I'd sew my new blue rakusu in the city on Mondays and then work with the students in San Rafael on Thursdays, so I'd always be one step ahead of them. But in the event, the students in the city needed help, and I've made very little progress on my own project.

What that means is that I helped my students sew their rakusus without the benefit of Blanche's special secret knowledge. And that's how I've gathered secret knowledge of my own. I wanted more than anything to be a great sewing teacher and to never make a mistake. But about the first thing I did was to confuse centimeters and millimeters, and there's a girl out there somewhere whose frame is way too big for her face. I'm sorry if she's unhappy about that, and send her nine bows for the lesson that even a teacher can screw up and things carry on.

Standing in the yard with Myogen after everyone had gone tonight, I told him that I was now ready for him to bring on some students who needed help sewing their rakusus. He laughed and said that was always the way, that you learned on the first few how to help the ones who came after.

As I walked back to my car, after bowing my good night to him, I thought of the difficulties we've had and the fact that I was one of the first three who he gave lay vows to. And on the day after the night of our very worst time, the night that his teaching and my reaction to it caused me to sob for hours, he looked me straight in the eyes and said "Please forgive me, I'm a new Zen teacher." Maybe he's learned on me, just as I've learned on Carolyn and John's rakusus.

July 28, 2001

There's a treacherous one-lane dirt road that winds up a mountain and then down into the valley that contains Tassajara. We own the house at the other end of the road, which is in a town called Jamesburg. The people who live in that house take care of the monks, including bringing mail in when they bring food. During the summer, mail comes over daily. During the fall and winter, it comes over a couple of times a week. I was like a Pavlov's dog when I'd see Keith, the guy who did this service for us — if he was in Tassajara, so was mail, and I'd run down to the mailroom to see what there was for me.

When the cold weather started setting in, some time in October, I started getting scared, and I started getting on the phone. There was an ad I'd seen in the New Yorker for forever, which showed a great black wool cape; I tried their 800 number, but it was only an answering machine. So I phoned a friend, gave her my credit card number and the URL for their website, and had her order it for me. I called Land's End myself and had them send a parka lined with Polartec 300. I also called the Vitamin Shoppe for calcium, multivitamins and toothpaste. Then I thought I was done. But the temperature took another dip, and I realized that I was still not prepared, so I called 1-800-Patagonia. It worked. I ordered expedition weight long underwear (forget the silk, forget the capilene) with express shipping. That was the sesshin where it got down to 28 degrees and the guys couldn't make the heat in the zendo work. Whooee was it cold.

Keith drove the Trooper over the mountain to bring produce, and the mail was sitting on the front seat. I could see the Patagonia package with my name on it. But we weren't allowed mail during sesshin. As it happened, I was cooking on that sesshin and not sitting the entire thing. Every time I passed the Trooper, I slowed my pace and went through the debate. What would it hurt if I just reached out - opened the door - grabbed the package - ran to my room - I wasn't really on sesshin anyway, why should I suffer - but I never did. I froze and waited for sesshin to be over, just like everyone else. That was a happy mail call. It was an even better opportunity to check the sincerity of my practice.

August 2, 2001

I started on staff at City Center yesterday. It didn't feel at all the way I expected it to. But then, what was I expecting.

This whole escapade feels like I had some cockamamie idea six months ago, and now it's turned into my life. Did I ever remember to examine it closely? What was I thinking?

I remind myself many times a day that if it were so wonderful and satisfying out in the world, I wouldn't have wanted to enter the monastery in the first place. But right now neither of the alternatives, 21st century life or Zen Center, seems possible. Is there a third choice? No, I thought not.

I want my cat. I want my car. I want to eat what I want to eat, when I want to eat it. I want to stay up late at night and sleep in in the morning. I want to be the glamorous one who lives on the outside and swoops into the building when I feel like it. I want to be able to go home and hide when I'm feeling grumpy.

I want to not suffer. I want to know the truth.

But I did make a decision, and set all the wheels in motion, and now they're pulling me forward. I'll work in the kitchen every morning and be Cathleen's assistant in the afternoon until the Intensive finishes on the 17th, and then I'll be doing office work full time until I go down to Tassajara with Blanche. I'll sleep in the "dorm" with two girls who are young enough to be my daughters until the Intensive's finished and they go home and leave me alone.

I'll keep saying "sure" whenever anyone asks me to do anything, and we'll see where that takes me. I said I would and I will, because I don't know what else to do.

August 3, 2001

I do believe it's this period with one foot in the old life and one in the new that's particularly difficult.

I want not to suffer. Last night, when I was leaving the building after my workday, after zazen, after dinner, after more tears, I opened the door to see the road crew who'd been working outside all day. They had scraped up the roadbed and now, at 7:30 at night, were pouring concrete down the entire block of Page between Laguna and Octavia. First the wet concrete grabbed my eye, it was so beautiful and shiny and smooth. But then I noticed the gang of guys who were downriver from the finished part, slogging around in the stuff that was pouring out of the cement mixer, up to their knees in it, shoveling it around. And I had a brief moment of getting things into perspective. *There* were the people who were having a rough day.

Norman said: the qualities necessary for a priest (or, I say, for any religious) are commitment and surrender. I think I'll try giving up today.

August 4, 2001

Today is moving day.

We took about two feet of hanging clothes, two boxes, and a duffel bag with my sleeping bag and zafu to City Center. We took about three or four feet of hanging clothes, all the art, the living room rug, and about 25 boxes to my cousin's garage.

Now I'm back in the old apartment to clean up. When I leave, I'll take one more suitcase of last minute things with me, and this computer. I am feeling so light hearted right now.

August 7, 2001

Today was the third day in my cycle of three days on and one day off. I woke to the sound of a roommate's alarm at 4:50, stumbled down the hall to the bathroom, and was in my robes and out the door before either of the other two women in the dorm was out of bed.

We start every day with two periods of zazen, a service that lasts about half an hour, and a period of temple cleaning before breakfast. My workday starts in the kitchen with an 8:45 bow-in.

There were six of us in the kitchen today, and we started with a short service at the kitchen altar. There are a few amazing things about a Zen kitchen. First, it's silent. I mean, no talking. If I have to ask the work leader a question, I walk over to her and speak softly. If someone's going to use a can opener or a food grinder, they call out "Noise" as a warning. There's also an extraordinary lack of hierarchy. Everyone cooks, everyone preps, and everyone washes lots and lots of dishes.

In the afternoon, I was trained into working the front office. The people who usually do it want to sit the upcoming sesshin, so I'll be filling in. The office is great, since everyone going in or out of the building stops by to say something. After the office closed I was finally able to go to my room and lie down. Now it's nearly time for dinner, and I can hear the chanting coming up from the Buddha Hall; the rest of the students are doing evening service, and I'm upstairs typing this note to you. After dinner I'll sit a couple of periods of zazen, take a shower, and then be in bed by 9:30.

This is my schedule for three days. Tomorrow is a day off, which means that I'll sit morning and evening zazen but the time in between breakfast and dinner is mine mine all mine. I wonder what I'll do with it.

I have little desire to go outside of the building, and none at all to drive a car. But tomorrow could be a different story entirely. Hell maybe I'll get in the car and drive somewhere else and start life over entirely under an assumed name. Maybe I'll get back in bed and sleep all day. Or maybe I'll go back to my old apartment and finish up more odds and ends from my move, as planned. We'll see.

August 9, 2001

This morning my little roommate didn't set her clock for ten minutes before the wakeup bell, so I really had to hustle to get my three-minute shower in and get down to the residents' kitchen for my half cup of coffee before zazen.

I was scheduled for dokusan this morning, so I left the zendo after the first period, when everyone else was starting the ten-minute walking meditation called kinhin, and went to the area at the end of Holy Row. There are five zabutons and zafus behind a small screen, and the students sit there mentally planning the big questions or bigger excuses for their practice leader. Teachers are sitting in three rooms in the area, and it's up to the student to recognize their teacher's bell ringing to summon them.

I know the sound of Blanche's bell quite well by now. As we sat facing each other in our robes, talking about my practice, we could hear the bonging of the big bell and then banging of the big drum from the Buddha Hall downstairs as the rest of the group did service.

Later in the morning, during class, Blanche read one portion from Uchiyama Roshi's translation of Dogen's *Instructions to the Cook* which seemed pertinent to my situation, and I wrote it down: "The degree of separation from the reality of life appears as struggling and suffering." The reality of life. Well, I guess that's the great matter that I'm here to study.

August 10, 2001

The commitment for living here is: two periods of zazen a day; participating in the Saturday morning program including oryoki breakfast and lecture; Wednesday evening lecture; one meal prep job and one dishwashing job; one bathroom job; one house job (keeping the sidewalk clean, watering plants, that sort of thing).

Last night I dreamed I was putting on my real estate makeup, but about times ten. My cheeks were flaming with blusher and powder was caked on my face. I looked beautiful, in a rather conventional and artificial way. I don't even look into mirrors any more, don't wear even the minimal makeup that I was using just a couple of weeks ago, and my hair is chopped off to about one inch long. If I'm going to be beautiful now, it's going to have to come from the inside — I just don't have the time or energy to fuss with the outside. But I can dream!

Now what I wanted to say is that it's dawning on me what a privilege it is to be able to live this way. It's easy to get my vision skewed and see it as restrictive or out of touch with the times or something, but the fact is that this schedule and this way of life is designed to *help* me.

Those guys who invented this stuff hundreds of years ago knew I was coming, and knew that I'd need tons and tons of help in quieting my mind and learning some new habits. Today I feel so grateful to them — and to all of you, bustling away out there on the other side of our front door, keeping the world humming so we can skim off this little bit of time and energy and investigate it thoroughly.

August 13, 2001

This morning was the start of the five-day sesshin. This means that the participants will be meditating from morning until night and taking all their meals in the zendo. I'll be cooking for them.

I had a wakeful night, punctuated by a bad dream. I got up in plenty of time to shower and grab a splash of coffee before the bell rang to get down to the zendo. As I was moving down the hall, the ino (head of the zendo) pulled me aside. She asked if I'd ever been "lighting chiden" and I said sure. She asked me to light the Buddha Hall, and as I happily moved in that direction I realized that this was a job that I'd only done a couple of times several years ago. But she was gone, there was no one to ask, and so I pressed on.

The Abbess, or whoever else is going to open the zendo, makes the rounds of several altars in the building before she comes into the meditation hall. First the breakfast cook meets her in the kitchen and they bow to the kitchen altar together; she does bows at Suzuki Roshi's memorial upstairs; and she finishes in the Buddha Hall where the chiden waits and rings the big bell while she does three bows.

I turned the chandelier on low and started lighting candles. I figured it was better to have too many than too few, so I got the place pretty well fired up. Then I sat behind the big bell and waited. She and her jisha (attendant) entered, the jisha carrying the lighted sticks of incense. Priests always put a cloth down on the bowing mat before they do their bows, and they bow before they unfurl the cloth. I know this. And yet, when Blanche did her preliminary bow, I hit the big bell. Damn! I remembered not to add the extra of a squinched face, and sat quietly waiting. Then I rang the bell - properly - on her first and second bows. Before the third bow, she turned to me and waved her hand to tell me not to ring it a fourth time. I remembered Mary saying that when you ring the bells you share your mind with everyone who can hear them, and was kind of sorry to not let the others know that I was so excited about sesshin that I'd rung the bell too soon.

Mistakes in doan ryo jobs (which is what lighting the Buddha Hall in the morning is) are to be observed and even expected. Those jobs are complicated and we're all nervous the first few thousand times we do them. My jumping the gun with the bell is not that unusual, and just a by-product of nerves.

When I first was a doan in the zendo, ringing the bell that would trigger movement in 50 people, I would be so horribly nervous that I'd do nothing during zazen but obsess about that one 'ding.' Then I realized that the nervousness I was feeling was the nervousness handed down through generations of first-time bell ringers, and ever since I've taken refuge and found solace in that lineage.

August 16, 2001

I got into a stupid beef with one of the girls here yesterday. Actually, it started the day before that. She works in the front office, and my afternoon assignment is to help out there. She asked me to do a task in a certain way that I thought was silly. The first time I did it her way, and I seethed. I thought about it obsessively during zazen, and on the second try I refused to do it her way. Kindly, but firmly. I said I'd do it my way or not at all. She, this inexperienced little pup with bad social skills, said I could leave the office. I did.

My boss came into her office several hours later. I'd been performing tasks for her left and right. As I gave her the results, I mentioned that I'd run into trouble with the pup. She asked whether I'd had trouble with Joe, the office manager. I laughed and said no. She sighed. I knew that other people had had trouble with the pup, and figured I was standing on pretty solid ground. When she said that she'd keep me out of the office for the remaining two days of sesshin, I figured it was settled. She put on her okesa and went down to the zendo. I remained in the office, doing her work and my own. When she returned an hour later I was looking at car sites online, preparing to sell my Honda.

She leaned against the computer stand by my desk and talked to me. She said that I'd come up against one of the hardest parts of practice in a place like this: being supervised by a younger and less experienced person who was senior to me, who wanted me to do a task inefficiently just because it had always been done this way. She said that this was the heart of practice, to let go of the ego and realize that there was no one there under these circumstances. I protested, said that it made a difference who was doing the asking, that I'd do it for her but - and she said there were no buts, that there's no real difference between that young girl and her and me. She said I was going to have to give up a lot more than my cat and my car, and this is where it started.

I was crying pretty hard by now.

She talked about clarifying my intention. She talked about how I'm apparently called to be here. I said that I only knew what I was moving from, that I'm so sure that it doesn't work "out there," but I don't know what I'm moving toward. She said that we're here to save all beings. She said that we're doing this because we want to wake up. I asked her if it worked. "Oh yes" she said. I asked her if she was sure we weren't just all crazy. She talked about the religious traditions of all cultures, and the spiritual seekers in all ages. I banged my hand against my forehead in a "D'oh" gesture. Right, I forgot: we're just spiritual seekers, and I've been one all my life. This is what I signed up for. It's just that doing it is so much harder than thinking about doing it and getting ready for it. I told her that I thought this was the hardest part. "You get corrected a lot" I said. She nodded. And she reminded me: be kind. "Be kind to all beings, including yourself."

Oh babies. If only this were about putting on a black robe and knowing which foot to use when entering the zendo. Apparently it's about more than that. Apparently today I'm to return to the young girl and do whatever she tells me to. I've had time to think about what I want to happen. Do I really want her to drop dead? No. Do I want her to disappear quietly? That would work. Or do I want her to change and do it my way? Yes. Is this how I've lived my whole life? Oh indeed it is. It is my way or the highway, and it is being damn sure that my way is the right way before I step out the door and begin demanding agreement from everyone I meet. Apparently it's time for a new idea. And the thing is, with a boss who leans against the computer stand having practice discussion with me, I can almost see what that new idea looks like.

I went back to the front office today, did the work as assigned, and it was no big thing. It had only felt like a big thing because I made it into one. That is the heart of the matter.

August 19, 2001

Things are looking up.   The sesshin ended Friday night.   Yesterday I ignored the wakeup bell (heaven!), went to the later public period of zazen and lecture, and then left the building and did errands, buying good coffee at Peet's for my private stash, pawing hopelessly through my boxes of stored stuff looking for mysterious pieces of paper, that sort of thing. My cousin decided to buy my car, which is obviously a great relief. It's the last hurdle in my leaving the outside world, and I had no idea it would be this easy to leap.

When I came back to the building in the evening, I was unsure of the protocol since the kitchen is closed on weekends. I crept downstairs when I got too hungry to put it off any longer, and found that there was a cart in the walk-in refrigerator with available food including a big pan of macaroni and cheese and some broccoli. So I got dinner together and went into the flop room (aka the student lounge) to eat - and there were four or five of my friends, and we could all *talk*. I quickly realized what a huge disadvantage it was for me to have moved in while the whole building was in silence. We had a great time, talking and laughing so loudly that people stuck their heads in the door to see what the party was. Whew, I thought, this is a situation I can live with.

Tonight the same set-up applied to dinner, so I reheated some soup and scrambled up an egg and went back to the flop room. Only Blanche was in the room, her head buried deep in the Sunday paper. We exchanged a few words and each went on with our reading. Then Peter and Jane Schneider came in. They were two of Suzuki Roshi's earliest students, and were here for a meeting of Suzuki Roshi's disciples. They greeted Blanche and sat down, she introduced me, and the three of them talked. The conversation was wonderful. Peter quizzed Blanche on dokusan as it's practiced here at City Center (they have lived in Southern California for many years) and Blanche talked about the various offshoots of SF Zen Center. I chimed in occasionally, mostly probably to prove that I knew who & what they were talking about, but really tried to get myself to be a little fly in the wall and absorb this wonderful meeting of the elders. Now this, I thought, this is really what I came here for. What a privilege. Peter is going to sew on his okesa for lay transmission starting tomorrow, and Blanche volunteered me to go over and sew with him. It feels as if I'm here now, the building is moving into its regular rhythm, and I can start to find my way of being a part of it.

August 20, 2001

Lay ordination is people like me — lay people who've taken the first step toward getting serious about this stuff. We're the ones in the blue rakusus. The next level is ordination - the priests - the folks in the black rakusus or okesas. Usually the final deal is dharma transmission, the brown rakusus or okesas. Those are the ones who are certified as teachers. Lay transmission is something devised for a couple of long time students, Leslie James at Tassajara and Peter Schneider who's been out on his own for a long time. As I understand it, it's a recognition of their eligibility for dharma transmission which also takes into account their being a little outside of the norm for that ceremony — Leslie because she never priest ordained, and Peter because he hasn't practiced as a priest for a long time.

I had occasion to quiz Peter on this because he came and found me after lunch and asked me to come to the sewing room with him to work on his stitch. He's a very easy guy to be around, and so we were talking and kidding around while we walked over together. He mentioned that Blanche had said that she'd wanted to have me sew with him "to set the hook." That is hilarious — has anyone ever met anyone who has the hook more firmly set already than me?!? And yet, it's this sort of kindness that's really done it, for someone like Blanche to turn me toward someone like Peter, I guess that's why I'm such a goner.

August 22, 2001

Today, in the line of duty, I enlarged a photo which will be on the altar for the funeral we're having on Sunday; began to assemble a computer stand (even though all of Zen Center didn't have a single good Phillips screwdriver); talked to the moving guy about getting the good Wedgwood stove out of one building and into another; and typed up a few memos and stuff. And all of this was done pleasantly, dealing with people I like, and moving at a humane pace.

At Tassajara, we have "town trip." The people in charge go over the hill and bring us back five items of our choice: deodorant, chocolate, cigarettes, books - just about anything but meat and alcohol. One of my friends asked for a bag of Reese's peanut butter cups and a six pack of Dad's Old Fashioned Root Beer. Since the town trip request sheet is seen by everyone, this got quite a few laughs. But one day off, when he brought four cans of root beer to the dining room to share, the laughter stopped. Glasses were filled, and a small group of us sat sipping and smiling. And burping. Then Ben walked in. He saw what was up, and went and got a clean glass. "Can anyone spare a little root beer?" he asked. Immediately there were four hands pouring the rare liquid into his glass. He looked up. "That's why I love my sangha" he said. That's how I feel tonight. Just loving my sangha.

August 23, 2001

This afternoon I was working in my office when Blanche came in and asked Cathleen if she could borrow me ("her" she said, gesturing in my direction) to make a call on a dying woman. The answer was affirmative, so I raced upstairs and changed into something black, and went with Blanche to a loft south of Market where a young woman was attending her mother who's dying of cancer. It certainly struck me that the setup was the same was it was when I helped my mom die 11 years ago. But we didn't have Blanche (and some monkish other person) chanting the Kan Ze On and burning incense. When we were leaving, the caretaker/daughter asked Blanche about reincarnation, and Blanche's answer was "I don't know, I haven't died yet."

September 1, 2001

There's not that much to say any more. I've settled into the life of the building and am glad to be here. I feel entirely supported by my teachers and friends. This past week was interim, so there was no wakeup bell and no required zazen, so I got lots of sleep, and that helps. I did meditation instruction this morning, and no one leapt up and yelled "you're a fraud!" so I guess it went all right. It's all just: life.

September 21, 2001

Now my time at City Center is nearly over, and I'm going through another round of goodbyes and tears and hugs as I prepare to move to Tassajara. I've been sending my stuff down in boxes for the last couple of weeks, so tomorrow I'll be able to put my bedding in a large duffle bag and my entire wardrobe in a small suitcase, and I'll hit the road.

The move from my apartment to City Center was the hard one because that's where all the thinking and organization took place. This one's just about the people who I've grown attached to in my seven weeks here.

I learned yesterday, almost accidentally, that I'll be kitchen crew during the fall practice period. There will be four of us working under the tenzo (kitchen head) and fukuten (work boss) to be producing three meals a day for the 46 people in the practice period. I was surprised to learn that this would be my job, and had trouble turning the juggernaut of my mental movie away from the image of me in a robe in the zendo sitting for long hours. Kitchen crew sits in the morning with the group and eats breakfast in the zendo, and then leaves to begin working. We'll work until lunch, which we eat in the kitchen in a semi-formal style, and then break until 4. We work again until after dinner, then rejoin the group for evening zazen. Our days off are different, though I will sometimes have the same day off as the larger group. The experience is much more one of connecting with the small kitchen crew than with the larger sangha, I hear. I feel concerned and disappointed about that, and also worried about how much physical labor this old body can do. More than that, I think I reacted to this strong reminder of how much I'm placing my life in the hands of Zen Center — because I really don't have any say in my job assignment. But kitchen crew is something that everyone has to do sooner or later, working in support of the sangha, and it's good that I can do it now while the tenzo and fukuten are good old friends of mine.

So tonight a friend will buzz what's left of my hair down, and tomorrow after zazen and lecture I'll take a bus to Monterey and begin stepping further in to my own monkhood.

September 23, 2001

Goodbye, my friends. Be well and take care of each other.

A Monk Faces the Tassajara World

Fall, 2001
2nd Tassajara Practice Period

September 26, 2001

It's the morning of the third day. For me, it's a day off. I'm sitting on my bed with two kerosene lamps burning and my laptop running on its battery. What a life.

I got a great room assignment. It's one of the pricier rooms during the guest season. It's called Yurt 1, and to me it's like a palace. The yurt is a wooden structure way down by the pool which has three rooms. It's insulated and my room has a wood stove, so the prospect is good for keeping from freezing over the winter. My room is round, probably 15 feet in circumference, with lots of windows and even a skylight that opens. It looks on to the hillside. It has two twin beds which I've pushed together to make one huge luxurious bed, but I've also told a couple of friends that if they get too cold during the winter they can come and stay with me so the bed may be split again. I also have a private bath. I'm sitting pretty here.

Unpacking was a trip because I sent so much stuff down. I really see my scarcity mind set in the way I packed. I have enough long underwear and neck scarves for two or three people. I also have enough chocolate for three or four people, but so far I'm not sharing it. I'm like a big old chipmunk stuffing its cheeks full of nuts for the winter to come.

Tassajara is a teeny tiny bunch of buildings tucked into the middle of the Ventana wilderness, and it could be that the animals think they got here first. Last night when we were sitting in the zendo one was gnawing away on one side and another was flinging itself against the screens on the other. They behave that way outside my room, too, usually around 1 a.m. Little buggers. I heard about the mouse problem when I was still at City Center, and a raccoon tried to open my screen door and waltz on in while I was sitting on my bed the first night. I laid awake last night listening to their noises and feeling the fear that it wakens in me. I have a long established habit of talking myself out of my fear, but last night I thought I'd try to explore it. I felt like Eve, all soft and unprotected against creatures who were armed with sharp teeth and long claws. My frightened mind/heart didn't care that the creatures were so much smaller than I am -- it was scared. My stash of cookies, power bars and candy is sealed in plastic and hanging from a hook where the mice and raccoons can't get at it. Tonight I think I'll put my ear plugs in and see if I can get some sleep.

There was a great thunderstorm the first night here. I think that's pretty unusual for September. It woke me and I laid in my bed looking at the lightning flash in my skylight. I wasn't the only one who wondered whether this was a sign of what the practice period would be like. The tangaryo students — people who are here for the first time — are sitting their five days. It's rough. There are no bells and no walking or standing except to go to the bathroom. They just sit from 4:30 a.m. to 8:30 p.m. with half an hour off after meals. I gave the ones I talked to the best advice I could, and now my mind turns toward them many times a day as the poor little things just sit and sit and sit. At the same time, I remember how much hotter it was last year and the flies that filled the zendo, and think, Kids these days, they don't know what hard is! I'm one of the three re-entering students who will do a one day tangaryo on Friday, so we'll see what I think about easy and hard after that.

The kitchen crew is on a three days on, one day off schedule, and this is my day off. Yesterday I cooked breakfast; we served oatmeal, orange juice, and tofu scrambled eggs. It all tasted pretty good. The Doshi (officiating priest) makes the rounds of the temple's altars before entering the zendo, so at a certain signal the breakfast cook dims the lights and prepares the altar, then stands to the side and waits for the Doshi's entrance. It's a sweet moment. The tenzo (head of the kitchen) told me that the most important things in the kitchen were, in order, 1) practice, 2) kindness to each other and 3) the food. This kitchen isn't totally silent, as it was and will be during sesshin, but it's very very quiet. There was a big fuss when I left City Center, with lots of hugging and sweet words from the residents, and my entrance here has been barely remarked on. What is there to say.

The strangest thing about being here is, it's as if I never left. Most of the people who I sat tangaryo with last year are still here, and I seem to have been inserted back into my class as if I'd been here the whole time. I know that the seven months I was away happened, and my heart and mind turn toward the people who I was connected to during that time. I remember working in the real estate office and then working and living at Page Street, I remember that the country's in a terrible crisis and roll the words Osama Bin Laden around my mind, but only this seems at all real. My friends who worked here over the summer have spoken of how happy they are to have Tassajara back, glad that the guests (much as we appreciate them) are gone and we have the place to ourselves, glad that we can now wholeheartedly move in the direction of studying the great matter together.

I see a little bat flying around above the deck, snacking on some tasty bugs before it calls it a night. The blue jays who decided to winter here are screaming in the distance. Most of the 45 people now in residence here ate their dinner in the zendo using formal oryoki, but I exercised my day off right and ate on a stool in the kitchen with the rest of the cooks; a couple of little mice ran by while we ate. The crickets are chirping, and if the deer haven't worked the area recently they'll be here soon. It's fall at Tassajara.

October 16, 2001

It's my day off, three weeks and one day from the start of the practice period. The great student body continues to move through its morning schedule of zazen, service, zendo breakfast, study, a work period, and then zazen/kinhin/zazen before lunch, and I scoot around here over on the side, sitting some zazen and then bolting down some oatmeal before driving a car to the top of the mountain to take pictures at daybreak (official Zen Center photographer yippee!), coming back to the valley and taking a long bath, and then charging my computer battery in the hair cutting shack (electricity!) while I lie on my bed and read a book in the silence. It's so lovely. I thought I'd hate being on a different schedule from the rest of the group, but instead I'm loving it.

Not long after arriving here, struggling with the physical demands of the kitchen schedule and my feelings about not being in the zendo with the Abbess, I saw the real price of renunciation: It's the people. Leaving behind the car and the television and even the cat is nothing compared to the people. I take naps on my breaks and have dreams that I'm with people on the outside and we're saying goodbye and we're hugging and kissing and tears are falling like rain. I had forgotten how isolated we are here. Yes there's a telephone and yes we get mail, but the phone is moody and the mail infrequent. And what is there, really, to say to anyone on the outside, anyone who's not a part of this one body with 45 hearts living this most peculiar life.

The five of us in the kitchen have become a tight unit, moving pretty easily through the cycle of the days. We have meetings on 4 and 9 days where we do a check-in, and it's surfaced that all of us went into this with some kind of reservations. We've started wearing dish towels as head wraps, as a sign of our team. One of us looks like a Middle European lady in a Babushka, one like a pirate, a couple look like sushi chefs, and I'm claiming a resemblance to Mother Theresa. One of my pals passing by, one of the guys who does jobs like pouring concrete and cutting foot thick pieces of wood, said "I can't tell you how relieved I am to know that my foods being cooked by people who are wearing dish towels on their heads." And that's the other side of the coin of renunciation, as we waltz around the kitchen together, whispering and muttering, teasing and laughing, providing three good meals to the group with some kind of spirit of kindness; that just as I left people behind, I'm finding people here. We all work so hard, and then I go to the zendo and see how hard the people up there are working too, and it brings tears to my eyes.

So there's all of this, the beauty of the place, the amazement of dealing with nature up close, the loveliness of watching the kitchen crew become a unit and the larger group settle in, and there's the big question on many of our minds of what it is we're doing here and whether it's reasonable to live like this when the outside world is going mad, or even when a good friend has been diagnosed with cancer. We've taken what steps we can: we've reactivated the Tassajara branch of the Buddhist Peace Fellowship, well be doing letter writing, we chant daily for the suffering of those who are under attack and the delusion of those who are doing the attacking, there is a card on the altar with the single world Afghanistan; I hold my friend in my heart and privately chant for her during service, and call her when I'm able to get to a phone. Is it enough? Would I be doing more if I were living in an apartment alone and listening to NPR while I drove my car around, either for the war or for my friend? This has felt like a great adventure, and its primary implication has been financial. It has seemed courageous, even, and I've loved the wholeheartedness and passion of it. But now we have to look at the world outside of the monastery and ask ourselves whether we're doing everything we can for it. This is no vacation, but it's selfish if were merely 45 people who have turned our backs on the world to try to heal our own wounds, calm our own hearts and minds, find a way of living that makes sense to us as individuals. That has seemed enough up until now, but it no longer does.

October 20, 2001

The end of another day off. Yesterday was the day off , the 9 day for the entire group, and they've started sesshin today so I have a very quiet Tassajara to myself.

Yesterday was difficult. Two members of our sweet crew have gone out, one for a conference and one to take care of a family need, and so we have two new crew members to work with. I cooked breakfast while they set out bag lunch (on 4 and 9 days we don't cook a lunch, but set out fixings for sandwiches and snacks so students can feed themselves) and there was a mix-up over serve up time. I had to produce breakfast for 60 people ten minutes sooner than I'd thought, and I was flying. There was a black mood in the kitchen for the rest of the morning, and I think I was its cause. I forgot that kindness to each other comes before food in a Zen kitchen. And once again, I ran into that part of the structure here that says the senior person is right no matter what. Once again I got reminded that all of my years of experience and fabulosity are worth nothing, and that efficiency isn't the point. It's a tough lesson. I beg myself to give it my best shot and let it go, but these moods have Velcro. Intellectually I understand that all this being right just strengthens the ego-driven sense of self that's at the heart of separation, that submitting to the organization is offered to me as a path to liberation rather than a punishment, but that news doesn't always make it the 18 inches from my head to my heart, and my stubbornness causes suffering for me and others. I doubt that I'll ever blindly follow whatever I'm told to do because that's our way, but I hope I can become more judicious in choosing between what matters and what's just about having things my way.

October 23, 2001

Day four of sesshin. The Soto Shu is here, a bunch of heavyweights from all over the country. They're getting together and staring at a wall. I'm still cooking. I have been working with such difficulty, so full of anger and resentment that I'm cooking instead of sitting.

Blanche summoned me yesterday for dokusan, and I explained carefully and completely to her the ways in which working in the kitchen was a bad deal. I concluded finally, after much back and forth (I knew she'd say it's practice and I was ready for her with It is not! It's just hard physical labor!) by telling her that the only thing that made it possible was the occasional flash of gratitude from some server standing across the counter while I served up the meal. In fact, I told her, all kitchen work was, was service. Service and love. It's the only thing that made any sense. "And you think that's not what we're doing in the zendo?" she replied forcefully. Whoa. We are?

And then again today, I had practice discussion with a friend who left Zen Center a year or so ago to head up a center in another state. She talked about realizing at some point that her practice had switched, that she was no longer doing it for herself but she really was doing it for others. Huh. I can take the vow to save all beings. In fact, there have been times when that vow seemed to be all that was keeping me connected to this earth. But her statement makes me see that I'm still seeing sitting zazen as some kind of self improvement project. This opens up a whole new field. An interesting one. Scratch that. Make it a vast one.

When I came back home after dinner I found a big spider in the bathroom. I took the lid off a glass jar, trapped the spider inside, slid it on to a card, and carried it outside. The standard spider catch and release. There's a box on my porch for firewood, so I set it on top of the box and turned the jar on its side. The spider clung stubbornly to the inside of the jar, so I gave it a few taps to encourage it to scoot. Too late, I noticed that there was a big giant ant walking by and I'd just skonked it with the jar. When I went back later, the spider was gone but the ant was staggering around in circles. Trying to save one sentient being, I destroy another. Yikes.

October 28, 2001

Another day off. Finally, finally, that sesshin is over. At the end of class last night, it was announced that daylight savings was ending and we could set our clocks back an hour. What joy. I already got to start an hour later than the schedule today because it's my day off, so I got a lot of much-needed extra sleep. One of the women who came in the kitchen to help us through sesshin told us at yesterday's meeting that we'd been spending 11 hours a day on our feet. I hadn't added it up because I didn't want to know; after hearing her figure, I double checked in my mind and am glad to say she overstated. It was only 10, since one of those hours was spent sitting in the zendo listening to lecture. But ten or 11, that's an awful lot of hard work to ask this poor old body to do. Any illusions I had of pursuing a kitchen practice in my Zen Center career are out the window. I can reach way down and find the stamina for this work, but I don't think I have the physical strength. My back hurts, and right now I just want to survive this three months and get my body back into the zendo.

November 4, 2001

Another day off for the group, another day of work for me, but a short one, and my full day off is tomorrow. I was down for two days with the flu, worked most of the day yesterday, and will do the whole day today. Having the flu wasn't pleasant, but being forced to lie flat on my back for 48 hours was just what my poor back needed. This is the first time in a couple of weeks that it's been pain free. For some time it was causing me such difficulty that I wondered whether Id be able to finish the practice period in the kitchen.

I've been doing some good reading down here. First I re-read David Chadwick's *Thank You and OK* for a hit of Zen life in Japan, and a reminder that Zen students don't have to be perfect. Then I finally read *The Endurance*, the story of the Shackelton expedition to Antarctica, which I'd been given for Christmas nearly two years ago.

I'd be scrubbing the burned oatmeal off the bottom of the pot, and thinking about those guys on that expedition and how any of them would have keeled over with gratitude to be living my life and scrubbing that pot. Right before sesshin started, the copy of *Shoes Outside the Door* which I'd ordered from Amazon.com arrived, and I devoured it. It's all about the abuse of power, both sexual and financial, that took place here 20 years ago, and I became quite upset by it. Re-reading Mel Weitsman's oral history of the early days at Zen Center was a good antidote to that.

On my first day with the flu I reread *Angle of Repose* by Wallace Stegner, a beautiful book about life in the early days of the settling of the West (mostly), and now I'm reading *Galileo's Daughter* by Dava Sobel. Funny thing -- the nuns in 17th century Italy lived on a schedule quite similar to the one we follow at 21st century Tassajara. There must be a reason for that.

While I was working in utter silence (the kitchen is always silent, but even silence is relative and it was much stricter during sesshin) and reading in *Shoes Outside the Door* about what a badly run organization San Francisco Zen Center was, my mind went some bad places. This last Friday night I was chatting with one of my old pals who was here for a meeting of the Board of Directors. I told him I was doing kitchen practice and that I figured that since both the tenzo and the Fukuten are friends of mine, this was a good time to get it over with. I thought the operative phrase was "get it over with" but he caught the "friends of mine" and said, And then they were mean to you, right? How did you know?! I answered. He gave me one of those looks and smiles and said, very quietly, Been there. There is no greater help for my unhappiness than moving my experience from the personal to the universal. So apparently I didn't just invent working in silence making up stories about how badly were treated by our so-called friends and then learning, after days of suffering (both for ourselves and everyone around us) that I made the whole thing up. It's a painful thing to go through, and also a powerful lesson.

November 5, 2001

I think it's time to finish these entries up and get them mailed off for posting. It has somehow been hard for me to do that, and I think it's because you all seem so far away. Writing for the Well, for living breathing people right there on the other side of my monitor -- people who I'd met in person and who were happy and even eager to share their reactions with me -- has been such a gift in my life. And now that I'm not online, and also now that some of my stuff has been posted on another part of the Web and is theoretically being read by eyes and minds of people unknown to me, the writing is a lot trickier. I find myself less willing to be as intimate as I've been in the past, and putting more effort into doing something wonderful.

So here, honestly, just as if it were 8:45 PM on a Sunday evening in my apartment on Edward Street, let me say this. This is hard. This is watching my suffering, watching where it comes from and the effect it has on my life, in excruciating detail. And working in the kitchen means also watching others' suffering arise and have an effect on them and on me too. We had a rough day today, with one of the crew flipping out and leaving the kitchen meeting sobbing, and the rest of us dealing with the fallout from that for the rest of the day. I went to a lot of trouble to arrange my life so that I never had to get along with anyone -- lived alone, worked as an independent contractor, answered to no one but myself -- and now I'm suddenly living in a place which is designed to stress us out and make us bump up against each other, and in the kitchen which is even more intense, and it's pretty rough. But I'm here by choice. Hell, not just by choice: I'm actually *paying* for the privilege of cutting broccoli florets and scrubbing oatmeal out of pots for ten hours a day. And I'm not here because I want to learn how to get along with any neurotic person who's put in my path (although I do think that's a skill that's going to save me a lot of difficulty if I can really learn how to do it). I'm here because I want to explore what Aitkin Roshi calls the three great questions: What am I, Where did I come from, and Where am I going. And I don't have the strength to explore those questions where I have the temptations of ice cream and television and new sweaters constantly in my face, so I have had to put myself into an environment of very limited options to see the questions more clearly. I don't think I've fully arrived yet. I just sat a period of zazen and the image came to me of a sci fi movie with a time travel machine where the person is only partially transported. Some percentage of me is here, I don't know how much, but the rest of me is still wandering over the Tassajara Road or maybe even window shopping on Fillmore Street. This will be easier when I'm all here.

I'm currently using two analogies when I talk with my friends. One is that when I used to ride buses and had a choice of a north/south or an east/west, I'd stand at the corner and look both ways, and take the one that arrived first. But I'd always walk to the back of that bus and look out the window to see whether the other bus was coming after all, to see whether I'd made the right choice, to see whether I couldn't have done better. The other analogy is that maybe returning to Tassajara is like getting pregnant for the second time: we do it because were in love with the results from our first time, but were so in love that we forget all the pain that was involved. The thing I can't talk about so well is having found a way to sit zazen with and for all beings. It's the easiest thing in the world. Try it, you'll see. Sometimes I think I can free myself from being a receptacle for every bad mood that passes through the kitchen, and find a way to chop carrots and wash dishes with and for all beings too, but that's still just a thought.

November 5, 2001

I dropped into it today. I don't know why, but I did. Kitchen crew is only required to sit the second period after dinner, and that's all I've been doing. But tonight I thought I'd sit both periods since zazen is pretty interesting right now. So after my dinner in the zendo (today was my day off) I went down to the dining room to pass my time by sewing. The break is so short and my house is at the far end, down by the pool, so it was easier to stay up in the heart of things. Heather, a tangaryo student who I gave some advice to back in September when we were both working at Page Street and she was preparing to come down here, was sitting over in one corner, some sewing in front of her. So I sat by her. She had the pieces of her rakusu in front of her and was expressing great dissatisfaction with her stitches. I told her that I'd had similar feelings about various sewing projects, and that Blanche had never allowed me rip out my stitches and start over. Heather remained dubious and continued to examine her sewing.

Greg came in. Greg isn't unsure of anything. He's sewing his okesa, and he got out his sewing box, rearranged the lights, and began sewing. Finally Ben, my most precious friend, entered the room. He's not sewing anything, but he stayed on the edge of our group and talked to us. Heather continued to fret. We found it pretty easy to tease her. It finally took the form of Heather accepting my help, Greg sewing, and Ben reading a passage from Dogen's *Shobogenzo* to us. Even though we're not so far from the full moon, Tassajara is very dark at night. Our lights in the dining room made a little island of pleasure as we passed the time together. Then we heard the han beginning for zazen, so we put our various projects down and moved, along with many other figures in long black robes, up to the zendo for zazen.

November 7, 2001

The kitchen is just a little Petri dish for watching suffering and the causes of suffering. I see the damage it does to me and the people around me when I'm suffering (= not wanting what I'm getting) and even more easily see the damage done when people around me are suffering and spraying their misery in my direction. Well maybe not more easily, because at first, of course, my reaction is that they're big jerks. Then as we continue to work, it occurs to me that they're acting that way because of their suffering. Yesterday afternoon while I was working, I was thinking about this suffering thing. I see us going to great lengths to stay asleep to avoid feeling any kind of suffering. But it gets through anyway, as it will in a place like this —since that's what this place is designed for, to let us see what's really going on. What it looks like is that we're constantly either running from suffering, or running on the fear that we will be suffering. It seemed impossible that it be the only motivation for all of our behavior. I went and found my friend Ben in the shop, and asked him whether he thought it possible that we could also find an alternative and come from love - if we could in fact transmute this suffering into love. Ben said absolutely he was sure that that was it.

Another crew member suffers. I'm not sure what the story is, she's either happy and laughing or angry and throwing things around. My first take on her was that she felt she was too good for us, that she should be in an important position and not working as one of the group, but I think that's just a show covering up whatever's really going on. Anyway, the cause of her behavior isn't my business, but the effect is. She is on occasion so rude to me that it leaves me breathless. She was today, and all morning I had the chance to work with it. My mind kept wanting to run the tape of our verbal exchange again, and I kept replacing it with a happier piece of tape, the news that Kathy's cancer was caught early and hadn't spread to her lymph nodes. All morning I kept choosing love rather than suffering. I couldn't love the rude crew member quite yet, but I could continue to choose to be a loving person. It was pretty good.

It's starting to get cold. I got a new wool robe and flannel kimono, and am now wearing them both every morning with silk long underwear. I think it's time to start adding the thermo fleece vest under the robe. We start the day by sitting for 90 minutes, during that cold time before the dawn. When we left the zendo after breakfast this morning, after the sun had risen, it was 35 degrees, so it must have been down near freezing during zazen. I'm using the wood burning stove in my room every day now. My windows face east but there's a hillside about 25 feet away so I get no direct sun at all and it stays cold. When I get home from work after lunch, I light one log and then let it smolder for the rest of the afternoon. It works well to keep the chill off. But I think the mice like it too. I have finally figured out that they're the cause of the noise near the head of my bed: it's mice in the walls. I thought it was raccoons trying to claw their way through the walls and eat me alive, but it's just little mice. Or maybe squirrels, there are enough of them around here. One of the girls who works in the garden slipped me a bottle of anti-rodent spray and I used it and had one quiet night, the night before last. But last night it sounded like they'd mutated and boy were they pissed. There was a constant tearing noise that I guess is their ripping off bits of insulation to make nests. I have a stick by the head of the bed that I use to pound on the walls to make their environment unpleasant and encourage them to move somewhere else, but so far they're staying.

There were several families of deer that were hanging around, but they left a week or so ago. My neighbor said she was coming home and they were galloping across our decks and nearly ran her down, so I suppose it's just as well. The raccoons are just awful. They know all of our bells and they respond too cleverly. If I don't keep the kitchen doors bolted when I'm there alone on the days I cook breakfast, they try to come in and have shredded wheat parties.

There was a woman here from Florida for the Soto Shu sesshin a couple of weeks ago who finally told me, after much hemming and hawing and looking over her shoulder, that someone had opened her door at 3 a.m. and then slammed it shut when she called out. She said "I heard footsteps, but when I looked out no one was there." I was sorry to tell her that it was raccoons and not ghosts. As far as I know, the ghosts confine themselves to the zendo.

94

There's an animal call that we hear before dawn that's just beautiful, sort of chirpy and fluttery and sweet. I thought it was foxes and told several new people that it was, but someone said it was raccoons. If so, at least there's one good thing about them.

One of my flip-flops was stolen from outside my door, and an old-timer guessed it was the foxes. When they get hungry they come down from the hills and steal shoes for the leather. The flip-flop is rubber, and whoever stole it discovered their error and spit it out - ptui! - behind a fence about 15 feet away. It's a pretty funny bunch of animals trying to find a way to coexist here in the Tassajara valley.

November 10, 2001

I had a terrific practice discussion with Leslie yesterday. She's lived here forever, rotated through all of the available jobs many times, raised a family here, and carries a feeling of ease and pleasure that's very appealing. I went to her to ask for her help in figuring out how to survive the dysfunctional family that is the kitchen crew. I started by telling her that since I intended to be here for a while, and since Blanche would be going home, I wanted her to get to know me so I could turn to her for help. That got a smile and an agreement. I wanted Leslie to tell me how to turn resistance into love. She said that wasn't it, that making it be love was a little extra. She suggested that I soften around it, whatever it was, and try to fully accept it. Where she got me was, when she said that the word or gesture made by the coworker that makes me crazy isn't what I need to work on, it's my reaction to it. It's not about negotiating with the coworkers so that they'll behave in such a way that we won't feel irritation. It's about feeling the irritation and letting it pass away. That's what there is to wholly accept, and even, she said, that's where Buddha is.

This morning I went back into the kitchen after my day off really understanding that my reaction was the only thing that was any of my business. And Blanche gave a dharma talk that told the group as a whole that we're halfway through the practice period, the honeymoon is probably over, and we're probably finding some of the other people here in the valley pretty irritating. She made it normal and funny instead of something that only I was doing, and only I was doing wrong. The afternoon in the kitchen was much nicer after the dharma talk. The one boss who's been giving me such a hard time apologized at the end of the shift, saying she was sorry she'd been snapping at us. Oh hallelujah.

It began raining today. It's supposed to continue for three days. The huge tree in the courtyard has been showering leaves when the wind blows, and the ground is bright yellow with them. I went to the baths on my break and floated in the hot plunge while watching the rain pound on the trees outside. It did seem like an incredibly privileged life.

November 13, 2001

When I arrived in the zendo this morning, I saw that Mel was there. Mel is such a great guy. He's a former Abbot of Zen Center, both of my teachers' teacher, and a wonderful presence. I've taken several of his classes at City Center and sometimes in study hall I read over my old notes and then run around Tassajara telling people "Mel says."

As kitchen crew I sit on the floor in the zendo, and I pick up my oryoki and sit wherever there's a seat available on the upper tan at mealtime. I ended up sitting next to Mel. Sometimes as I travel around at mealtime this way I have the feeling that the person who I've landed next to is checking me out, maybe even judging me some, but not old Mel. It was like I could just ease into his presence and: eat breakfast. Very nice.

Since my day is free after breakfast on days off, I went right down to the baths and had a shower and hung in the plunge for a while. On my way back, I saw a friend who's an ardent student of Mel's coming my way. We're still in silence until after lunch, so I had to whisper and lean close to his ear to say "I got to eat breakfast with Mel." He was laughing. He had been jealous.

Now, back in my room, I see the temperature's staying at 43 degrees outside. It's 8:30 in the morning, the sun's been shining brightly, and Tassajara is absolutely gorgeous. We had two good days of rain and everything is still dripping. The creek is up about 2 feet and running very fast. The sun hitting the wet mountains makes a beautiful mist. Since it's 62 degrees inside, I've put another log on and am settling in for the morning. More sleep? Probably.

I have one more four day cycle in the kitchen, and then volunteers will do the cooking and we'll be able to sit sesshin. Thank

God. We are so on each other's last nerve, I think there might be violence if we didn't get a break from each other. I get to be Blanche's anja, the assistant who takes care of her personal needs, during sesshin. Although it will mean more work and longer hours (the anja gets her up in the morning and tucks her in at night) I'm very pleased to have that job to do. She is very tired and cranky this practice period, and that's slopped over into our interactions during dokusan so I'm glad we can have this chance to hang out together in a more casual way. I think that's when she gives me the best teaching anyway.

November 23, 2001

The five day silent sesshin is over, as is my time of being Blanche's anja. God it was great. The anja job meant knocking on her door 20 minutes before each zendo event, and spending about the same amount of time with her when we left the zendo. I woke her, made her bed, brought her hot water, kept her supplied with firewood and built her fires, and cleaned her cabin. After meals I'd slip out the back door of the zendo so I could be in her cabin when she arrived; I'd stand behind her and receive her okesa when she removed it, and fold it and put it away for her. During work period I did repairs on it. This schedule meant that I got six hours of sleep a night and three 25 minute breaks a day. While everyone else was resting, I was taking care of Blanche.

We had a closing ceremony last night where I told the group that the job's hours were terrible, but the pay was great. Because while they were resting alone, I was with my dear Abbess. The duties would vary with different Abbots, and so would the personal part of it. With us, it was all very sweet. Once I knocked after work period and, instead of knocking back, she called "Come in." The sesshin was totally silent, and I think she called out because she was still asleep. So I opened the door. She was sitting up in her bed (a futon on the floor with a quilt) in her long underwear with her little bald head. She looked at me and said "Don't you think day three is always the hardest?"

There was just something about the energy this woman in her mid-70s finds to keep up with this grueling schedule, and also her admission that it's still hard for her. When she was teaching me how to fold the okesa, she teased me by remarking that this was good practice for me, implying that I'd have one of my own some day.

Our oriyoki sets of eating bowls have a stick for wiping the bowls clean called a setsu. The tip is wrapped with cloth, which has to be changed frequently. About a year ago I switched over to a small rubber spatula, and she teased me then, too (because priests can't use the spatulas) that I'd have to sew setsu tips some day. Taking care of the Abbess's oriyoki set is part of the anja's job, and so indeed I found myself sewing a setsu tip for her. I did it three times before I got it right, and it took over an hour. I was working on it in the dining room and she was aware of my struggle. She handed me a note on the second day of sesshin that said "Nice setsu tip. Thanks." The note's still on my altar.

I love abandoning the clock and going by the bells, but I couldn't do that this time since my schedule was slightly different from the group's. One morning when I heard the wakeup bell ring I said "Oh shit," hopped out of bed, and sprinted for the bathroom. If the wakeup bell was already ringing, I was late. I poured my thermos of hot water into my basin to wash myself and then saw that it was only 12:30. I think the creek was playing a joke on me by creating the sound of the bell. I told this story at lunch today, and several other people agreed that they hear wakeup bells and the densho in the creek. Too bad I'd already poured out my hot water, though; it was stone cold when I got up to my alarm at 3:30.

My back began to hurt again. Once when the teacher sitting behind me was facing out and toward my seat, I found myself trying to sit up straight and remain still to impress her, even though I was in great pain. And I had one of those bolts to the brain that said there was no one else for me to be but me, that I didn't have to look like "a Zen student" to impress anyone. In fact, that's the last thing they want me to do.

A few days before sesshin began, we had skit night. My two dears Greg and Ben sang the song they wrote based on Chapter 20 of the *Lotus Sutra*. The chorus is

"I would never disparage you, or keep you at arm's length.
You only see your weaknesses, I only see your strength.
I would never despise you, or put you down in any way.

Because it's clear to me, I can plainly see, You'll be a Buddha some day. I love you."

They first performed it at the July 4th skit night, and it was such a hit that this time, when they got to the chorus most of the people in the room already knew the words and spontaneously sang along. It was one of the sweetest things I've ever heard. That song got stuck in my head during this sesshin, and just went around and around and around. This is not uncommon, but it's usually something like a Bob Dylan song. In fact, initially I was running a version of Bob Dylan singing it, but it finally settled into just the song and finally became background noise. Which is when I realized that I was thinking hard about what was wrong with someone sitting near me at the same time I was singing "I will never disparage you," and realizing that disparaging him was exactly what I was doing. That was probably day four.

The closing ceremony was the shosan, the one where each student asks the Abbess a question, and it's more a matter of inquiry than receiving an answer. When it was my turn, I told her that I didn't understand what I was turning to when we take the refuges; I understand taking refuge in Dharma and Sangha, but what Buddha is this. She said it was the one mind, and the funny thing is that I finally understood. And yes, I can take refuge in that. Tomorrow: back to the kitchen. I hope I can remain enough, and I hope I can remain non disparaging. As if!

November 26, 2001

The next day, I was summoned to dokusan with the Abbess before I even got to the zendo. For the third time, we talked about my ordaining. I initiated the topic, and she very matter-of-factly agreed. The next step is to talk to the other Abbots and get their approval, and then (if they do indeed approve) I can begin sewing my okesa. The whole process usually takes about a year. She agreed that my original Zen teacher, Myogen Steve Stücky, should and could be involved.

We talked about what it means to be a priest and she, as usual, quoted Suzuki Roshi saying he didn't know. We've touched on the celibacy requirement in previous conversations. Learning to be a priest takes total attention and energy, and people who meet someone and fall in love are required to put their priest training aside for a year while they work on the new relationship. The entire period of close training is about five years. As far as I know, the other requirements are to be kind and try to see the Buddha in everyone. She asked me to begin acting like a priest immediately.

My mind was blown.

This is what I came here for, but it seems too daunting to undertake. On the one hand, I feel entirely inadequate to the task. On the other hand, and that hand is currently the stronger one, it seems like something I must do. My mind wants to compare myself to other people who are in the process of preparing for ordination and say "better" or "worse" and I'm trying hard to step to the side when it goes in that direction. I can only do this if I stay focused on who I am and what I want and need.

So I did something very unusual for me: I only told one person about this for two days. Only today did I begin whispering to friends "Blanche gave me permission to start talking to the Abbots" and none of them has laughed with derision or looked startled. So that's a reality check. There's a wonderful young Italian priest here right now, and we had a conversation after dinner. He asked whether I was going to ordain without my bringing the subject up, and when I said yes he was very pleased. I indicated that I was nervous about it and he said that ordaining was like riding in a plane through turbulence and then rising above the clouds into the clear sky. That's useful information.

We always talk about celibacy a lot down here, and last night after our Thanksgiving dinner (nut loaf, three days after the rest of the world ate theirs because we're Tassajara and we do these things when our schedule permits) a small group of us sat in the back of the dining room over our final piece of pie and continued the conversation. I'm currently trying on the idea that total celibacy would free up a lot of energy for pursuing the dharma. Others say it's unnatural and a denial of an important life force. That same Italian priest joined the conversation and told us that in his life he tried to hold to the rule that he only became sexually involved with someone who he felt serious about and he talked about how a couple in a strong relationship can be a living example of the dharma.

Blanche's regular anja became very ill, and so I helped out over the last few days while I was working in the kitchen too. I did her laundry two days ago, and the weather's been so heavy and the air so moist that it never dried out. That's why right now I have Blanche's underwear hanging all over my room and am burning logs like mad to keep the temperature up so it can dry.

We live so close to each other that sickness travels like wildfire, so I have the head cold that's going around myself. I was breakfast cook today and Blanche came in to show us how tofu cabbage grill should be cooked, so I only had to cook the cereal, warm the juice and do serve-up, and it was an easy and sweet morning.

Once the regular shift started, though, I got into it with the boss again. I tried a new way of communicating my distress "It hurts my feelings when you talk to me that way" instead of the "You piss me off" or "Why do you always" that are in my head, and it apparently worked. The whole mood of the day changed, and our small crew (one member was out entirely with the flu) had a lovely lighthearted time of preparing the lunch for the group. Interesting that it could change so much.

December 1, 2001

Five days ago I had a very difficult telephone conversation with someone back in San Francisco. I talked to my friend Ben about it briefly, and the next day I saw him, downcast, walking toward the baths. "I made a mistake and someone else got hurt" he said. "That's exactly what I was talking about!" I answered. "No," he said, "I mean I left a hole in the floor open and someone fell in and twisted her ankle." Oh.

So when I stopped in the hurt girl's cabin and saw that she was wearing her jacket in bed because her room was so cold, I invited her to come and stay with me while she healed. I have the extra bed, and I have heat. What I liked about it so much was that the invitation was entirely spontaneous, that I didn't have to bargain with myself and weigh the pros and cons. Probably, too, I felt so unable to do anything for the person who I hurt in San Francisco that I was glad to be able to do something for the one Ben hurt here at Tassajara.

Now, on my day off, I've spent the morning hiding out in a vacant room, waiting for the dear hurt lady to find another place to stay. No hard feelings on either side, but four days was enough. She had a great time, lying in bed, receiving company and drinking Peet's coffee in the warm room. We're all so exhausted down here that a few days laid up in bed with a twisted ankle can be a boon. I enjoyed her company too, until the time yesterday when I needed to be alone and there wasn't room for me in my own little house.

There was another incident with my boss yesterday, this one so bad that I actually left the kitchen before the end of my shift. After my tears had dried, I talked to Blanche and then tried to set up a meeting with me, my boss, and a mediator. This feels like old stuff to me, probably family situations being replayed on both sides. It appears that my assignment is to keep my eye on the suffering that causes such behavior in both her and me, and try not to escalate the situation. Or at least I think that's what it is.

It's quite a contrast between being everyone's hero for taking the injured girl into my space, and being the identified problem in the kitchen. Three more weeks.

Someone asked me why I'm writing these reports since the interaction that's so much a part of the Well is missing. Interesting question. One answer is that I'm writing them to make a record for myself. I wouldn't keep a journal if it were only me and my computer, and I love reading back myself in the journal that I've created for you. Another answer is that typing up these words, rearranging them, stopping to think about them, helps me to clarify what's going on. So I think I'll keep it up for a while longer.

There's also the fantastic fringe benefit of the gift boxes that arrive. Karen sent nearly five pounds of homemade fudge, Sweeney sent her leftover Halloween Tootsie Rolls and also some pralines and chocolate for when I got tired of Tootsie Rolls, and another friend sent some Paul Newman's chocolate bars. Everyone at Tassajara sends you heartfelt thanks, even the mouse who grabbed one of the Tootsie Pops and tried to run out the door with it!

December 2, 2001

This morning I was called to dokusan, right after the woman in the kitchen who I've been having trouble with. It appears that a resolution is in sight. When Blanche and I were through talking about the specifics of the kitchen conflict (which Lord knows we've talked about plenty in the last two days) I told her that I wanted to be porous the way she is. Stuff happens, and it just blows right through her. With me, I can feel the shield form around my chest, feel myself clamp down on my idea of who I am and what I must have. As I said that to Blanche, I began to gesture to the empty zafu sitting off to one side, ready to say "I know that I just have to spend more hours in zazen to get that way" but she was already saying "We get that way by going through exactly the kind of situation that you just went through." So Zen really doesn't just take place on the cushion.

December 4, 2001

Last August, I rented my apartment furnished, and about two weeks ago got a message from my tenant saying he'd be leaving at the end of December. I put my personal stuff in boxes in my cousin's garage and about a week ago got a letter from her saying she was selling her house. I heard about a self-storage place in San Francisco and learned that I could get a good rate from them for long-term storage. I found my mover and he's available the day I need him. I even arranged to have my white couch cleaned before I put it away.

I have no desire to live in San Francisco right now, or to live anywhere but at a Zen Center place. Still, this afternoon, when I got mail from my landlord confirming receipt of my 30 day notice, I found that I felt sad. It's like getting a divorce from someone who you don't much like: relief that it's over is temporarily outweighed by sorrow over such a good idea turning out so badly.

Last night I woke up to find that I was lying in the center of a circle of moonlight, flooding through my round skylight. When I was walking up to the kitchen to start breakfast while everyone else was still sleeping, I was surprised to see that the moon wasn't even full. I've wakened other nights to see it shining other places in my room, but this is the first time it's been on me. I wonder if it does that every night. I suppose so.

December 6, 2001

Yesterday I had the "mediation" meeting with the boss with whom I've had so much trouble. It was really eye-opening. She's not just a meanie, and I'm not just a troublemaker. Work today was very sweet.

I popped my head into the office of the woman who handled the meeting to thank her: "It's things like that that make living at Tassajara so great" was her response. Yes. Watching enmity turn to affection is really moving.

Tears rolled out of my eyes during the meeting. I was thinking about them later during zazen, and it occurred to me that the bottomless lake of sorrow is no longer the source for my frequent crying. These tears were fresh. That lake might be finished.

Some people put together a scheme to chant the entire *Lotus Sutra* from 3 a.m. until noon, and of course the senior staff enthusiastically gave them permission. We used the kaisando, the little building dedicated to Suzuki Roshi. When I entered at 4:30 there were about 20 people sitting on zafus arranged in two rows on either side of the room, chanting along at a good clip. There was a note outside explaining that we were chanting seated for 40 minutes and then while walking around the room for 20 minutes. We each had flashlights and our own copy of the text. So today I chanted for three hours, then helped someone finish sewing a rakusu for his ordination tomorrow, and then happily went to the kitchen. Any one of those things would have been interesting to me today, and it felt like an abundance of riches to have all three available at the same time. I think we're all very aware — I certainly am — that we're down to the last two weeks of this practice period, and everyone's jamming in everything they can.

December 9, 2001

Myo Lahey, the tanto (practice leader) down here, has begun offering brief dokusan -- five minutes, in and out, and I've taken him up on that offer.

The first time we talked, I came back to my room and wrote "Liberation from the illusion of a separate self" on my calendar.

The second time, we talked about renunciation being the primary quality that makes a good priest. He defined renunciation as being free from attachment to stuff and free from a separate sense of self and I asked, "Who wouldn't want that!"

The leaves have nearly all fallen from the trees, and when I walk back to my room at the end of the night I can see the stars in the sky. Yesterday was a work day and one of the crew was out sick, so we were really kicking it. Toward the end of the morning I was getting something from the walk-in, and this thought streaked through my head: What's the difference between doing this and sitting in the zendo. I thought: Nothing! and laughed and kept on getting lunch ready.

Sweeney has been printing out Life 134 and sending it to me, so I saw someone's question about the phrase "sitting for and with all beings." I initially approached "saving all beings" from an angle of making myself into a better person and thus helping the world become a better place. But this is something else. This is moving zazen, moving all the teachings, away from being concerned with what kind of person I am. It's a way of sending my heart/mind out while I'm on the cushion to all beings and knowing that there is no separation between us. It takes remembering to do it, but that's all it takes. And then we're all sitting together, and we're all sitting for each other.

Rohatsu sesshin starts tomorrow. The schedule sounds grueling. Then there's one more great ceremony, a lot of running around, and we're done. And after that: we start again.

December 20, 2001

Well, that's it. One suitcase, two boxes of laundry (because I didn't want the funky kitchen stuff to contaminate the rest of my dirty clothes), and the rug I brought down which turned out to be too fragile for this place are all waiting to get loaded on the truck for the ride to the city tomorrow. My room is both clean and tidy, thermoses and flashlights have been returned to their rightful owners, and I've even done my Christmas cards. It's been pouring rain all day. I worked my last shift in the kitchen yesterday morning. The shuso ceremony was yesterday afternoon. This is a big ceremony where the shuso (head student) is asked a dharma question by each person. Former shusos come from all over Northern California to participate. After the ceremony our group photo is taken and then we have dinner in the dining room. Tomorrow morning we have zazen and a closing ceremony, and after a bowl of cold cereal we hop into cars and leave Tassajara. Some of us are leaving for good - a few who came for just one practice period, others who've been here for a while and are now going back to Green Gulch or City Center, and even one or two who are just getting the hell out of Tassajara.

A lot of tears were shed today. Romance happens here, and failed romance too, and one person is leaving because of it who doesn't want to go. Some foreign students are feeling far from home now that the holidays are on us, and feeling blue about that. Some of us just don't handle endings well. I am so glad I'm one of the ones who's just leaving for vacation and will be coming back. Three months is much too short a time for this thing we do here. Apparently I'll be staying in the same room, which is great. I don't yet know what my job will be. Today I couldn't stand it any longer and asked the director where I'd be assigned, and she said that was usually decided during the first week of the practice period so I just have to wait.

December 23, 2001

I've been back at City Center for a day. I've done my laundry and walked to Safeway to get shampoo and hand cream. I went into the Gap and didn't even get greeted — that's how other I've become. I walked in a big loop from Church and Market down to Flax's and then back through Hayes Valley. I didn't see very many happy people. I was surprised by how many versions of the same thing were available, and how much they all cost.

I helped Blanche make her Stollen for her family last night, the two of us chopping and mixing and washing, chatting along as we did it. I mentioned that I didn't know whether I'd be able to talk with Mel and Reb while I was here, since neither of them had returned the messages I'd left for them earlier. She casually replied that there'd been an Abbot's meeting the day she returned, and she'd told them to find time for me so I can get their permission to start sewing for ordination before I leave the city.

I phoned my friend who was so enthusiastic about the kitchen practice she did during her time at Tassajara. I told her that things had become so difficult for me that I'd actually left the kitchen during the middle of my shift. She laughed and told me that she'd thrown a pot at the fukuten when she reached the same point. Hah. Now she tells me.

December 29, 2001

What I'm doing now is called "interim," the period between practice periods, and I'm staying at City Center while I take care of my business here in San Francisco.

I'm dealing with two primary concerns. One is getting all of my possessions into deep storage, and that's the source of much anxiety. I paw through carefully-packed boxes looking for books and sweaters, shift things from City Center to Tassajara to my cousin's garage and to my old apartment. I shop for plastic storage containers and batteries, Peet's tea and power bars, books and Polarfleece socks. It's endless. So that's one job.

The other is connecting with the abbots and former abbots to talk to them about my ordination. That one's a lot more interesting. After I got Blanche's approval, I think it was November, I placed calls to both Mel and Reb asking for some of their time over the holidays to talk about ordination. Absolutely no response from either of them. I placed more calls, same result. Finally last week I got the word from Reb that it wasn't necessary for us to talk. Blanche and I discussed that with puckered foreheads. Did that mean I was so impossibly bad that there was nothing to talk about, or did it mean that I was such an obvious choice that I should just go ahead? I went over to Green Gulch, where Reb lives, for a ceremony a few nights ago and talked directly to his assistant. She laughed: he meant that he approved.

Last night I took BART over to Berkeley and met with Mel. I got there early and so had to time to sit in the garden in the rain and think again about whether this was what I wanted to do with my life. The answer was yes. Mel and I just sat on chairs in his office and chatted. I started by explaining my lineage, showing him my rakusu which was given to me by his good student Myogen Steve Stücky. Mel asked to see the rakusu and as he held it and stared at it in silence, it was as if he was falling into it. It was quite wonderful. After a bit he handed it back and we talked for about half an hour, when he said "You seem old enough and sober enough to know what you're doing." I said "Is that a yes?" He laughed and said it was and I hollered "Yahoo!"

Today I met for quite a long time with my original teacher Myogen. I've always thought he was hard on me, and wondered what I would do if he denied my request, but our meeting wasn't like that at all. We talked a lot about my experience of the last practice period, and about why I want to be a priest. I told him about my meeting with Mel and he admitted that he'd called ahead and talked to Mel about me. Since I'd brought a letter from Mel back to Blanche by arrangement between the two of them, I knew she had too. I guess the fix was in. When Myogen said that I had his blessing, I hollered again.

On a completely different note, I just ran into a girl who lives here in the building who went down to Tassajara for a few days and stayed in my room. She found a dead mouse under my pillow! I left some vitamins by the sink which I forgot to take on my last morning there, and one of them was pulled apart and scattered around, so the theory is that the mouse ate the gel cap, crawled under the pillow, and died. Euuww.

But that euuww is much softer than the ongoing yahoo.

December 31, 2001

City Center has been a beehive of activity today.

We did the Full Moon Ceremony at 8, and the Buddha Hall was packed. The ino asked me to stand in the front row since I'm familiar with the ceremony and many of the people had never done it before. Fine, but I've just tapered myself off of Premarin, I'm having one continuous hot flash, and the only zendo clothes I brought with me were a wool sweater and fleece pants. We do about 40 full prostrations in the ceremony, and on some of them I was wiping the sweat from my face while my head was on the ground.

After the ceremony (which is beautiful no matter how hot I am) we had temple cleaning: swarms of people in the kitchen and scrubbing the Buddha Hall and cleaning bathrooms and every other inch of the place.

I spent most of the day working at my old apartment, packing up the many things I left behind when I rented the place furnished five months ago. I don't feel sentimental about the place or the stuff, just tired of this move and wanting to get back to the peace and quiet of Tassajara.

January 2, 2002

Tonight's my last night at City Center. This time tomorrow I'll be back at Tassajara — back home. I'm going to try like anything to get something written up about the last few days while I still have Well access.

January 3, 2002

I was so proud of myself for arranging for my move from Tassajara's one telephone. The move was yesterday. Nothing went as planned.

Today my lifetime's accumulation of stuff went into a very funky storage unit in Hayward. I know that State Farm won't insure belongings in storage units, and it's an odd feeling to put everything I own into a little metal building, put a $15 padlock on the door, and drive away for five years. Very odd indeed. I think it will take some getting used to. My mind keeps turning back to everything lumped together in the darkness, the couch, the art, the clothes, getting used to its new situation, settling in in a new configuration for a long snooze.

During my first Tassajara practice period, I had a profound experience of "no coming or going." As I was working up to being quite upset at having to leave, I understood that that was impossible. That I couldn't leave Tassajara and Tassajara couldn't leave me. And that has indeed been the case. In the same way, I understand that I can't leave Blanche and she can't leave me. At our parting this morning, I told her that I didn't have words to thank her with, and could only thank her with my life.

Waiting to Enter the Zendo

Winter 2002
3rd Tassajara
Practice Period

January 8, 2002

Only by typing that date do I realize that I've only been back at Tassajara five days. Once again, leaving the city and coming in here it feels like I never left, like the two weeks in the city was a dream that happened while I was asleep in my bed here by Tassajara Creek.

The tangaryo (first time) students have arrived, and are sitting their obligatory five days. It's rough: just sitting, with no walking meditation to unkink the legs, no dharma talks to distract or inspire the mind, just the self and the wall for five days straight. During my second practice period last fall, my mind was always turned toward the zendo and I felt great appreciation for their effort. This time I just feel sorry for them, and make as much noise as I can around the zendo to give them something to listen to.

Returning and continuing students are working around the place for this time before the practice period begins. I've been mostly working in the garden, pruning roses and hauling old berry vines up to the burn piles. Tassajara has two "benji trucks," so named because they're driven by the benji, who's the assistant to the head student, when they haul garbage to the compost area. They are horrible things, old beat up blue Toyota mini pickups, and I've really enjoyed roaring around in the one of them that's currently running. When we couldn't get the truck to start this morning, my partner and I lifted the hood to take a look, and found a teabag sitting on the carburetor. I wish we could say we removed it and the truck started, but no such luck. It took a push and popping the clutch to start it on compression, with a great roar of noise and fumes right under the zendo.

As these days pass, it's becoming clear who's going to be on the doan ryo, and I'm not one of them. These are the five people who are the big cheeses in the zendo: they hit the han (the wooden board outside the zendo) to call everyone to the zendo, hit the bells to start and end zazen and guide us through service, head up the serving crews, and so on. These are the glamour jobs, to my way of thinking at least, and it's amazing how much I wanted to have one of them. I'm watching my mind work it, noticing how the disappointment feels, watching it lurch forward to the next bit of glory to want. Here in this practice of non-attainment, there seems to be an ample supply of things to want to attain. And here in the land of monastic living, we aren't freed from ambition and competitiveness: being here just gives me a better shot at seeing them for what they are.

January 9, 2002

I didn't know what a habit I had of looking in the direction of the Abbess's cabin until I came back to Tassajara without Blanche. How I miss those shoes outside the door.

I've mentioned the shuso a number of times, but probably haven't said that much about what it is. The shuso is the "head student," and there's one for each practice period. A shuso is someone who's been around for a long time and knows the forms thoroughly. They're usually a priest, and hopefully have some knowledge/wisdom about the teachings. They sit next to the abbess in the zendo and, if the shuso's a priest, s/he does morning service on a regular rotation.

The shuso ceremony is held at the end of the practice period: everyone in the zendo, including past shusos who come in just for the event, ask him/her a dharma question. Once the shuso has completed that ceremony, they're considered qualified to teach.

The shuso lives in the first cabin across the bridge from the zendo, a highly visible spot, and the cabin's small and unheated. The work of the shuso is always cleaning the toilets and tending the compost. The shuso's assistant, usually a younger student and hopefully young and strong, is called the Benji.

Our last shuso, Marta, showed us what it means to be a monk/shuso, down to and including leaving the door to her cabin propped open all day, even in the coldest weather. Marta's originally from Colombia, and she's a rascal. But when she was shuso, she was totally straight ahead good. She talked about it toward the end of the practice period, of the relief of being submerged in the role and letting go of "Marta."

Last night I sat and chatted with our new shuso-to-be (since the installation ceremony hasn't taken place yet). He's one of the Green Gulch people, one of those big easygoing guys who I like so much. He last lived here four years ago, and so of course I asked about his re-entry whether he, like I, quickly had the sense that he'd never left. He said the most striking thing was his realization of what a privilege it is to be here. I had that strongly at the end of the last practice period (just a few weeks ago?!?), a sense that there were myriad beings supporting us here, and that those of us living here are unbelievably lucky to have the combination of time, financial resources, and interest that have led us to this place. Our new shuso and I agreed that it was a significant flip of the mind from grousing over how uncomfortable we are to gratitude for being here, and then we laughed and went our separate ways.

Putting everything into storage meant that I brought a lot more stuff back down here with me. Boxes and boxes more. I keep thinking about "renunciation" as I watch myself being unable to part with one of my multiple sweaters, flashlights, sleeping bags, robes, hats and so on. All I can do right now is put away some of the duplicates in storage here, figuring it'll be like a free store when the stuff I'm using now is worn out or lost. I keep thinking about the mind that needed to buy all this stuff. I also keep remembering a guy at City Center saying "The more you have, the more you have to take care of."

January 14, 2002

Linda Ruth said yes.

She was the last of the Abbots whose permission I had to get before I could begin the next step in ordination. Since I knew she'd be down here to lead this practice period, I didn't try to get together with her over interim.

I was the second person in to see her for dokusan after she arrived.

I started crying immediately. I've been doing this every time I see her, simply because she's not Blanche. First I got used to the Abbots' cabin without Blanche's shoes outside the door, and now I have to get used to the Abbots' cabin with other shoes outside the door. I really didn't want to cry in front of Linda Ruth, especially to start this discussion, but my tears are stronger than my willpower. So first we talked about missing Blanche, and about coming and going. Then we talked about me and why I want to ordain.

Linda Ruth's was the scariest of these discussions, because she emphasized the dangers I'll face after ordination. She talked about the way people, even our close friends, project things on us once we're "a priest." She said that we also become more sexually attractive to some people then, too, and the dangers this presents. I talked with her about the difficulties I've had in this area, calling sex my "Achilles body." I told her, as I've told the others in these interviews, about the affair I had when I was back out in the world between my first and second practice periods. The way I like to tell it is, The Buddha sat under the bodhi tree and Mara tried to distract him with sex and the Buddha said "no thanks"; I decided to come to Tassajara, Mara said "sex?" and I said "sure!" with disastrous consequences. Linda Ruth and I therefore talked about ordaining being too hard to do without help. When she asked whether I had any questions for her, at the end of our conversation, I said, "Yes. Will you help me?" She said she would.

When I left the cabin, I thought service had started in the zendo because I could hear scores of voices chanting "All Buddhas ten directions three times" but they were still sitting zazen up there and it was totally quiet. It was my trickster friend the Creek again, putting sounds in my ears that weren't really there.

My dear Ben is Linda Ruth's jisha, the person who accompanies her to and from the zendo and arranges her dokusan appointments. We wait to talk to her in the founder's hall, which is called the kaisando, a small building dedicated to Suzuki Roshi that is just about 20 feet away from the Abbot's cabin. When I went back in the kaisando, because we wait there after dokusan until it's time to re-enter the zendo, Ben and another guy were sitting. When it was just the two of us, I leaned over and whispered to Ben "She said yes." A couple of minutes later, when I was heading toward the zendo for lunch, Greg came running up on tiptoe -- because the paths are gravel and every step can be heard by the people sitting zazen -- whispered "Congratulations" and hugged me.   In the 60 seconds between my telling Ben and walking toward the zendo, the news had begun to spread. I returned the hug and whispered "Will you help me?" "Until the day we die" was his answer.

But up by the zendo, waiting for the bell to ring to enter, I felt scared by what Linda Ruth had said. Can I really do this? Is it really what I want? Then I thought of Marta talking about the relief in being "the shuso" instead of "Marta" and I remembered that being less of This and more of That is what I came here for. So yes I want it, and with help I can do it.

January 16, 2002

First, the weather report. It's cold! The mornings have been in the low to mid-20s for the last few days, and last night was the first time I woke up and thought I needed another blanket. Right now it's 9:30 in the morning and the thermometer says it's 53 degrees here in my fancy insulated room.   I'm sitting right by the fire, which has been burning since about 7:30, wearing heavyweight thermal underwear, flannel lined pants, a heavy wool sweater and a hat. I have on cashmere socks under Polartec 300 socks, and my feet are still like blocks of ice. It's cold!

So here's what happened on the job thing.   During tangaryo week, when we were all doing general labor, I spent two days hauling old blackberry vines to a burn pile down in the flats. My partner was a 21 year old girl. I of course kept up with her. Even enjoyed it. But of course this screwed up my back again. So I told the work leader I needed a non-physical job, and she put me in the library for a couple of days.   The library. Warm. Quiet. Full of books. Yes.

While I was waiting to find out who was going to take the sixth doan position, hoping desperately it would be me, I mentioned to one of the seniors that I wouldn't mind being librarian. It's always been a part time job, and I figured I could work it in. Besides I surely wanted it to look like I didn't care about any big fancy jobs.   The morning after the Abbess arrived, we had the opening ceremony and the jobs were announced. I'm the librarian. And the first thing the woman who got the sixth doan seat said to me when were out of the zendo was "You lucky dog."

And of course she's right. I putter around on my own, getting familiar with the stock, even sometimes lying down in a patch of sun to read a book, finding miscategorized books and getting them where they belong, thinking how the place can be improved (a section on sex and spirituality! a section on work and spirituality! a section of spiritual biographies, which I happen to love!). People know where to find me during work period and stop by to say hey.

It occurred to me that when I came to Zen Center in the first place, I was running away from the overly responsible position I held at the very small dharma center I'd been a part of, and all I wanted was a chance to sit down in the back row and do some zazen. Now, three years later, I have that chance. This job thing is really just more Taking It Personally. Waiting to hear what job I've been assigned is really just waiting to hear whether or not they love me. When I already know that they, whoever "they" are, do. Entirely. And I already know that this one, just as she is, this body and mind, however anyone on the outside feels about her, however I on the inside feel about her, is my best vehicle for awakening, and is totally adequate to the task.

January 20, 2002

Hard. Hard hard hard. Tears for days.

It's about people. It's about expectations and desire and open hearts walking into sucker punches. It's about being called on my shit, both by others and by myself. Aren't you tired of this? Doesn't this sound like just where I was during my practice period in the kitchen? Isn't it, like, This again? Well, me too.

I came here for mystic revelations and deep insights into the nature of all being, and I get girls blowing me off on personal days and boys calling me rude. And so, the way I'm wired, I brood and I cry. And that's what I've been doing.

When I came back to my room mid-day, I wrote on a card "It's not difficult because you're here, you're here because it's difficult." Then I had a pb&j in the courtyard with a friend who's a very young priest. When I told her that I was suffering, she said that it helped her to remember the emptiness of all things, and that there's no one here to suffer. I told her that telling myself stuff like that in the middle of the event just made it worse, since I was then not only in pain but also being a Bad Buddhist.

Linda Ruth taught on the *Sandokai* last night and explained that the character "*San*" stood for the absolute, "*do*" is the relative, and "*kai*" is their overlapping; so I told my friend that maybe it's like that, that we have to both admit our pain and also remember that there's ultimately no-self to be in pain, to hold both of those truths at the same time in the same place.

Wendy Johnson, the longtime head gardener at Green Gulch, is here for a month and has been coming into the library to write in the afternoons. After letting her get some work done, at the very end of work period, I asked her my question this way: "We all come here to study the Buddha dharma, and yet once we're here we spend a lot of our time and energy on getting along with other people. Does that mean that getting along with other people *is* the Buddha dharma?" Wendy said yes, just as I thought she would, and she reminded me that there is nothing that's not Buddha dharma. I saw the fallacy in my thinking, in creating a universe where *this* qualified but *that* didn't. What a disappointment!

Don't you wish just as much as I do that there really were a monastery I could go to where all we did was swan around in beautiful black robes and everything was peace and love all the time? I don't know, maybe that really is the monastery I got, it's just really hard to see it sometimes.

Tomorrow we start a three day sesshin. I was worried about carrying these tears and fears into the zendo for extra long sittings, but now I think I'll be all right.

We got a little sun after lunch, and everyone stripped off their Polartec and then we all froze when we went back into the shade at tea time. I wonder whether being so cold all the time is contributing to my touchiness and tears. Could be.

January 24, 2002

The three day sesshin is over. On the first day, I talked with Myo Lahey, tanto (head of practice) here and someone I've been gradually forming a relationship with. I got scared of carrying that black mood into sesshin, so I bleated for help, and I got it.

As I described the mood, the events, the stuff with people, it became clear that what I was looking for was a trick to use the next time that (very familiar) mood came on, a trick so that I wouldn't have to feel that way. So we talked about that, and about remaining upright with the feelings that are arising (or coming at me, as it sometimes feels).

We talked about my confusion between psychology and Buddhism, and he said there was no real difference, but that modern psychology had just given us a new vocabulary for dealing with the same old problems. And finally he said, "And, as you know, all of these words are just a raft and have to be thrown away anyway." It was electrifying. I didn't know that at all! What was he talking about? He reminded me of the teaching that all of this is just a raft to get us across the river, and once we're there we get rid of the raft. It then seemed that all I was trying to do was build a better raft with all of my thinking and scheming and planning. So my slogan for the rest of sesshin became "No new rafts."

Myo's helping me with my move toward ordination, and one thing he said in passing was that after ordination we have less private life and a more public one. He also said something about "Becoming not *a* Buddha but becoming Buddha" and something about all beings in the universe rejoicing when one ordains. The next day I pissed off someone again, one of the doans during a doan/librarian exchange. When I pissed off a guy a couple of days earlier, he called me rude and I burst into tears. When this one said he felt I hadn't shown him respect I felt the tears come near and then instead rushed to defend myself. The first one said "I just wanted to get this off my chest" and the second said "I'm telling you this because I care about you." This gave me a lot to think about when we went back into the zendo. What am I here for? Am I here to learn social skills? Am I supposed to learn a way of behaving that will never irritate anyone again? I worked up a good head of steam about being myself and they could all take it or leave it. But that leaves out kindness, so that's not the answer either.

Linda Ruth gave dharma talks every day. She's emphasizing a very precise way of using the forms, talking to us about using old fashioned setsu sticks instead of rubber spatulas in our oryoki, about keeping our robes clean and in repair, about how we bow, and so on. She does this in a very general way, and it's easy to absorb, easy to feel it as being aimed at the assembly as a whole and not right at me. Still, I heard it when she talked about the injunction against idle chatter. And so while I was talking to Myo I made a commitment to do that. There's more to Right Speech than just not gossiping.

Today's dining room lunch was strange indeed. Just as Linda Ruth said, there were great silences. I watched the stuff race through my head that I'd normally say to liven things up, mostly stories about myself, and just let them go and held my tongue.

During sesshin I watched myself spin stories about the other people here, and then watched myself plunge into suffering over those stories. I watched it but I continued to do it. Today I talked with Kathy on the phone and she said that her teacher Katharine said that the third practice period at Tassajara is about just that: learning that the one who makes me miserable is me. Buddha dharma. Being upright.

February 4, 2002

One personal day to prepare for a nine day sesshin. Just typing it makes me shudder. Nine days. The longest sesshin I've ever done is seven days. I used to do 16 and even 30 day retreats when I was a Vipassana student, but those are much easier than this thing we do.

During zazen last night, Linda Ruth spoke. "Pace yourself" is one thing she said. Her sesshins are in the old style, and they're easier than the totally silent "sesshins without toys" that Blanche prefers. There's a dharma talk every day, tea is served (with a cookie!) in the zendo in the afternoon, and we rise and go to bed at the same time as on our regular schedule. Still, they manage to stretch the day out and insert extra zazen (cutting study hall and shortening work period) and there's all that silence and no reading or writing to deal with. Okay. I'll stop whining and do it, one period at a time.

In general, these last few days I've been overwhelmed by gratitude. This way of life is so amazing, and being allowed to live it is such a privilege. I've been waiting and waiting for my okesa fabric so I could start the long process of sewing that leads to ordination, and finally gave up and cut myself a black rakusu during the last sewing class. The okesa is the large rectangle that gets draped over our robes, and it takes months to make. The rakusu is the simpler bib-like rectangle that lay people wear in blue and priests wear in black when they're not wearing their okesa. It's usually sewn last, or sewn by members of the sangha, but I went ahead and started mine because I so feel the need to do *something*.

After I'd marked the black fabric, coming at it with scissors was quite a moment. Having started, there's no stopping, no unfinished rakusus or okesas, no room for second thoughts. I bowed to the fabric, blinked my eyes to clear the tears, and cut.

Did I tell you that it snowed for 36 hours? Fantastic! I was a server that morning. We put the pots of food on tables set on the porch behind the zendo, and bring them in at the signal. There's always lots of standing still, hugging ourselves and shifting from foot to foot in the cold outside air. That morning there was standing and staring at the landscape as the snow fell. The minute the last serving chore was finished, I ran to my room and got my camera and shot off a roll of film. I even got some shots of the Abbess building a snowman with the children.

One afternoon I took a walk down by the flats for exercise. There was still a thin layer of snow on the ground in the shade and I saw blades of grass poking through little tiny melted spots. It looked to me as if their energy had melted the snow, and I hoped to run into Wendy so I could ask her about this. It didn't take long: I stopped at the baths on the way back, and I was in the plunge when she walked out on the deck. I hopped out and we had a conversation about grass and snow and energy, me naked and steaming, she fully clothed. Conversation over, I went back to the plunge. She slid the door open and handed me a pelargonium leaf she'd pinched off: "Here, goddess, smell this." I still have the leaf in my room. It certainly smells good.

Having the little kids here is such a blessing. I think I told you there are two young families participating in this practice period, sharing child care and zendo time. The little girl, Olivia, is 2 ½ ; the little boy, Lucas, is a little less than a year older. I found myself in their vicinity with bubble soap in my pocket one day, and we all learned together that if I blew bubbles the puppy would jump for them. Now I have little bottles of bubble soap in all my jacket pockets. One night I was coming down from serving dinner, rushing through the dark, in my robes, hat pulled down to my eyebrows, and Olivia, riding past on her father's shoulder, called out "The Bubble Lady!" Amazing.

Last night she topped that. I happened to be heading in the same direction as Olivia and her mother and walked alongside them. Olivia was crying: she'd fallen in the dining room and hurt herself. I said some words to her as the three of us walked together, she continued to cry, and then she said something through her tears. Her mother translated: it was "How's your booboo?" I scalded my hand filling my hot water bottle a few days ago and got a spectacular burn. The hand has been wrapped in gauze and is just now recovering. I've found it all pretty interesting. The amazing thing to me was that this little baby found a moment in her own pain to reach out to me and ask about mine. I think this must be what good parenting brings.

It's getting increasingly hard to find time to write these reports. One day during zazen I began to wonder whether this is the best use of my time. I also wonder about my photography, in spite of a current spate of recognition in that area. Both the words and pictures can too easily be used to shield myself from experience rather than open further to it. For now I'm going to try writing less frequently and photographing more selectively, and we'll see what happens in the future.

February 14, 2002

End of the nine day sesshin.
Whew.
Linda Ruth is a wonderful teacher. She lays out the dharma very clearly and invites us to take a look. She also is impeccable in her own practice and invites us to be the same, and so during lectures she continues to talk to us about oryoki and bowing and posture/breath, the things that you'd think people who've made it to Tassajara would know all about already but hey we don't. Today is the day that Shakyamuni Buddha went into nirvana (also known as: died) and so she read to us from the *Parinirvana Sutra*. All these elements were woven into her daily lectures. They were pretty stunning.

A burned hand doesn't hurt so much at the time of the accident, but the recovery is grueling. I sat with considerable pain while the poor thing went through its changes.

I had dokusan on about the third day of sesshin. First I told her that I was having trouble breathing, that I felt like I was strangling. I told her that I thought that we'd put the snake in the tube (a common expression of what we're doing here, though I still don't know why we want straight snakes) and then stuffed an okesa in too, and there wasn't enough room to breathe. We talked about that. And then we talked about my hand. I told her that I kept thinking "My pretty hand! All scarred!" She replied that someone had once said to her, when she was having similar thoughts, "What do you want to do, have a good complexion or be a Zen master." I want to be a Zen master.

Later the same day, I was sitting out on the deck in the sun trying to write to you, a friend came along, another friend appeared, we had lunch, we cut each other's hair, and buzzed around with all the other details that seem necessary on a personal day. Suddenly it was time to robe up and race to the zendo for service and dinner. While I was there I remembered there were two more packages for me on the shelves that I'd noticed and forgotten to open. So I went back down after dinner and there were the fabric for my okesa and six pounds of homemade fudge from Karen. Now that was a good mail call.

Back to the nine day sesshin. My energy came and went. It's common to be tired at the start of sesshin and then to pick up some mysterious energy from the zazen and find that the practice is more interesting than sleep or food or even a pain-free body. My body seemed surprised to be asked to keep sitting after seven days, since that's the usual length of sesshin.

I had a practice discussion scheduled with Leslie on the 8th day, and asked her if there was really any point to sitting on my zafu doing nothing but being tired and grumpy. She talked beautifully about following the schedule completely, and about how doing that breaks our idea that we can and should control our lives. She also said that zazen is way bigger than some idea I might have of what it should look like, and that it's plenty large enough to contain my temporary discomfort. It was inspiring enough that I could go back to the zendo and finish out the schedule without a problem.

When sesshin finished this morning, I went right to the stone office to look for mail. My teacher Myogen printed out some of these reports that I sent him, and wrote comments on them. So when others came into the office they found me holding his letter and howling with laughter.

February 22, 2002

The loneliness has really been getting to me. We're all sleep-deprived and irritable and I'm trying to find the line between being kind to others and taking care of myself and failing, failing, failing. The romantic bubble I built around someone sitting across the zendo from me has burst, and it's come home to me that I'm here to study Buddha dharma and not to find romance. And that I really do have to choose between those two, at least as long as I'm in priest training and committed to remaining here at Tassajara..

Yesterday at work meeting Leslie announced that she'd be unavailable for a couple of weeks. Later that day I asked whether I could have practice discussion before she left. She explained that last night and this morning were the only possible times, thought it over, and set a time. But when I showed up this morning during the second period of zazen, after a first period spent planning for our talk, she said there'd been a mix-up, she was waiting for someone else and wouldn't have time to see me.

I took a fast walk in the dark, adjusting my head as best I could, got back into the zendo in time for the second period, and spent it with my head in the crook of my elbow crying. When the robe chant came, I didn't put on my rakusu. When the bell rang for service, I quickly walked out of the zendo. I went into the kitchen for sick food about half an hour later, and talked with Anke, the day's breakfast cook. She said "Are you sick?" I said "Mentally." She said "A lot of people are feeling that way." I talked about feeling unsupported here, being out on my own without a teacher to talk to. Myo's away, another one seems to have taken a dislike to me, and Leslie stood me up. And that's the selection.

We talked about Blanche, of course, and a light bulb came on over my head. I ran to my room, got my Palm Pilot, and ran to the phone in the stone office. Since everyone was still in the zendo having breakfast, the phone was free and I could have some privacy. Blanche answered. She wanted to talk about setting up further calls, but I asked if we could talk about the difficulties of the moment. She told me the story about dealing with her internal needy little girl and I pointed out that I'd done that to a large extent. I hate being pop psyched when I'm in despair, even if it's Blanche who's doing it. But she hit the mark when I cried, "This is too hard, I don't think I'm strong enough to do it." "You are" she said, "You are."

We concluded the conversation by trading information about other people, including several who are having health problems both here and in the city. I was placated but not satisfied.

I roamed around a bit. The student body was now out of the zendo and on their break. A couple of women, the ones who'd heard the sounds of sniffling and nose-blowing in the zendo and paid attention when I exited, whispered encouraging words in my direction. One of the ones who are chronically ill suggested going back to bed and getting some sleep. But that wasn't what I needed.

A walk, I thought. So I set out toward the flats. But instead of going straight by the bathhouse, I hung a sharp right at the small sign that says "Path" and went up to the Suzuki Roshi memorial. It's a sharp climb on a narrow dirt trail, with a gentle nearly-straight stretch just before the final bend. It was on that stretch that I started calling to him. "Suzuki Roshi, help me. Suzuki Roshi, it's me, it's too hard, I can't do it. Suzuki Roshi I'm lonely." I walked in circles in the clearing in front of his memorial as I talked. Finally I knelt down -- no, it was more of a crouch than a kneel — I was still doing none of the forms, no bows, no rakusus, no incense, no chants — and put my head on the rock that serves as his altar. Before I did, I noticed that one branch above the large rock that stands in tribute to our founder was gently nodding up and down. I checked: it was the only branch in the clearing that was moving. I'm just saying.

"It's all zazen" is what entered my head. "Nothing is excluded from zazen. This right here, kneeling in the dirt and crying, this is zazen. zazen is much bigger than you can imagine, and it's all there is for you to do. Come back to this moment. You don't have to worry about being a priest, being poor, having or not having romantic attachments. Just relax into the zazen of this moment and let the other stuff go." Thank you Suzuki Roshi.

The rest of the morning continued strange, almost dreamlike. My boys came to my side with their own brand of helpfulness: Greg asked how my burn was doing ("How's your owie?" he whispered) and Ben asked whether I still had a good supply of the jasmine tea I like so much. Mostly I felt protected from likes and dislikes, from abundance and lack, by the immense bubble of zazen that included it all.

February 28, 2002

I talked to Blanche again yesterday, quite by accident. When we got to the part where I whispered into the telephone about going up to the Suzuki Roshi memorial and receiving his help, she boomed out "Did he talk to you?" When I said yes she again, she boomed "Lou" (her husband) "does that all the time!" Oh. Maybe it's just that easy.

Yesterday was a workday, and we always have dining room lunch on workdays — left over soups, some starch, some salad, either leftover or fresh. I got my food and went out to the lawn in front of the stone office and ate on the grass with a group of people. The families were over on the other end of the lawn, and the kids ran back and forth between the groups, begging bites of cake and dodging the boys playing hacky-sack. There are clumps of daffodils everywhere and we were sitting under an old tree that was covered with sweet-smelling white flowers. People began to move away, and eventually Greg and I were left alone, leaning against the old stone wall, watching our friends playing. "Oh yes," I said to him, "This is certainly hell."

March 1, 2002

I went out to the chiropractor yesterday; a whole minibus full of us went. Kosho drove and all the rest of us were women. I said we should have a sign for the side of the Suburban saying "Transport for the Institutionalized Mentally Ill" because that's probably what we looked like anyway. When I called out, "Do we have to go back so soon Dr. Kosho?" in front of the Monterey Whole Foods, he didn't think it was funny. But the point I started to make is, the world looked just awful. We were at Del Monte shopping center, which is one of those upscale places that people work all their lives to be able to shop at, and it looked like the living dead driving Porsches and Mercedes to me. It was really a shock. I'd become bored and restless here in the valley, but my excursion (we hit two or three other shopping centers in our relentless search for *stuff*) made me very very grateful to be here. I will say this: the chiropractor fixed my back quite nicely.

March 3, 2002

I just had a blowup with another woman one who I'd been becoming friends with, who'd been cold to me lately, and this was the time she chose to tell me why. At the start of the conversation I said "I have a feeling I'm not going to like this" and I was right. It was brief because I walked off. She came to find me and apologized for the last thing she'd said, the thing that set me off, but by that time I was too angry to talk. So frustrating.

As I was walking back to my room, the shuso came along. "I want to practice in a cave far away from all these irritating people" I told him. A standard Tassajara opener. We talked about it in the courtyard, and then as we walked toward his cabin. "What is it?" I asked for the millionth time, "All we want is to be kind to each other -- no, that's not necessarily true. What is it we want?!?"   "The way I see it" he answered "Is that what we want is to be loved. But since that's grasping, and love is ungraspable, we take what we can get, and that's attention, either positive or negative."

It certainly makes sense to me. It certainly jibes with this strange thing we do here of stopping people in their tracks to tell them what's wrong with them.

March 7, 2002

In between the two chunks of time we spend in the zendo in the morning, we have a one-hour "study hall." It's become one of my favorite parts of the day.   Study hall takes place in the dining room, and we're asked to read Buddhist books but we're also allowed to sew sacred things. At first I read *Branching Streams Flow in the Darkness*, Suzuki Roshi's lectures on the *Sandokai*, then I listened to tapes of Reb Anderson's famous sesshin where he lectured on sex, and now I'm sewing on my okesa.

There are two parts to the dining room: the front part, which is where everyone sits because it's heated, and the back part, which is where a few of us sit because it has lots of elbow room. It also has sun streaming in the windows at this time of year, and sometimes I get in the downdraft from the stick of incense that the servers have left burning and I look up from whatever I'm doing and utter a little sigh of gratitude at how beautiful it is. The windows look east toward the back of some dumpy little cabins, at a huge rock which is covered with moss, at lots of trees, and at the creek. While I was listening to Reb's tapes I stationed myself at the window and gazed and gazed and gazed.

But now I sit at a special sewing table that's kept clean and has two lamps for the sewers to use. The okesa joke is that we take a perfectly good piece of cloth, cut it up, and sew it back together again. okesas were originally made from fabric found in the charnel grounds, but that was a long time ago. Now they're made from the nicest cotton we can afford. Blanche found me a cotton that's so fine it feels like silk. Since this is Zen, our basic okesas are black. It will be a rectangle with seven panels, and I'll wear it over one shoulder, wrapped around my body over my priest's sitting robe. It's all sewn by hand, with tiny little stitches that appear like dots. I'm sewing with a medium gray thread, so the stitch is evident but it doesn't shout for attention. Every time we put the needle into the fabric we say "Namu," every time we pierce the fabric in the next spot we say "Kie," and when we pull it through we say "Butsu." Which means, "I take refuge in Buddha." This is said, of course, only in our minds, since we sew in silence. I'll take thousands of these stitches and take that refuge thousands of times before the garment is finished. Some of sewing has to do with how you work the needle, but at least as much has to do with how you hold and move the fabric the needle's going into. My left hand -- my holding hand -- has a fresh big angry red scar from my accident with the scalding water, and working with the fabric right under the light gives it such prominence. It's quite a contrast between the beauty of the garment and the scar on the hand holding it. Sometimes I stop sewing and look at it closely, and I think of Linda Ruth's "Do you want a good complexion, or do you want to be a Zen master." I still want to be a Zen master.

Yesterday was rainy and warm (probably around 50 degrees). Greg sat across the sewing table from me, working on the ties that will hold his okesa together. He's nearly finished sewing, and his ordination is on April 20th. I was putting the short seams in my second of seven panels. Myo was sitting at another table off to my left. Sonja, the head of housekeeping, was sitting behind me, laughing quietly at whatever she was reading. Julia, a tangaryo student, was over by the window, head on the table, softly snoring. The puppy came rushing into the room, tired and bored from being cooped up in the rain. He's about ten months old now, and it looks like he's going to work out. Last September I was predicting otherwise, but Sonja took him in hand and got him trained and he's settling in. But yesterday morning he was anything but settled, hopping around the room with his chew toys, looking for a pal. Myo, of all people, our elegant and strict practice leader, grabbed the end of the toy and pulled it and the dog back and forth. The rest of us looked up from what we were doing, smiled, and then went back to our work. This is sangha.

I've been given permission to step outside the schedule and call Blanche during breakfast once a week. With two phones, one of which is often broken, for 61 people, calling her while everyone else is stuck in the zendo is the only way I can be sure of being able to call, with the bonus that I'll have a bit of privacy. It's a good time for her, too, between service and breakfast at City Center. I had to get the permission of the practice committee, and I like to imagine someone saying "Yeah, let her do it, maybe it will calm her down a little" since it's unusual to be allowed to break ranks with the group, but who knows. It was sweet talking to her this week. We talk a little about her (she just had a cataract removed from one eye) a little about me ("Ordaining just makes you a bigger screen for people to project onto") and a little about sangha members both here and there. I'm very lucky indeed to have such a relationship with such a woman.

People are starting to talk about the summer, about where we'll be living and what our new jobs will be, and I'm not taking it very well. I'm so pleased with things as they are, I don't at all want to rush into changing them. Yesterday I went down to the barns, which is where students live in the summer. They're not used for housing during practice periods, when we live in the rooms that our rich guests occupy during the summer. If I get my choice (and I probably will), between April and September I'll be living in a roughly finished room about 7' by 10' with a screened window facing the creek. I'm going to ask if I can keep looking after the library, but that's not a fulltime job during the summer, so I'm also going to ask if I can work in the office. But that's nearly a month away, and now, at 7:15 at night, it's 45 degrees outside and I have a cozy fire burning in my wood stove in my large luxurious room while I write to you. And now the han's started for zazen so I have to go.

March 10, 2002

I did my taxes yesterday. It looks like Uncle Sam is going to give me the big lesson in renunciation. This is the 16th year I've paid taxes as an independent contractor, and I never got good at it. So the government is going to take the final pittance I still have in the bank, and I'm going to be, at age 58, back to zero or even (because the return's not entirely done yet) slightly in the hole.

This was a shock to me. I knew I'd owe money, but not this much. So this money is – was -- my escape money, my rainy day money, my money I'll need if I have a health problem. Wow. And now it's gone. Many people my age become full time monks thanks to pensions or inheritances, and then they can afford to live on the $150 a month that Zen Center pays us and still have nice clothes and cars and maybe smaller fears about their future. But this really is what I had to do, and this was really the only way I had to do it.

On the zafu, of course, this is all much on my mind. Now, half a day later, it feels as if I'm beginning to see a way to let this be all right, and to even more completely take my daredevil high wire self and throw her into her heart's desire. Once again, my bluff has been called.

March 11, 2002

This morning my head was still blab blab blabbing away for the first two periods of zazen, so I took Pema Chodron's book *When Things Fall Apart* to study hall. What a great book. On the page I happened to open it to, she's talking about her first years in the monastery, and she says, "In the first years it was like being boiled alive. In a place where there was so much practice and study going on, I could not get lost in trying to justify myself and blame others. That kind of exit was not available." But then she goes on to talk about how things falling apart is the best thing that can happen, that we can be given a chance to see beyond the illusion of security and control, and that finally we can learn to become the calm point in the middle of chaos. So the section has a happy ending.

So let me stand up and say this about myself: I've never been good at taking care of money. I'm a greed type (the other choices being anger or delusion) and my style is to want-take-have or, more exactly, want-charge-have. I thought I could neatly deal with the fruits of this way of living in one bold stroke, but not so. I'm going to be paying the price for my long attempt to buy happiness for some time to come.

I'm writing this during the break between lunch and work meeting. I see my reflection in the glass on a Myumi Oda print across the room. I'm lit by the sun from the skylight, I have on a straw hat from the Amish people (quite natty actually), my Dogen Zen t-shirt, and I'm working on my laptop. The rest of me is in shadow. That must be what I look like, and this must be who I am.

March 12, 2002

Continued signs of spring abound at Tassajara.   Outside my window, the huge Maple still has blossoms. The old-timers said that they used to have maple blossom tempura in the zendo at this time of year. Then they all laughed. I guess we don't eat like that any more.   The gardeners stuck a bunch of willow sticks in the ground down by the baths, part of a project to suck the soap out of the water from the bathhouse before it returns to the creek. A few days ago I noticed that those twigs had signs of life, and yesterday those signs of life turned into little green leaves. What an agreeable tree the willow is!

Once I was inside the bathhouse, one of the women was pointing and gesturing, making her hand go quack quack quack. In silence, dripping water from the showers, five or six of us moved over to the wall of windows to see the two migrating ducks that were swimming on the creek.

After we eat a meal in the zendo, we all stand at our places while the priest leads us through three bows and then gracefully exits through the door that's been opened for them. Last night after dinner, a little bat flew in the open door and swooped and glided around the room. I actually managed to bow once just as he was heading toward my corner, but there was nothing I could do to disguise my instinctive fear when he came at me again while we were filing out. There were grins on many faces and I was smiling too, at the same time as I was cowering.   I'm not afraid of the bat, just of the unpleasantness of having him come too close and get caught in my 3/8" long hair.

Best of all, during zazen last night the frogs started croaking. Tassajara is built along Tassajara creek, and it's intersected by Cabarga Creek. Cabarga has been flowing since the heavy rains started, and it's nearly dried up now. That's where the sounds came from; there must have been tadpoles waiting in the mud for the mud to warm up. If the frogs are back, can the crickets be far behind?

March 13, 2002

I was listening to the tapes of Reb's March 2001 sesshin again today. He offers celibacy as a chance to "be committed to something without being attached to it." It just occurred to me during the last period of zazen before lunch that this is true, too, of the renunciation of material wealth. If I grab onto that particular form of renunciation and use it as another way to solidify a sense of self ("Hi, I'm willing to be poor!") then I'm grasping and I'm entirely losing the point. Thanks, Reb.

March 16, 2002

This is the end of the second day of being off the schedule with the flu. It's just a little flu with chills and fever and being very tired, and it's also an epidemic (at first there were two of us, and by dinner time today there were six) so I know it's not all in my head. I've had a pretty pleasant time, lying in bed and reading books, listening to tapes (of dharma talks), and receiving visitors.

Today I read *Cave in the Snow*, the story of Tenzin Palmo, an Englishwoman who became an ordained Tibetan nun and stayed in a cave for 12 years meditating. It's full of good stuff. There was one passage I wanted to find to quote to you but couldn't, so I have to do it from memory. She was talking about renunciation and said it's not stuff like hair, clothes, or a home that we renounce. It's ideas. It's our very sense of self. I of course thought of Cathleen on the day I gave my cat Blue away telling me, as I sobbed, "Oh it will get much worse than that." Maybe that's what she meant.

March 20, 2002

I've talked about the problem we have at Tassajara with mice and raccoons, but I haven't talked about the blue jays yet. The first time I came here, about ten years ago, I got a sandwich from bag lunch and sat by the pool eating it. A blue jay landed on the back of my hand, grabbed the sandwich, and flew off. That's how bad they are. Any time we get a little piece of anything to eat and want to carry it from the back door under the open sky, we carry it with one hand holding and one hand covering. They're a plague. Not only do they harass the people, but they eat other birds' eggs so the ecology of the valley has become very lopsided. Lots of them go away for the winter, but now they're starting to come back. This year we're taking action. One of the guys is luring the blue jays into the shop with bread crumbs, shooing them into the little office, and then catching them with his bare hands. He says they hardly even fight him. Then he puts them into laundry bags, although he thinks he's going to change to pillow cases, and drives them Salinas, which is the "big city" one valley (about two hours) away. He told me that they remain entirely quiet for the drive and then fly away happily when he releases them. Last time he put duct tape on the legs of two of the Blue Jays to see whether the experiment was working. This place.

This is the same place that's been suffering a plague of mice, and where we have periodic announcements about putting the pieces of plywood back on the basins of water that we put our dirty dishes in so the mice won't fall in them and drown. This place.

March 21, 2002

I've been thinking about the line from Dogen's *Genjo Koan* (the magnum opus of the founder of this school of Zen) "To study the Buddha way is to study the self / to study the self is to forget the self" and I've been wondering what self he's talking about. I managed to slip in a little question to Myo the other day while we were talking about library stuff: "He doesn't mean Jack and Mary Bunce's little girl Judy, right? Isn't he talking about something like being human, and the greater self that we all share?" His answer, if I heard him correctly, was that Dogen's "self" is about the relationship between those two, about finding what it is to be human by looking at this particular manifestation of that state.

As I was walking to the zendo for the first period after study today, I felt like crying. I felt like doing one of those big cries that I and a few other women do from time to time. "Why?" I wondered. What is there to cry about. Another line from *Genjo Koan* popped into my mind: "The depth of the drop is the height of the moon." In that line, the moon is Enlightenment and the drop of water is, oh, for instance, me. So that's how far down it goes, and that's how far down I have to go in my pursuit of it: to the height of the moon. Simultaneously, I understood what there was to cry about and why I didn't need to bother shedding a tear.

During kinhin, the ten minutes of walking meditation that we do between periods of seated meditation, I ran down to the coffee/tea area to get some hot water with honey for my throat. We keep silence from the time we go to bed until after lunch the next day, and people who break the silence, particularly people who whisper around the coffee/tea area like it's a free zone, really bug me.

Except Ben. None of the things that bug me about other people bug me about Ben. He came up and whispered, "Bunce have you lost weight?" I have, 10 or 15 pounds worth, so I nodded. Then I whispered back the phrase that was on my mind: "The depth of the drop is the height of the moon." He got it, smiled, nodded back, and whispered "All Buddhas are in one atom, and all atoms are in one Buddha." "Whoa" I answered. We grinned, exchanged a hand touch that's halfway between a high five and a clasp, and went back up to the zendo to sit the second period.

March 23, 2002

I worked pretty hard on getting something in shape for my third entry in Slow Trains (www.slowtrains.com, <sindigo>'s online literary journal). I take all the Well postings I've done since my last submission, and then edit them down to make one big essay. I found in this one a theme of renunciation. Here's the introduction I wrote there:

Seven months ago I gave up a normal middle-class existence to become a fulltime monk at Tassajara, the mountain monastery of San Francisco Zen Center. I had done one practice period (a three month period of intensive meditation) here the year before, and left determined to do anything necessary to return. Last November, I received permission from my teacher, Abbess Blanche Hartman, to begin the steps that lead to priest ordination. At that time, I asked the head of practice here what he thought the most important quality in a priest was, and his answer was "renunciation." That's a word that I've been studying as I've moved through this, my third practice period. It's talking about the home, it's talking about the people, it's talking about the hair, it's talking about the stuff but it's talking about something even harder to give up: it's talking about my very sense of who I am. That's where renunciation lies, and that's what Zen practice is about.

And here's the ending I posted there:

I have to be here. It's not just that I don't want to be there, it's that I have to be here. Just as I can't turn myself into "a priest" but am going to have to stretch "priest" to include me. Neither being here nor ordaining is a turning from. They're both a turning to. And if my finances are such that I'm even more thoroughly dependent on the triple treasure of Buddha Dharma and Sangha to take care of me: good. If pinning my hopes on romance with someone led to heartbreak: good. Because there's no point in doing a thing like this if there's any holding back at all. And I am so doing a thing like this. I still want to be a Zen master.

Tomorrow is the start of a seven-day sesshin, then we have a few days of ceremonial stuff, and then this practice period is over. If you want to know how short three months is, come on down to Tassajara and do a practice period. We're all scratching our heads and asking Where did the time go? But it's gone, and now I have 25 minutes to get this finished and in the mail before the bell rings for dinner and I'm once again caught up in the schedule. This morning I had many things to do: finish this, wash my eating bowls and cloths, clean my room, write some notes, see some people.

Sesshin is so intense — no writing, no talking, three very short breaks a day — that getting ready for it does give the feeling to Tassajara of getting ready for a storm. But this morning I didn't do any of those things. It's been raining for the last day or so, and as I walked back to my room after breakfast I was pulled further down the road by the beauty of the rain drops on the bamboo and the roar of the recently fortified creek. I ran inside and got my camera, and then kept walking. And I found myself, down by the barns and all alone, doing something that was halfway between singing and chanting, making up a song about how right this moment is, how there's no need for regret over not getting here sooner because I'm here now, and how it's all so beautiful.

So don't forget: the depth of the drop is the height of the moon! See you later –

March 31, 2002

It's 7:00 p.m. Sesshin finished at 7:00 a.m. and I'm just beginning to come to. It was a tough one: a lot of sitting and a lot of aching in my body. I'm glad to say that I followed Leslie's advice that she gave me on the nine day sesshin and showed up for every period of zazen. On the sixth day, I did have to bug out after morning service, eat granola in my room, and catch an extra 40 minutes of sleep. It helped. Seven days of six hours of sleep is pretty intense for this old body.

Linda Ruth did a shosan ceremony on the morning of the seventh day. This is the ceremony that I've talked about before, where we each ask a question of the teacher in front of the whole group. She told us the night before that she'd be doing the ceremony, and asked us to ask what was in our heart. I said something like "Irritation and irritability are such an astoundingly large part of living in a community. Can you help me find a way to deal with them?" Everyone laughed. They always do. When I ask a question about freaking death they laugh. So I added, "They're laughing, but I'm serious." She said some words and I started to respond, and then while my mouth was flapping and words were coming out, I heard what she said and I stopped myself. Because she said that the irritation I feel is a gift, and a gateway to undiscovered parts of myself. I checked that with her, she said yes that's what she'd said, and she said some more words that I didn't hear. I was amazed to see how I'd come asking for an antidote, a way to not feel what I was feeling, and how she'd turned my question and shown me that this unpleasant feeling, this emotion that I've spent a lifetime trying to keep a secret (when my mouth was flapping, what came out was "But I've been pissed off all my life" and boy was I embarrassed about that later) is *not excluded* from Buddha dharma.

At this point, I've been through quite a few shuso and shosan ceremonies, and I've asked many "questions from the heart" but I've never had so many people stop me the day after the ceremony to talk about my exchange with the teacher. I'll bet they laughed because they feel irritation too and were embarrassed to hear it mentioned in public.

Tomorrow's a work day, the day after is the shuso ceremony (same format, different questionee) and then we're through. Amazing. Three months, just like *snap!* that.

April 5, 2002

The shuso ceremony was on the 3rd, yesterday we had a quick breakfast and then half the students zoomed over the mountain to return to civilization. The 30 of us who are left here are mostly moving and getting settled in our student housing. Tomorrow 70 new people arrive, volunteers who come to work on Tassajara during this month before the guest season opens.

Yesterday I got settled enough in my new room to spend the night here. I'd had two sleepless nights worrying about how I'd fit all my stuff into this tiny space, so I wanted to get on with it. Student furniture is very old and battered, and there's not that much of it, so there's a kind of gentle furniture grab that goes on during moving. I got a bed with legs so I can store stuff under it, and a good firm foam pad to put on top of it. Then I found a little dresser, a nice short bookcase to use as a bedside table, and finally a nice bookcase for the 6' of books I'm still lugging around. My altar's on top of it and it's where my eye rests when I sit on my bed, as I am now. The bed is placed along the window wall, and mostly my head is turned to look out at the wall of maple trees that are now in full leaf. The freshness of the green at this time of year is exhilarating. I'm now about 30 feet from the creek, so its noise is always a presence. I slept here last night, and I slept like a rock. This teeny oddly furnished room is quite a change from the swanky guest room I've been living in for the last six months, and it could be that this is more appropriate to a monk than the other one was.

I've continued to click away with my camera, even though the processing is expensive and I'm broke. I covered a counter in the dining room with the best of the images from this practice period on the morning of the final breakfast. The images are about half of Tassajara itself, and half of other students. Someone asked me -- someone usually does -- why I took the pictures. What are they *for?* Myo and I were talking about them and I mentioned the question to him, and he said "You take them because you're a photographer." Precisely.

We had a meeting of continuing students on the final night, to go over guidelines for the summer. We were told about proper dress (spaghetti straps: no; lasagna straps: okay), proper decorum (at the Narrows, a spot down creek which is coed nude, we're expected to keep our bathing suits on), and proper sexual behavior (no sexual involvement with anyone, guest or student, who hasn't been here six months). My favorite was the little speech that said "Guests will fall in love with Tassajara, but they'll think they're falling in love with you. They're not. In fact, once they get to know you they might not even like you." Okay.

Walking to the Zendo

Work Period/Summer 2002

April 25, 2002

So now it's three weeks into the work period and four days after my return from a short vacation. It's 6:30 a.m. and my compatriots are in the zendo sitting, but during the summer we don't get up at the bell and go to the zendo on our day off; in fact, we don't do anything at all. It's a real day off. The hardest thing to get used to is that there's no silence at all. Oh, and that there are 70 people here, working hard on Tassajara.

We're getting major construction on the kitchen, on the drainage project down by the baths, and on one cabin. There's minor construction everywhere else: cabins are getting painted, floors are getting refinished, and gardens are getting weeded. The people who come and go during this month of work period are the angels. They're mostly Buddhist or Buddhist-friendly, and the majority of them come to the zendo for morning and evening zazen. They come down and do this hard work for nothing but room and board and the love of Tassajara.

It was a shock when they first arrived (and some of them camped in the parking lot waiting for it to be time to come in on the first day) since we'd been so locked in here alone for three months. Once that shock settled, the only hard part has been the noise. People talk! Zen students nod and smile. Actually, by this time, many Zen students talk too. The real introverts among us are having some trouble with the social interaction. I, being just barely an introvert, talk some and sneak off alone some. Everyone eats every meal together in the dining room but there's always a silent table for the times when I just can't stand the sound of my own voice one more minute.

We're all pretty well assigned to our jobs by now. I'll be halftime in the library and halftime in the front office, which is great. I'm still ripping the library apart and putting it back together in what I consider to be a better way, and I'm also beginning to get trained in the office. There will be four of us working there, all women I like and get along with. It's always been how I've seen myself in the summer at Tassajara, standing behind the counter in the stone office and taking care of the guests, so we'll see how having that fantasy comes true plays out.

Sweeney came through for five days just before I went out on vacation, and it was great to have her here. I think that happens more now, that the world begins to come to me. In this case, the world also brought me ginger snaps!

At this time of year we get a six day vacation. A truck goes out shopping twice a week, so I caught a ride over the hill that way on a Tuesday. A friend met me at Jamesburg and drove me into Monterey. First we ate restaurant food, then I hit Walgreen's, and then she took me to her dentist. I was in such a good mood that I even loved the dentist. The rest of the vacation was time hanging out with her and then, in the city, visiting people, going to my storage unit and pawing through stuff, photographing an ordination in Berkeley, and zooming back here. One night I stayed in Walgreen's so long that the security guard started following me around. God I love Walgreen's. I got skin lotion, sunscreen, suntan lotion, toothpaste, a photo album, and a battery operated fan. I found the city much too noisy (why does every shop and restaurant in San Francisco play crappy music over fuzzy speakers?) I also got much too over stimulated by it, and I was glad to get back here.

May 1, 2002

Last Sunday, the director came up to me at afternoon work meeting and asked if I wanted to drive out in an hour and pick up Blanche at Jamesburg, the little cluster of houses at the other end of the 14 mile dirt road that separates us from the world. I of course gave her a very enthusiastic yes.

Once a year, we do an event in between work period and guest season called "sangha week." People who are members of small groups all over the country — about 100 in all, I think — come here and do a combination of work practice, study, and vacation. That's what Blanche was coming down to lead. While she's been here I've been both her anja (the personal attendant who takes care of her and her cabin) and the jisha (the rock star attendant who follows her into the zendo with incense and schedules her private interviews with students). It's been wild.

My other two jobs and my personal maintenance have gone to hell, because Blanche has kept me running from the time I wake her in the morning until I prepare her cabin for sleep. The first morning, I woke her five minutes before the wakeup bell (that's the anja part) and then got ready to start our incense offering at four altars plus the zendo (the jisha part). It was raining, of course. I dropped one of the sticks of incense on the ground and it went out. She waited patiently while I got it together. We're supposed to be doing a formal procession, she sweeping along six feet in front of me, but since we were sharing an umbrella we walked with our arms around each other. I did something wrong at every altar. It's the way it's been with every other job I've had at Zen Center: they give me about two minutes of training, tell me I'll be fine, and then I learn how to do it right by doing it wrong. But no one ever gets mad at me or chastises me. Blanche just gives a little blink and I know that I need to pay attention to whatever caused that blink.

The interaction with her has been wonderful. I'm in and out of her cabin all day, tidying up, putting her bed away and putting the mats down for dokusan (private discussion with students), lighting the fire, bringing in cups and cookies and hot water for the teas that she gives, bringing the students to her for private talks, and throughout it all we're talking talking talking. This morning when we set out for our little parade I smiled and said to her "I'm having so much fun." After we'd lit our first altar and were going down to the stairs toward the kitchen, she paused and said "I'm glad you're having fun, I was afraid I was working you to death." She moved ahead, and then I caught up with her for a step and whispered in her ear "It's both."

May 4, 2002

Working for Blanche threw me back into practice period, but without the protected environment that we create when it's just us monks here. I crashed hard after she left. I was so tired. Normally I work four days on and one day off, but I didn't take my day off while she was here and ended up working seven days straight. I promised myself that I could take off after she left; when I heard at work meeting that I was assigned to get up an hour early today and light the lanterns, I nearly cried. After all, it wasn't that hard to find someone to switch with, so I stayed in my room last night and slept in this morning and still, I was weepy and sad during the morning work period.

The official guest season started yesterday. During the four weeks of work period we all ate in the dining room. During Sangha Week we ate partly in the dining room and partly in the student dining area, a screened in space with dirt floors and picnic tables that's between the kitchen and the office. Now we eat entirely on the student side, our schedule's shifted slightly, and our entire practice is about serving the guests.

In the office I discovered a serious fact about summer at Tassajara: practice may have made me raw and vulnerable, but there's no time for tears and facing your feelings when there's an office full of people who want to buy their cook book and check out of their room. I splashed cold water on my face and did my time on the cash register, and then ate my lunch alone at the silent table in the student dining area.

May 6, 2002

Reading back over these last month's worth of postings, I see that two important things got left out, both things I saw on my vacation out of Tassajara. First, there's how easy it was to accept people's kindness.

I've led my life by keeping track and maintaining control, striving to never be in any person's debt. I was always the driver. Now people drive me around and drop me off places like a six year old. My stepmom even slipped me a twenty when she left me at the San Rafael bus depot, and I enjoyed it. I first saw this change with the favors that Sweeney and Kathy have been doing for me while I've been in Tassajara, and I saw it even more strongly when I was in the outside world. I'm a monk. I'm poor. I'm trying to save all beings. And there are people who can help me with that by driving me around and buying me restaurant food, and it's easy to accept that help.

Second, I finally saw what a strange thing I've done by moving into the monastery. The ladies in the dentist's office gave me my first hint on this ("She's a monk!" "No way!") and so did my stepmom. When I was moving down here, I was entirely driven by necessity. Now that I'm living it, I still have no regrets, but I'm also pretty amazed at what I've done.

May 17, 2002

It's strange to me that I'm writing less now that we're in the guest season. I would have thought I'd write more, since we have more spare time now than we did when we were in practice period. For instance, evening zazen doesn't start until 8:40 and our dinner's over at around 6:30, so you'd think I'd be doing something with that two hour chunk of time. But I'm not. I'm lying on my bed reading New Yorkers, or going to the baths, or I'm just hanging out. Maybe I'm not writing so much now because I don't have much to say. It still feels like I'm pretty quiet.

My birthday was yesterday and my sangha really came through for me. It was also my day off, so I didn't go to morning work meeting but someone still announced it, so that throughout the day many of the people who I saw wished me a happy birthday. We eat in partial silence now: five minutes or so after we serve ourselves, someone hits the clackers and we all bow and greet each other and begin talking. At yesterday's lunch, after the clackers hit, everyone burst into the happy birthday song. It was finally enough. Enough attention, enough affection, enough presents (thank you again Sweeney!), enough enough. I do love my sangha.

It's starting to get hot. The end of my room on the creek side is about half screened in, and those screens have been covered with heavy plastic for insulation. I pulled most of it off this evening — it's 74 degrees at 8:10 — and my room's even more full of trees and the sound of the creek. I also put a discarded puppy gate across the door so I could leave it open for the cross-breeze without inviting in the little wood rat that lives in this building.

May 19, 2002

Myo gave me a sign to hang outside the library that had been living under his bed, waiting to find its place. It's a smooth half-round piece of wood about 20" long, silvered by age and exposure to the elements, with the kanji for "Namu Amida Buddha" lettered on it. The other day I noticed that something seemed to be falling from it; assuming it was the powder post beetles that threaten the library, I left a note with the head of the shop asking again for him to call the exterminator. Yesterday there was such a pile of stuff below it that I pulled the sign off the wall to take a look. I brushed it and finally, to try to knock off whatever was eating it, I gave it a little slap. Was I surprised when a big bee flew out of it. I turned it upside down and saw the hole the carpenter bee had made, burrowing in to create a nest. These are the biggest blackest slowest bees in all creation, and they eat buildings. And also little signs. I asked the guys in the shop to put some putty in the hole so the bee would move on. When I told Gaelyn about it, she asked if the bee was humming *Nammmmuuuuu Ammmmmida Buuuuuudha* as he flew by.

I think about the movie *Groundhog Day* a lot as I show up for days that look like they're going to be a lot alike and turn out to be quite different. Every time I go to the office after work meeting I have that "here we go again" feeling. There are four of us who work there. Two cope by getting very energetic, and two cope by getting very quiet. I'm one of the quiet ones. It's interesting to watch how the varying combinations interact, since there are usually three of us working together. It seems that life gets so damned simple here that I can see how it's always been with me and other people. I greatly enjoy the part of dealing with the guests who are checking in and out and buying stuff (we sell books, statues, t-shirts, incense — that sort of thing). I'm enjoying dealing with my co-workers too, now that the initial few weeks are past and we're all finding our ways of dealing with each other.

It appears that I pulled the plastic off my screens too soon: it's raining today, and the temperature's dropped to 60 at 8 p.m. But putting on another sweater is a small price to pay for how beautifully green Tassajara looks.

May 21, 2002

I think I'll finish this group of postings with a description in the day of a life of a monk during the guest season at Tassajara.

Yesterday was a busy one for me. My alarm's set to go off slightly before the 5:20 wakeup bell. We have to be on our seats in the zendo by the first roll down or they're considered available for visitors, and my commute from the upper barn to the zendo has been timed at three minutes, so I have to be washed and dressed and on the path by 5:38 or I'm late. Morning zazen is a one hour period followed by a shortened service and bang we're outta there. During soji/temple cleaning I go down to the office, tuck my rakusu in and tie up my robe sleeves, and sweep the floor and clean the windows. Then it's 7:30 and time for student breakfast. I'm hungry this morning, so I don't bother to walk home and change into jeans before eating. The first seven minutes are in silence, and then someone hits the clackers, we bow and greet each other, and the talking begins. One of my side jobs is to schedule the body workers who come throughout the summer and work on students in exchange for room and board, so this morning things are quiet enough in the office that they don't need me on the cash register and I can go up the library, spread all the little bits of paper with vital info scribbled on them out on the table, and get the schedule in order.

I was supposed to drive the noon stage to Jamesburg, but it rained all night and I'm too nervous about the road to be comfortable with the idea of driving nine people out, so other arrangements are made.

After student lunch it's back to the library to finish my project, then down to the office at 3:00 to relieve the woman on duty, then over to the zendo at 4:00 to give zazen instruction to new arrivals, then down to my room for a few minutes until I go back to the zendo for a very quick evening service. Then it's 6:00 and time for dinner.

After dinner I go down to the baths where I hang around and chat with a few other students. The 109 degree plunge feels particularly good on this cold day. I'm the jiko (hold the incense for the priest who's opening the zendo after everyone's seated) for evening zazen, so I have to get my robe back on and get up there by 8:25. The priest is my friend Marta, the rascal from Colombia, and we huddle together under the overhang of the roof by the Abbot's cabin, talking quietly, as we wait for the han on the zendo porch to give us the signal to open our umbrellas and start our procession.

After zazen, I give myself the small pleasure of staying up reading until 10:30, snuggled down with a hot water bottle, a wool sweater over my flannel nightgown, and my hat on my head in my cold room. Then it's lights out (at least our tiny funky student rooms have electricity!) and time for sleep.

Everyone talked endlessly about how hard the summer is, but no one ever told me that: this is a practice period, too, even though we're no longer the only people at Tassajara and even though we work more than we sit. There's a lot less zazen than in practice period, a lot more opportunities to watch self clinging as I interact with both friends and strangers throughout the day, and also a lot more time for reading and staring out the window thinking. I think I'll turn this infernal machine off and do some of that right now.

May 31, 2002

They call it "getting a date." First your teacher says you can ordain, then the other abbots and former abbots agree, then you start sewing the thousands of stitches it will take to create your sacred robes, and then, finally, your teacher says when the ordination will be.

The phone situation here goes from bad to worse in the summer (more people and less phone access) and the only time I can reach Blanche is a little 15 minute window between morning service and breakfast. Often she's away from the phone at that time, talking to the real live people at City Center.

Today, after several frustrating misses, I talked with her. Once we got the conversation about logistics out of the way, I moved right in with my request. I knew that often ordinations were held at City Center in January, and that traditionally in Japan they're in the winter. So I asked "Could I be ordained this winter?" Blanche suggested that we have the ceremony down here at Tassajara just before the last sesshin of the winter practice period, the long and serious and cold rohatsu sesshin. She laughed and said that then I'd have to struggle with my okesa for the whole sesshin, and I told her that I'd welcome the practice.

So the date is set.

If I waited until January, I'd probably be part of a handful of people ordaining at the same time. I could have a big public whoop dee doo in the afternoon with plenty of guests from the outside and a big party after. Down here, there'll just be the people in the practice period attending in the dark quiet Tassajara night as Blanche and I face each other, one to one, in the zendo. After the ceremony's over, we'll all silently fill our thermoses and hot water bottles and stagger off to bed. Even though waiting a couple of weeks and doing the big thing in the City is tempting, the intimacy of doing it here is irresistible. So that's what we've agreed on.

I have a date.

June 5, 2002

People have been stealing stuff from the library. I know because they return the stolen goods to the book return box, cards still in the books' pockets. When I complain about it, I'm asked "Don't you think it's guests?" And I say "Guests don't know how to open the door to my closet, take the key to the locked cabinet, take a book out, lock the cabinet and replace the key and then walk out without filling out the checkout card." My startled fellow students are forced to agree.

And the Walkmen! We have a few grungy old portable tape players (for listening to tapes of dharma talks) that are checked out through the library which are disappearing rapidly. I locked them up to stop the outflow, and today saw that they too are disappearing from my closet. I happened on Myo on my way back from the library and aired my grievance; after work meeting (which I didn't attend since it's my day off) several people told me that he'd made a short speech to the group about not taking things from the library. Then I could see how personal it all was. I like to fume about how this is a monastery, that we're living by the precepts and one of those is not taking what's not given, but my reaction is really centered around the feeling that this taking is disrespectful to me as the librarian. And I saw that that Myo's little speech made me feel cared for — not the library, but me personally.

Yesterday I got a package from Sweeney, and when I saw a check from her I thought Oh my goodness, but when I read her note and saw that she was just passing on an anonymous gift, and read the card from the anonymous person on the Well who'd sent me money for my photography, I cried. Rereading the card just now, I cried again.

This is a new realm. I recently spent some time during zazen running through a list of people on the Well I haven't heard from, brooding over the nature of friendship and so on, and that adds an interesting layer to this experience of generosity.

This morning Ben was in the screened porch, trying to read last Sunday's *Times* while I was talking to him. First I talked about the thing with the library thefts, and then I told him the story of the anonymous gift. He asked "And can you not take that personally either?" Well, no! May I please choose *this* and not *that*??? Thank you!

June 8, 2002

I had this dream last night. I was a man in the dream, and I'd just woken from my third suicide attempt. I'd tried to kill myself and my children by setting fire to the house. When I woke in my dream, I looked at the wick made of strips of paper and felt such joy to see that it had failed. I knew that would be my last suicide attempt.

My alarm went off early today (in real life) because I had to get up and light the lanterns. The sun rises so early that we only light a few now, the ones on the porch around the zendo and down in the courtyard by the coffee/tea area. It's lucky that my schedule in the office got adjusted so I could take the morning off. I've spent the morning dozing on my bed. I'm quite frazzled by all of the blah-blah-blah that my several jobs require. I'm used to living in such a way that I can come back to my home, whether that's an apartment in San Francisco or a bed at Tassajara, and recharge, but that time is lost during the summer. It's hard on me. So it's great to be here right now, stretched out and alone with only the sound of the creek filling my ears.

There are four of us in the front office, rotating through different combinations of two and three. One of the other women, the one who's doing her first Tassajara summer, weeps constantly. I want her to overcome her despair because I care about her, and also because it's so hard on me. The boss thrives on chaos and, it seems to me, creates it if it isn't already there, and that's hard on me too. More and more I'm getting assigned afternoons when I can work behind the counter alone, talking with the guests and students who straggle through, and that's suiting me quite well. If I say to other residents that the office is hard, they assume I'm talking about dealing with demanding guests. That's not it at all. Our guests self-select for mellow, for the most part. It's just that the work in the office is so constant. I'm seeing how badly I react to noise and confusion, and wondering how I ever stood it out there in "the world."

June 11, 2002

Tonight a guest summarized the entire season of "Buffy the Vampire Slayer" for me. I just cannot believe that Buffy had sex with Spike!

After waking Blanche at 5:15 (she was here for a couple of days and I was her anja again), working in the office in the morning (insert sound of teeth gritting here), seeing Blanche off on the 3:00 stage, and getting bodywork for the third day on a row on an injury created by the damned chiropractor last Saturday, I did the closing shift in the office. A guest came in at 6:30 and we were talking. He said he was a television writer and I of course said "Television! We don't cater to your ilk around here — unless, of course, you write for a good show like Buffy the Vampire Slayer." He wasn't one of the Buffy writers, but he was a recent Buffy fan, and so he told me, as probably only a writer could, everything that had happened on the show since I moved here and lost contact. It was quite a Tassajara moment.

Everyone streams through the office, all the complaints and jokes and people who have to feed their shopping jones. The day started with two separate couples who'd booked for one night and wanted to stay longer and a woman who wanted to move from the dorm to a private room because her bed was too hard. One of the couples gets to stay, the other one is going to drive over the awful road and sleep in Carmel Valley and then come back tomorrow as day use guests, and the woman with the hard bed realized that she'd accidentally moved into student housing and that's why her bed was a foam pad on the floor.

A woman came in today who I've known for 21 years and haven't seen for two or three. She hadn't heard I'd moved here and kept saying things like "Your hair!" and "I can't believe it!"

July 20, 2002

I say "Tassajara is so hard." I want to retire the last word of that phrase, and have been trying to find a replacement. It might be "challenging" and it might be "relentless." They're both true. Still, I don't think either catches the essence I'm reaching for in the way "hard" has up until now. But words are too powerful, and I need to let go of that idea.

Maybe "Tassajara is so "Tassajara."

Part of that is the summer weather. It's been up to 113 degrees already, and the only way to cool off is to go sit in the creek.

Looking for a replacement word, I asked the young summer guy who I ate lunch with what he would put in that space. He gave me about 20 minutes of disappointment in this place as a monastery. He's in the place I was in during my kitchen practice period, I think, where I felt more like a set of muscles to be used in keeping Zen Center going than a monk. The longer I listened to him, the more I felt like the old tea lady: listening, nodding, allowing, and not needing to voice my disagreement.

Reb Anderson, the former Abbot, was down here about a month ago and someone asked him whether he thought Tassajara was a monastery during the summer. I loved his answer, which was essentially that if two or three people treat it like one, and live as monks, then it is. There are about 60 students here during the summer, maybe 20 holdovers from the practice period, 20 young people who've come down here to live and work for the whole summer, and the rest are short term people who come and go. That allows for a big range in commitment to monastic practice. It's my intention to be one of the people who's way way over on the monk side of things.

I've asked Blanche if I can change my ordination date from December at Tassajara to January at City Center. Although I loved the idea of doing the ceremony here, which would have meant full-tilt intensity, I began to see how many people would be excluded from attending. Blanche agreed. And then, the next day, I'll come back here and start the next practice period.

I was up in the city recently and just managed to cross paths with Blanche. She began reading to me from the new book of talks by Suzuki Roshi, reading the part where he talks about watching your teacher rather than listening to her words. I thought I heard a hint, and asked "Should we think about my finishing the summer and the next two practice periods, and then coming up here with you?" and her answer was no. Oh.

Movies, a temperate climate, and the telephone make living in the city so much easier than living here. But I stayed at the Jamesburg house (the outpost on the other end of the road into Tassajara that's our link with the outside world) for two nights on my way back from vacation, filling in for other vacationing folk, and found I'm just as restless and hungry for distraction now as I ever was before I moved here. Damn. I thought maybe I'd acquired the discipline to voluntarily sit down with a good book after dinner and meditate for 45 minutes in the morning, but not so. So I guess Blanche is right. Again.

July 23, 2002

I've decided on a name for this feeling. It's: homesick. I talked on the phone with my original teacher Myogen Steve Stücky this morning, and when we hung up I cried and cried. Rather than putting on a happy face for the sake of the younger students, I got my mush and tofu hash and went to the silent table and ate with tears running down my face. Our conversation was nothing but good news, and the tears came from missing him so much.

Similarly, when I was up in the city recently I spent the night with my stepmom and, in the morning, we were playing some music and I opened the cabinet to find another CD. I saw all of the CDs I'd given to her last fall, my complete Beethoven sonatas, Mozart concerti, Bach cello suites, and was overcome with great gusting sobs.

I came to the monastery because I found life so difficult, but on those mornings when the sun was coming in the window and I was playing music, it wasn't difficult at all. I do miss comfort here, and I do miss certain pleasures. Music is primary among them. In the conversation with Steve, we agreed on the January 4th date for my ordination. He'll be one of the preceptors in the ceremony. The group at Dharma Eye will be in sesshin, and I'll sit with them all day on the 3rd, then they'll all pile into a little bus and come over to City Center for the ordination on the 4th. Nice plan.

July 30, 2002

Someone left a beach chair out on the deck by my room. The kind with plastic webbing and aluminum frame. I took it down to the creek and sat in it while I sewed on my okesa. It worked very well, and my feet are still cool and comfy. Someone who I passed on the way down said "Don't drop it!" I could only think that I should drop the self and save the okesa.

These measures are necessary because it's so damn hot. Right now, at 4:50, it's 90 degrees in my room. Most days the temp gets up to 100, and during our heat spell it was up over 110. At those numbers, it's like walking around in an oven. Ah, a little breeze just started blowing. That, and the fact that there's virtually no humidity at all, makes it bearable. But still — *damn* hot. The nights get down to 45 or 50, so it's jackets in the mornings and shorts in the afternoon. Yikes. Too hot to write.

Work Circle

Fall 2002
4th Tassajara
Practice Period

September 24, 2002

I wondered whether I'd keep writing. I didn't know whether it was the energy of the guest season, the heat of summer, or whether I just didn't have anything left to say anymore. Now it's the second day of the fall practice period, and here I am again.

I'm partially moved into my winter quarters. I had a choice between a warm room and a private bathroom, and I went for the bathroom. I again have a cabin with a wood-burning stove, and I'd rather wait an hour for heat than live in a dorm again. I realized toward the end of the summer that I hadn't had a minute's privacy for six months, and I realized how very wearing that was. So here I am in wildly cute Cabin 12, snug up against the side of the mountain and away from the infernal noise of that relentless creek. This is one of the original summer cabins that were built in the 30's, and which we've improved over the years but not much. I have windows with screens (originally the windows were just screen and in the winter we'd tape on plastic to winterize them) and the beloved wood-burning stove. The room's about 12 feet by 15 feet, with a little rectangular space along one end creating the bathroom and, in the nook left over from that space, a little writing area with a built-in desk and a beautiful oval window looking onto the hillside. I'm sitting on a dainty blue velvet chair as I write, which is kind of wild. Cabin 12 also has a *real bed* and I'm already sleeping better here than I ever did in my little horse stall by the creek with its worn out student futon. This cabin is famous for its built-in altar, which is formed from a tree branch. I'll try to take a picture of it for Sweeney to post.

This practice period we have 12 returning students (an unusually large number, probably because this is the last practice period Blanche will lead at Tassajara), 24 continuing students, and 20 new students. The new folks, many of whom I already know, are "sitting tangaryo" this week. Remember when I did this two years ago? They sit for five days from 4 in the morning until 9 at night with three short breaks after meals. They can only move to go to the bathroom: no walking meditation, no standing by the seat, no stretching.

Yesterday was so hot, and those of us who were working around the place whispered to each other how bad we felt for the people in the zendo. Maybe it's because I went through the same thing that I know just how hard it is. It got up to 100 degrees yesterday. So far this morning it's clouded over, and I hope it stays cool for them. Another thing I remember about my tangaryo was how wildly disappointed I was with Tassajara. I thought I was coming to ceremonial Mecca, and what I heard were wobbly chants and missed bells. Now I'm on this side of the looking glass, and I see how those of us not sitting are scrambling around to get Tassajara back into monastic shape. There are some things I'm supposed to do this week that I haven't done for six months, and they exist only in my muscle memory. When I ask my brain about these forms, as when I was supposed to demonstrate oryoki to a group of tangaryo students, it goes Buh??? I have other jobs I'm supposed to do this week that I've never been trained into (in the true Zen Center style) such as shadowing the priest (jiko, it's called) during the longer form of service that we use during practice periods, and I'm trying wildly to figure them out as I go. I wonder if these tangaryo students are as disappointed as I was, and I think, Probably so, probably so. So may they also stick around long enough to be moved into positions of responsibility with little training beyond watching others do these jobs and no feeling of being a senior student. A long time ago, when I went through my crushing disappointment with the Episcopal church, I was standing watching a big fancy procession with guys in brocade dresses and medieval hats, and it came to me, They're just people! Same thing here: it's just people.

I took the Greyhound from San Francisco to Monterey earlier this month, returning from my vacation in the bay area. I looked out at the early morning world, gas stations and liquor stores and taquerias whizzing by outside my window, and I wondered, What do you all think? What is the meaning? Is life about survival? If so, is that enough? Of course that thought had a snooty little aspect of monks having the answer to that question, when in fact now that I'm back here I don't see much particular meaning going on. I used to, but I don't any more. However, I do see a way of passing my days that suits me better than the getting and spending (and deliberate time wasting) of the life I spent there, so I guess this will have to do.

It seems that every practice period I have one big injury and one big understanding. So, let me talk about how that was during the summer. Actually, since the summer's twice as long as the fall and winter practice periods, I offer two bits of insight. The first came right after I returned from my mid-summer vacation. That is, I can be homesick and grateful to be here at the same time. I believe there was a kind of grief that I'd been pushing away because it felt too dangerous: if I missed the comfort of my previous life, this whole thing would be a big fat mistake. But that's not so, and I can and do have both. But oh some days what I'd do for a couch and some Beethoven CDs, you know?

The other bit of understanding that I had seems larger than that, maybe because it's fresher. It's something like this. By the end of summer I saw how much time I spent being grumpy. I was hot and tired and critical. First I saw how embarrassing this was, how strongly my mom had taught me that you don't come out of your room until you can come out with a smile on your face. Then I realized what a bummer it was to be the grump. Here I am living in this place that people travel hundreds of miles and pay hundreds of dollars to visit, and I'm stomping around it with a scowl on my face. The biggest surprise, I think, was that it was my criticism of others that was creating the grumpiness. Okay. Now we're getting to the good part. One evening I was standing in the zendo after zazen, waiting for the signal to troop on out, and one of the people who were on my list did something irritating, and I watched the criticism arise, and then finally I knew it was just a thought. *Just a thought.* Not some concrete truth. Did you read *Crooked Cucumber* where David C. asked Suzuki Roshi to sum up Zen practice and Suzuki R stops, thinks, and says, "Everything changes"? That's what I'm talking about here: it's just a thought, and it just passed. It is not, as I had been telling myself, The Truth.

I asked Leslie at lunch yesterday (the few of us working around Tassajara eat in the dining room while the poor tangaryo people eat in the zendo) if she knew how many people had come here as guests this year. Her husband Keith was with us, and he did the numbers: 80 a night times 129 nights at an average stay of two nights makes 5000 people. I interacted with a ton of them, since I checked them in and out in the office and also drove some of them over the mountain and back. There are more, too, in the people who live and work with the students for periods ranging from three days to three months, and the people who come to work on Tassajara during the spring and fall, all requiring some degree of interaction. I wonder what number we've gotten up to. A lot. A really lot.

What I least liked was being an object of curiosity for the guests. Our monastic life was pared way back, but it was always there, and sometimes as we'd go through one of our rituals around the zendo, there'd be guests standing and staring at us as if we were animals in a zoo. I really didn't like that. What I liked most was hearing from people about the effect their annual visit to Tassajara has on their lives. I liked that even better than I disliked being objectified. In fact, my favorite job (next to continuing my reorganization of the library) was driving the stage. I really enjoyed spending an hour with a small handful of guests, explaining our life to them and finding out about theirs.

Now the place is quiet again, and my life is my own until Blanche arrives tomorrow afternoon when it will be hers. My job this fall is to serve as her personal assistant (anja) which is one of the most non-stop jobs there is. I spent yesterday cleaning the Abbot's cabin, today is a free day for me, and tomorrow I finish cleaning her cabin and raking her garden and then drive over to Jamesburg to pick her up. Tangaryo finishes in four days and then, finally, the practice period begins.

I went through the transition from spring to summer, from being one of a small group of silent people to being part of a very large and very noise horde, and all summer I wondered what this transition would be like. Now I know. It feels exciting, and it feels inevitable.

October 9, 2002

We've been through a few cycles now (a "Tassajara week" is five days long), enough to get a feel of what this practice period is going to be like.   It's going to be busy. It's going to be very very busy, because of my job as anja. I asked our new director whether he'd ever been an anja.   He said he had, thought about it, and then said that it was the happiest practice period he'd ever had, and also that it was more work than any other job. "It's devotion," he said. Yes. I am in and out of Blanche's cabin all day, waking her, bringing her hot water, serving at the teas she holds (that's a hard one, being a shadow and keeping my mouth closed while discussions are going around about things I either know something about or think I do), putting her bed away, putting her bed down (it's a tatami cabin and she sleeps on a futon in the middle of the single room), cleaning, and sometimes just chatting with her. It is the job of intimacy. Sometimes I get a little frantic because I don't have the time to take care of my own life -- our personal days seem to be one of my busiest doing stuff for her -- but mostly I'm in the groove and it doesn't even feel like work.

The two things that Blanche is having me do that are new are taking her okesa and folding it and storing it when she leaves the zendo, and shaving her head on personal days (every fifth day we have "free time" between breakfast and dinner). I shaved her for the third time today and am finally gaining some confidence in it.

Our new tanto, Meiya Wender, is the tea teacher at Green Gulch. She's giving tea classes here on 4 and 9 days, and I'm doing that too.   Blanche says that priests who've studied tea know how to move better than those who haven't, and she wants me to learn this. I have no interest in picking up another Japanese skill. I want American Zen! But I trust her so I'm doing it. It's actually pretty interesting, and I like Meiya a lot and am glad to hang around her.

I already know everyone here with the exception of about three people who came from Green Gulch, and that's making my entry into the practice period a lot easier. I also find myself not caring so much if a doan misses a bell or a server slops cereal on the outside of my oryoki bowl; there's a kind of keeping track, a "who was that?!" that's missing in my reaction this time around. It's just early days, just people who are trying very hard to do stuff that they've never done before.

An extra thing on this personal day was scattering the ashes of two sangha members up on the hogback ridge. It was powerful. Life is passing so swiftly, and soon enough we'll also be a couple pounds of powder in a cardboard carton marked "temporary container" and then dust in the wind. Soon enough.

October 19, 2002

At the start of the practice period, Blanche did chosan — a formal tea in the Abbot's Cabin — every few days. The guests were organized by crew: first the senior staff, then the doans (six people who ring bells and hit drums and lead chants in the zendo), then the shop, the gardeners, and so on. The last groups to come through were the tangaryo (first practice period) students. Since it was my job to make the tea for the group, I attended all of them.

The groups of senior students were quiet, deferential, accustomed to these events. The newer students in the final groups were by far the peppiest. Some of the students brought their questions with them and presented them to Blanche as soon as the first sip of tea was taken.

I remember being a tangaryo student, thinking I was pretty good at the forms, and then arriving here and being horrified at the way we were apparently being asked to act just like medieval Japanese men, how Tassajara seemed to be all form and no heart. There was a tangaryo student this time who was apparently having the same reaction. After some discussion, she told the story of the bride and the hambone — you know the one, the punch line is that she always cuts the 4" off the ham because her mother always did, and her mother always did it because her pan was to small for the hams the store sold. Much laughter in the Abbot's cabin. But then Meiya Wender, our new tanto, told a story about the two schools of Tea. Both use a little metal teapot to bring hot water into the tearoom. In one school, the teapot has a cover over the spout that flips up. In the other school the cover fell off the founder's teapot and so they only have a hinge. When you're buying your supplies you have to specify which school you're a part of so you get the right teapot. This can sound stupid, like the hambone story always has. But Meiya said that this metal teapot with its tiny hinge flapping uselessly ties the students back through the years (centuries?) directly to the founder, that what he learned and taught is preserved so precisely from student to student that, in fact, the student becomes the ancestor. To me, that put a whole new light on what I've seen as mindlessly following an old form.

On the days that Blanche does chosan, I leave the zendo before breakfast, eat a hurried meal in the dining room, and then go to her cabin to set up the tea, cups, cookies, maybe get fresh flowers for the altar, and so on. For the last few days she's been involved in a Dharma Transmission ceremony which has been a lot of work for everyone involved. I'm a little tired and cranky, a little put upon, everyone in the practice period is no longer unconditionally beautiful, the anja job's a little too hard and I want to have time to hang out with a cup of tea and stare at the wall -- and then I get over it.

We start sesshin tomorrow and I don't know whether that will slow down or speed up my duties as anja, but for sure today, our personal day, is my last best shot at getting both Blanche and me ready for five days of intensive sitting.

October 30, 2002

Laid up in bed all day today from another fall and damaged foot. Unfortunately I was carrying my computer to the haircutting shack to charge its battery (the computer's, not the shack's) when I fell, and my computer took a hard fall. It's working all right, but the space bar's broken. I am currently typing one long mother of a word. There are several refugees from Silicon Valley here, and maybe one of them can do something with this.

It's not been entirely bad to be sick at Tassajara — to ignore the wakeup bell, lie in my cabin all day and have food brought to me, and talk about life and the dharma with my visitors. Right now, at 5 in the evening, I'm looking out of the window past a dormant lilac bush, over the roof of Cabin 13 and the Maple that towers over it, toward a huge tree in the lower garden that's gone entirely yellow since the last time I looked. What a beautiful time of year this is.

I started the day yesterday with tears which came from the frustration that's a part of this way of life. Following the schedule completely and dropping preferences is a part of the training, and it's a part of monastic living that I've come to love. But its evil twin, powerless-ness, gets me down. It can be so hard to get anything done here, take so many days to even make a phone call, and there's inertia around stuff (one iron for 60 people who are required to present themselves without wrinkles???) that drives me nuts. That drives me to lie face down and sob every once in a while.

Blanche saw what was going on and came to my cabin to see what was up after breakfast. While we talked, she idly picked up a piece of paper lying near her, then the one under it, and then the one under that which was face down because I was hiding it from her. Unbelievable. My little room is stuffed full of things, and her hand goes to the one that I don't want her to see. I talked as she read, explaining how an e-mail to her came to be laying face down under some other papers on the table next to my bed. She looked at it for so long that I grew alarmed. Was she pondering the way she'd found it? Was she mad at me? Was she asleep? Finally, when she looked up, her face was neutral, she commented on the content of the e-mail, and our conversation went on. Sometimes I think she's a Zen master, and sometimes I think she's a psychic.

I didn't feel the tear storm hold over into the rest of the day, but I also don't think it's a coincidence that this is the day when I hurt my foot and had to take to my bed.

November 2, 2002

Back in my room after morning zazen, service and breakfast, settling in to stay here and elevate my foot, fire burning in the wood stove, getting ready to settle down and there goes another scorpion, trundling across the floor. I did the old inverted glass trick, but these things are so nasty that, instead of slipping a piece of paper under him, I dragged the whole rug outside. Yick. This one actually wasn't as bad as the one I found on my pillow this summer, maybe because I saw this one move and saw how slow he was, but this is one critter that I really don't like.

I was going to write about two things: sex and the weather.

It's cold again. 43 degrees out now at 8 a.m. on a sunny morning. I'm gradually upping the ante in my zendo wear: today I progressed from the silk crewneck to Daddy's old v-neck cashmere sweater as my first layer. I've been in both the flannel kimono and wool robe for quite some time now. Before I go outside, the hat and wool shawl are added. The tangaryo students are already bundling up with full thermafleece turtlenecks under their robes, and those of us who've been through Tassajara winter before tut tut "I wonder what they're going to do when it gets cold." One happy piece of news is that this little cabin heats up a lot faster than the cavernous Yurt 1 did: I can feel the effects from the wood stove here within 15 or 20 minutes. Like: now!

The public rooms of Tassajara, and some of the residents' rooms, are heated with hot water that runs under the floors. We're in a drought year and the rains haven't started yet, so we can't use the little water we have for heat. I've always been skeptical about how much difference the heat in the zendo makes, but now that the outside temperature's getting down to the high 30's and there's no heat at all, I'm a believer. Heat was added to the courtyard rooms a couple of years ago; before that, they were thought to be among the coldest at Tassajara and no one wanted to live there. I feel sorry for the guys who're stuck there now in their private little refrigerators.

Okay, that's it for the weather. Now for sex. Haven't any of you wondered about sex in a place like this? I've noticed that no one's ever asked about it. Well, I may have said, for the first part, that we're all under "the six month rule" which is that we're prohibited from having sex with anyone who's been here less than six months. There was one cute thing who arrived at the start of the summer who proved irresistible to the baker and they eloped to Monterey after about a month. They were asked to leave Tassajara, so that rule is serious. Once the six month period is past for both parties, though, sexual relationships are allowed. It's hoped that people will talk with their practice leaders before becoming intimate, but I don't think there's a punishment if the act comes before the discussion.

This practice period we have seven couples in residence. One thing this means is that there's much less social life in the dining room on off days and in the break between dinner and zazen, traditionally a time for visiting together. Once we were through with our formal teas with all the crews in her cabin, Blanche had the couples in for an informal cup of tea to discuss areas of practice around being coupled here (exclusivity, maintaining silence, etc.) One of the lesbians heard this was going on and registered a complaint, so Blanche's next tea was for lesbians and gays. I thought this was pretty silly and told her so. "Aren't we all celibate monastics here? What difference does it make who we'd be sleeping with if we had the chance?" She smiled, had the tea, and reported that it was a good tea and informative for her. Finally yesterday I was one of nine self-identified celibate monastics who went to the Abbess's cabin for a cup of tea. We started by defining terms.

"Celibate," it turns out, means no sex without marriage. "Chastity" means no sex at all, and is probably closer to the mark of what most of us had in mind. I was one of the first to speak, saying that since I had to stay out of new relationships for the first year after my ordination, I was looking at chastity for at least the next 15 months and, in fact, was interested in remaining celibate beyond that. Sexual energy has driven so much of my life, I think I'd like to give some other energy a chance; working on the addiction model, since I can't control sex, I can only try life with no sex at all. Another woman who's ordaining with another teacher said that her reasoning was similar, that her teacher had initially requested four years' celibacy but "the sentence had been reduced to two years." A third woman who's ordaining will have to commit to five years. Which is when Blanche popped up and said that in fact she doesn't have any celibacy requirement! News to me! But I'm still interested in trying something else.

Several other people spoke of turning to celibacy after finding themselves either heartbroken at the end of a sexual relationship or "not liking who I became" in the midst of one. My turning isn't that active, I think. I feel more of a quiet discouragement over the whole thing after 35 years of giving it my best shot.

When the other six people left at the end of tea, I stayed to clean up and Blanche and I chatted while I did. This is one reason I'm not getting any breaks this practice period: while the other students are relaxing in their rooms or having a nice cup of coffee, I'm sitting on the floor of the Abbot's cabin talking things over with Blanche. Not a bad deal at all.

November 6, 2002

Once again I'm tucked into my bed with my foot elevated, heat radiating from my wood stove, and all three kerosene lamps lit. It's just 6 a.m. and still entirely dark outside. I sat the first period of zazen but my foot's hurting too much today to stay in the zendo.

After breakfast I'm driving Blanche over the hill. She's going up to the city for a week. I'll have a chance to do some deep cleaning in her cabin, and also to take care of some of my own stuff. I hope this foot gives me a break.

One of the young guys (not one of the Silicon Valley refugees, who are all a bunch of dainty software geeks, unable to contemplate dealing with hardware) got my space bar back on. What luxury. I'd been thinking of asking Sweeney to look on eBay for a cheap used laptop, but there are other things I need to do with what little money I have (like paying off the IRS) and this one's entirely adequate. In the "don't know what you've got 'till it's gone" department, I'll tell you this: a space bar is a wonderful thing.

One of the ceremonies we do is called nenju, and it takes most of us a long time to learn to love it. At the end of each day before the day off, we all line up on the porch that surrounds the zendo and stand utterly quiet and still for about half an hour while the Abbess goes and presents incense at all the altars and then does bows in the zendo. When that's all through, we enter three at a time, present incense, and do what's called a jundo: first we bow to the Abbess and the head student, then we put our hands in gassho and, with our heads and upper bodies bent down, we walk all the way around the zendo. When we're through, we go to our own places and stand in the same position of reverence while the rest of the students pass by. It's a ceremony of expressing gratitude to each other for our practice.

Standing on the engawa (which is what the zendo porch is called) this week was too much for my foot, so I went around to the back and sat in a chair and waited. The ceremony takes place at the end of the day, and the fall twilight was beautiful. More trees are turning blazing red and bright yellow. My friends the little bats zipped by. One star winked on the end of a tree and then disappeared. When I heard the shuffle of feet behind me through the thin zendo wall, I went back around to the front and entered and did my bows, heartfelt bows of gratitude to be living this life.

There was another part of the ceremony that took place at the kaisando (founder's hall), and then Blanche stepped into her cabin to change from her ceremonial okesa to her everyday one. I nipped in after her and folded the one while she wrapped herself in the other, and then she, her jisha (the ceremonial attendant) and I hustled back to the zendo for our dinner.

Ah, in real time I hear the bells from the zendo telling me that morning service is going on, and I see the sky has lightened enough that I can see that big yellow tree again. I think it's a Walnut. Jeez my foot hurts.

Yesterday morning as I was settling down to the first period of zazen, Blanche came up from behind and whispered that she'd be doing a formal tea during study. So I left the zendo after service and ate my quick "anja breakfast" alone in the dining room to get up to her cabin and get the tea set up.

It turned out that the kitchen crew had been having some problems. Remember when I was in the kitchen a year ago? Remember when I had to put my knife down quietly and go home in mid-shift because I was afraid I'd stab the kitchen manager if I stayed there one moment longer? That's the stage they're at. So I got to sit in my corner, making the tea and then settling back to watch and listen as Blanche tried to help these eight people find a way out of the difficult spot they found themselves in. It was brilliant to be able to watch the movement of the group from the sidelines, and heart breaking to see the initial resistance. It would seem that monks in a monastery would be eager to support one another in their practice, yet I saw, I heard, that it's not always that easy. And if monks in a monastery can't readily agree to this, what does that say for the people on the other side of the hill. After they left, I tidied the room while Blanche rested, and tears streamed down my face while we talked about it. What a sad and difficult thing it is to be human.

Now that there's more light, I see that that yellow Walnut tree has already dropped most of its leaves, and the ones that are left are more of a deep gold. Time is passing, right before my eyes.

November 7, 2002

I was walking down to the baths after work, and saw my friend Katharine coming the other way, wearing a green raincoat and carrying a bucket. She's the one who read *Higgledy Piggledy Pop* by Maurice Sendak to me back when I was first getting ready to come down here over two years ago. She brought it with her when she came down in September, and loaned it to me while I was laid up with my hurt foot.

"Katharine," I said, "I don't get it. Jenny the dog has everything, leaves it behind, goes through an initiation, and then ends up with everything again, only in a more mysterious and glamorous form. What's the point?"

"But you've just described your path toward the priesthood" she answered. "And it looked like Jenny's new life was more fun than her old life. She found Sangha." Well all right then!

We're finally getting our first rainstorm, and Tassajara is incredibly beautiful. There's a big tree in the courtyard whose leaves turned a bright yellow a few days ago. Those leaves are now covering the ground, as are the deeper gold Sycamore leaves around the cabins. There's a tree down by the bathhouse whose leaves stay a bright fresh green but all go whomp and fall at the same time. It's been one of those days where I've carried my camera and mixed snapping pix in with my regular routine.

Driving Blanche out yesterday was lovely. There are usually little afterthoughts or questions that get lost in the shuffle when primary contact with the teacher is a formal dokusan every week or two, but as anja I'm able to pull out anything and everything and look at it with her. I thought, driving back, that one thing about her, and one thing about the way she and I are with each other, is that she switches back and forth from chit-chatting to dealing with the most weighty matters without batting an eyelash. She likes to tell me about the old days, and I like to hear those stories. And there's nothing I can't tell her, nothing that she doesn't meet with a friendly curiosity. I recalled my therapist saying that the experience of therapy for someone like me was an experience of finding someone I could trust. That's how it was with her, and that's how it is with Blanche.

When we passed the road to the Observatory — a metal gate with a No Entry sign on it — she mentioned that the old fire lookout is now open and that I might be able to get some good photos there on my way back. My foot was hurting and I asked how long a walk it was, and she said "Farther than the Hill Cabins but not as far as the Suzuki Roshi memorial," and I thought that sounded doable. In fact, I hiked and I hiked and I hiked, limping along on the sore foot, until I reached a really big fire lookout that was closed up tight. I took a few shots and walked on back. I had, of course, taken a wrong turn and gone all the way to the Observatory. That is a very small Observatory, I must say, more like an executive's second home than a place with huge telescopes. But on the way back I saw, for the second time, a strange round puffy thing on the road. When I picked it up and turned it over, I saw it was a bird's nest, teeny tiny, maybe 4" in diameter, and exquisitely made with one little feather sticking jauntily out the side. I brought it back and one person said it was a hummingbird's nest. Beautiful.

November 8, 2002

The rainstorm continued all night. Leaving the zendo, I found a blanket on the engawa that felt really soft and nice and then realized it was my black shawl, blown off its peg and lying in a big rain puddle. Branches thumped against my roof as I prepared for bed, and there's lots of fallen debris on the paths.

My little cabin is set back against the hill, so I walk about 30 feet past two joined cabins to get to the main path. Since Blanche is out of town, I'm waking to the bell and moving with the group instead of getting up early to get her ready for the day. This morning I dressed in my robe, pulled on my little black "fur"-lined boots, put on my shawl and hat, stepped out into the 5 a.m. darkness, and opened my umbrella. Past cabins 10 and 11, I joined a stream of black-robed figures with big black umbrellas moving through the wind and rain toward the zendo. This is what we thought a monastery would look like.

There's a creek bed that runs between the cabins and the zendo that has been dry since maybe March. When it runs, it's called Cabarga Creek. It's running today, roaring in fact. The zendo was built as a temporary structure about 25 years ago after the original zendo burned down. It's about 60 feet long and 30 feet wide, two large doors front and back, a row of soji panel-covered windows above eye level running all the way around the room. It was built in such a rush that we can see cracks of light between the upright pieces of wood and the white-painted panels of the walls. Its roof is corrugated something. When it's raining like this, between the sound of the rain on the zendo roof and the roar of Cabarga Creek, I feel like a very thin-skinned beetle. The noise is so great that it throws our chanting off. We "chant with our ears" but when the water's pounding, the people in one end of the zendo can't hear those in the other, and we begin to chant in different time zones.

Today's a work day (thus the sitting at 5 instead of 4) and I'm going to continue my thorough cleaning of Blanche's cabin. Thank God I have an inside job.

November 28, 2002

One evening I was walking back from the baths and saw a couple of friends up ahead examining something in the road. They called out to me that it was a tarantula, and to be careful not to step on it. Okay! Talked me into it! They walked on slowly, and when I came up to the big furry spider I felt the fear. Spiders are fast. So I was faster, running until I caught up with and then passed my friends.

The next time I saw a tarantula was during the four-day sesshin. I walked behind it and watched it negotiate its way along slowly, all those legs going this way and that. Although there's a restriction on reading and writing during sesshin, I went to the library and got a spider book. Tarantulas are not poisonous. They even make good pets! While I was at it, I went ahead and read up on scorpions, black widows and brown recluses. I held the pages of the book gingerly, by the edges, not even wanting to touch the pictures.

I know where there's a black widow. It's inside a warm cabinet at the bath house that only a few people ever have access to. The woman who cleans the bathhouse told me about it, and as soon as I could, I opened the door and took a look. Sure enough, there she is, and there are the remains of two of her ex-husbands in the web below her. You know, it's possible, just possible, that we go too far in this live and let live thing around here.

Today is Thanksgiving, and we had nut loaf as usual. Nut loaf and pumpkin pie with whipped cream and no place to be and nothing to do. I felt a little moody and blue on general principles, but am loving the big chunk of free time.

I'm nearly through sewing my okesa. Blanche helped me do the first corner in the last sewing class; when I finish the other three, I'll hand it over to a kind woman here who's going to do the rest of the small fussy stuff for me. I did the math: took an average-looking 10 centimeters, counted the stitches in it, figured how many centimeters there were in the whole okesa, and came out with 13,000 stitches. Since we have a tradition of sewing on each others' okesas, I haven't done all 13,000 but I'll bet I've done 12,000 of them. My zagu (bowing cloth) is being sewn up at City Center, and so I just have to finish my rakusu (the little biblike version of the okesa) and I'm ready. I finally got my invitations together (as usual, trying to do something like get cards printed from here at the end of beyond was frustrating and took much longer than I'd expected) and they've gone out.

So what is this ordination thing I think I'm going to do. It means more clothes (the big okesa instead of the little rakusu is the usual sacred garment, and the priest's sitting robe – the black robe under the okesa -- has about a third again as much fabric as a lay person's) and less hair (I'll have to stay bald — hello, bald! — for a year). It's pretty common to concentrate anxiety on the baldness, but what about the rest of it. What about the, for instance, lifetime commitment!?! What about how I'll actually be a priest with whatever the expectations are around that on my part and others'. I can't think of any other experience in my life that so combined inevitability and fear.

December 4, 2002

One of the tangaryo students, a guy in his 30s, saw a tarantula and then, a couple of days later, when he slid his foot into his shoe and felt something, kicked out reflexively and the shoe flew over the railing of the stairs down from the zendo and into the puddles that are still sitting in the bottom of Cabarga creek. Insect fear.

Not a piece of wood enters Blanche's cabin or mine that hasn't been thoroughly inspected on all six sides. That's a lot of inspecting. I'm okay with the tarantula but I so much don't want to encounter another scorpion.

After the rainstorm, a huge old oak tree fell down. We heard about it in study hall, and later in the morning we all trooped down there and did a ceremony for it. Mel was here, and he said a few words after we'd finished chanting. All I remember is "there's a lot of life still left in that tree, a lot of toothpicks and chopsticks and furniture and winter heat." I photographed it and the pictures came out fine. I'd always admired the tree for its burl, and so was disappointed to see that, rather than being uprooted, it broke off at the base, the victim of some sort of rot. Probably it fell because the tree itself was so water logged. The great part is the way it fell. It was right in front of the old bathhouse bathroom, about 15 feet from some guest rooms (the Stones and Pines) and it fell exactly between them, just puncturing the roofs but nothing worse than that. A few feet either way and it would have demolished a building. This is the Tassajara magic, and I think it's the same magic that led Blanche's hand to pick up the one piece of paper that I didn't want her to see when she came to my room. It's magic, but it doesn't necessarily always make things go the way I want them to go.

December 21, 2002

The practice period is over. There are only 12 of us left here. The rest hopped into a variety of vehicles this morning to make their way out over the road that's covered with mud and snow. Of course it was hard to say goodbye to Blanche. I cleaned her cabin this morning for the last time, and tears were shed. It doesn't matter that I'll see her in the city in a few days. This period as her attendant was so precious, and it's over.

I'm exhausted and am really looking forward to catching up on my sleep, reading some novels, and listening to some music for a couple of weeks. But that doesn't mean I wouldn't have been willing to go on taking care of her forever.

We have "open kitchen" during interim. I went in for lunch with my heart set on a grilled cheese sandwich. We were low on bread, so I got some frozen tortillas and made a quesadilla. As people drifted into the kitchen I kept on making more. Someone else made a salad, a pot of tea appeared, and someone brought a bag of M&Ms. For dinner a few people heated the leftovers from the big shuso dinner night before last, and we all carried plates over to the dining room and sat around one table together. All grudges and problems were forgotten and we were the happy Tassajara family.

We light a bare minimum of lanterns on the paths, and the place is incredibly dark without them. It's 40 degrees out but my wood stove's got it cranked up to 64 inside. I've just graduated to two hot water bottles. Oh hey it's the shortest day of the year, which means that this valley gets no direct sun at all.

A year ago we had a good rainstorm that made the creek rise enough to float the giant tree stump down stream about 30 feet, from the new bathhouse to the old bathhouse. It was created when a tree was felled about six years ago and bears the marks of the chainsaws where the crew tried, and failed, to chop it up. It's about the size of a Jeep. I thought it was so exciting when it moved last year. This year the rain was so violent and the creek rose so high that the tree stump is gone entirely. It happened during rohatsu sesshin, the most intense sesshin of the year. During one of the breaks I went up to see if the stump had moved again, and then walked down past the cabins, past the pool, and past the barns, searching for it. After sesshin I went even further and saw that it's gone entirely. We can't cross the creek at this time of year, so we'll have to wait until the spring to see how far it's gone.

For all of the exhilaration of living in nature like this and practicing so intimately with my teacher, I still got into quite a dark place during sesshin. Ordination is bringing up a lot of fear, which manifests as a distrust of the organization of "Zen Center" and a dislike of some other monks, particularly those who dare to mirror back the parts of myself that I least like. The darkness is gone now, and I don't doubt my right to wear Buddha's robe or my desire to ordain.

December 22, 2002

During cleanup this morning, one of the guys found an old copy of *Vogue.* I snatched it and spent the morning sitting on my bed reading it. At first my attitude was "Oh how superficial, how materialistic," and then gradually I lightened up and relaxed and enjoyed it. And I love love loved the interlude of lazing around doing nothing. Because soon enough it was time to get off the bed and get to work, cleaning my cabin and packing for tomorrow morning's early departure. This is such a great way to do Tassajara, I'm sorry I have to leave so soon. Still, working seemed fitting. We are still monks.

I wanted to tell you about the photo project I did this fall. Melissa, the ino (head of the zendo) was an art major in college, and she thought of a gift for Blanche, which involved my taking a portrait of each of the 55 people who were here. Some of the pictures I took were so-so (I haven't yet found a way to photograph couples), and a handful were absolutely sensational. There's about a two-week turnaround time between putting film in the mail to the lab and receiving prints back so I didn't have much time for do-overs. It was nerve-wracking. I still have no confidence that I've gotten the shot until I'm holding an acceptable print in my hands. These were acceptable enough, and they were each pasted into a beautiful book that Melissa made and we nearly all wrote something by our picture. It was a gorgeous thank you gift. I received some praise from some people and some silence from others, and contributions of about $100 to defray the $130 lab costs.

One night I was roaming around in the Abbot's garden, waiting to escort Blanche to the zendo, and it occurred to me that the project was a dream come true. I took extension classes at the SF Art Institute after college, but I couldn't keep up with such an expensive and demanding craft. Years later, after my first long meditation retreat, it came into my head to go back to the art school and start taking photos again. However, for years I was too shy to ask anyone if I could take their picture, and made only black and white landscapes. Eventually I did do some formal black and white portraits. Packing my photography stuff away was one of the hardest parts of moving down here, but when I got here I found there was a way for me to continue taking pictures using color film, which I mail to a lab in San Francisco. And now, I realized, with this project my initial desire was being fulfilled. I had the chance to photograph some beautiful people who trusted enough to give me their faces for that second of the camera's click.

Next practice period I'm supposed to be on the doan ryo (the people who hit the bells and so on in the zendo). It's a pretty big job, but it'll be a walk in the park compared to this practice period. Being on call for Blanche all day every day, sewing my okesa, and taking 55 good photographs as well — it makes me tired just thinking about it. Now what's ahead is two weeks of ignoring the wakeup bell, finishing my preparations for ordination, going to some movies and seeing some friends, making some phone calls from a phone that actually works, and the ceremony itself.

Procession

Winter 2003
5th Tassajara
Practice Period

January 8, 2003

Usually when I come back to Tassajara after spending interim in the city, it rapidly feels like the whole thing was a dream, and that this place, this schedule, these people, are the only thing I've ever done. This time it's different. This time I know I went somewhere and something happened, because I have a whole new set of robes, and I'm bald as an egg. Well, at this point, maybe the egg has a little stubble.

January 9, 2003

I'll tell you this: I sure don't feel like a priest. I have a robe I can't get into and oryoki bowls that crash onto the meal board when I try to open them. The wrapping of the okesa takes three times as long as it should, and then the whole thing falls apart. People have been making jokes about this part of the process to me for months, and now that I'm in it I know why. I don't feel like a priest. I feel like a baby. Or an imposter.

The day of the ceremony, Tova (the other person receiving ordination) and I went to the dokusan room after breakfast. There, two people shaved our heads down to gleaming baby skin. The night before we'd buzzed our hair off in hilarious parties with friends. This event was more serious. After we'd been shaved, we left to bathe and then, dressed in new underwear, jubons (the white blouse that forms the base layer) and new kimonos, we spent the rest of the day locked at the hip. We were dressed during the ceremony (these shavers and dressers are honored positions, given to close friends) first in our new black koromos (the priest's sitting robe) and finally in the okesas that we'd sewn ourselves.

Somewhere in the morning it occurred to me that I could do the rest of the day full of tension and anxiety (I'd had a stress dream earlier in the week that I was in the Buddha Hall with everyone watching and I couldn't get my bowing cloth down), or I could do it with joy. Praise be to whomever, joy won. Tova and I were relaxed as we sat together in the zendo before the ceremony, chanting a little, whispering last minute questions about the ceremony a little. As soon as the tanto came to get us, I began to smile. We went around to the various altars in the building and then waited at the entrance to the Buddha Hall as the last of the seating was arranged. Finally we entered.

The room was jammed full of people. Every person in the hall was there because they loved us. Some were there just for me, some were there just for Tova, and the vast majority were there for both of us. There were huge turnouts from Green Gulch and Tassajara (people made the four hour trip up, attended the ceremony, and made the trip back the same day), as well as from City Center. Everywhere my eye rested, I saw love beaming back at me. It was a dream come true.

The first thing that happens in the ceremony is that the teacher shaves off a nickel-sized patch of hair called the shura that's left on when the rest of the head is shaved. First it's done while the student is in the kimono, then again in the new koromo. That was the most intense part. When it's done the new priest-in-training chants

"Freed from my ancient karma
Freed from my worldly attachments
Freed from form and color

Everything is changed
Except my deep desire to live in truth with all beings."

Then the teacher gives the student new bowls, a new dharma name (I kept my jukai name, Ren Shin Ji Ko which means Lotus Heart Bound-less Compassion), and, finally, the precepts. Then it's done.

The ceremony started at 2:30 and we partied and ate and opened gifts until 9 that night. When I came out of my room at 3 a.m. there was another gift propped against my door. When I came out again at 6 a.m. there was another. When I came back from breakfast there was another. When I got back to Tassajara on the 5th there were more cards and gifts. The joke is that we leave home (Shukke Tokudo is the ceremony of home leaving) and are given expensive new clothes and showered with gifts. There are lots of books and incense, a few malas, and even some really big checks.

The next day, believe it or not, I drove Blanche down to Monterey for another priest ordination. We changed into our robes downstairs, three established priests and me, and I felt like the little girl wearing her mother's high heels, coat, and hat.

So maybe imposter's the wrong word. Maybe I'll stick with Baby.

The first morning back here at Tassajara, I thought I did pretty well in getting the okesa on (I snagged a nearby priest to come and help me). Then during service I looked down and saw that it was inside out. Slick. That afternoon the three new priests had a training session given by the work leader and oh it was sweet. Getting the okesa off (remember, this is a rectangle about 4 feet long and 6 feet wide) involves putting it over your head and I particularly liked the part where all four of us had our okesas over our heads like four storybook witches.

But we're not witches. In the ceremony we're called Baby Buddhas. I like that.

January 11, 2003

This morning during service and breakfast I was struggling with my okesa. The flap that goes over the left shoulder keeps falling forward. I thought about Linda Ruth (co-Abbess of Zen Center, just arrived yesterday to lead this next practice period) and I thought how naturally she wore her okesa. It was just there, without all the pulling and fussing. And then I thought what a great reflection of our inner priesthood the garment is. I'm so new to it that I can't wear it at all; she's so accustomed to it that it's not even anything extra.

I'm not a priest, I'm telling my friends. That ceremony was an affirmation that I have permission to begin finding out what a priest is. Nothing more and of course nothing less.

March 4, 2003

Aha, by a coincidence, today, the day when I finally have the time and energy to fire up the computer and write, is two months since the ordination. It's also 2/3 of the way through the practice period.

I'm just starting to write now because I've just come out of my usual mid-practice period depression. I really do think this is the way it always is. First I'm elated, then I'm depressed, then I come out the other side of the depression having learned something and I think to myself, That was nasty but it was also really worth it, and then I cruise on through to the end. I cannot believe that I'm looking forward to the summer, since I clearly remember how hard the summer was and how I spent most of it yearning for practice period to start. And there it is: suffering. Human nature.

My job this practice period is to be a doan. There are six of us, and we cycle through the four main zendo jobs. I had done all these jobs when I was at City Center, and thought being on the doan ryo at Tassajara would be an honor and that it would be easy. I also thought I already knew how to do all these things better than some of the doans I've heard during my previous practice periods here. As it turns out, I only knew the mechanics of the jobs, and when it's my turn to do them I seize up and make all kinds of mistakes. The mistakes are killer. Dealing with making mistakes is something I've never been interested in working with. Either I do something perfectly or I don't do it at all. Making my mistakes out loud for everyone to hear has whipped me to a pulp. Making my mistakes out loud while wearing an okesa is even more difficult.

First I tried to get good enough to be a priest. Then I fell into despair over ever being able to measure up. Now it's somewhere in the middle. I hope. Just for today. I mean, this practice period we're studying karma, cause-and-effect, and lack of inherent self, so it must be noted that this idea of who I am and what I can do and how it will express is subject to change on every moment, and subject to forces that are waaaay out of my control.

We did a four-day sesshin early on. I caught the cold that was going around right after I got back down here and got well in time to sit that one. Then I went to the city for Blanche's stepping down ceremony, marking the end of her seven years as Abbess, came back here, and got sick again. I recovered from the second bout just in time to sit the nine-day sesshin. This is unusually long and it's pretty interesting to stay silent and sit extra periods of zazen for so long. The difficulty for me is that there are no days where we get the extra hour's sleep. Our normal Tassajara week is three days with six hours sleep and two days with seven hours. Those two extra hours really help. We're supposed to be tired and ragged, but I don't think we're supposed to be so exhausted that we injure ourselves. Being a doan during sesshin is an extra strain, too, since our breaks are shorter than everyone else's. So I have Linda Ruth's permission to sleep in (= one extra hour's sleep) halfway through the seven-day sesshin that will close the practice period at the end of this month.

The thought that began to consume me during that time of exhaustion was, I'm too old for this. I just can't take this any more. Neither of those things is true, but neither can I keep up with people who are in young strong bodies. Staying at Tassajara for another year is still my first choice, and I think I'll be able to do it if I start being able to admit that I'm older and weaker than most of the people here. And with that, I think I'll turn the computer off and take a little nap.

Spring is beginning to burst out, with little green leaves spurting out of the ends of the tree branches and daphne, daffodils and narcissus blooming. It's still cold in the morning (in the 30s) but it warms up in the afternoon (to the 60s). I already took a hike today, so now it's time to enjoy nature through the window and catch up on my *New Yorker*s.

March 9, 2003

An advantage of staying here long term that's emerging is that the same challenges keep rolling around, sometimes with the same face and name and sometimes not, and I get to work on them again. The connection to the story that goes with the event gets a little looser each time. When I had an emotional collapse a month or so ago, there was a little peep peep in the back of my mind saying, Haven't we been here before? because the cause of the collapse, the little trigger that pushed the first in the string of upended and vulnerable dominoes, was so familiar. When I lived in the world, I'd become good at sheltering myself from these feelings, but here there's nothing to do but experience them.

Those who have been reading this journal for some years (and oh how I thank you for that, most dear and faithful friends) will remember that when I did my practice period on kitchen crew there was one particular woman with whom I had trouble. So much trouble that we went to mediation. And the mediation worked: we saw through the misunderstanding that had arisen, talked it out, cried, hugged, and so on.

But I would now say that the karmic formations that were behind the misunderstandings were still there. Are still here. I'd say that because I'm again on the same crew with the same woman (yes, same face and name this time) and am having very much the same reaction to her now as I did then. One important difference: she's not my boss this time. Another important difference: about a million more hours of zazen. So day before yesterday there was another incident between us, sharp words, stomping feet, hurt feelings, and then yesterday there were various conferences between her and the ino (head of our crew), the ino and me, the two of them and the tanto (spiritual head of all crews) and then the tanto and me. It was so cool to move our difficulties from the realm of she said/I said conflict mediation to hard-core Zen practice. What I've been trying to study is what it is in this woman (and a couple of other kind souls who provide me with the same opportunity) that pisses me off so much — not to put a label on it so I can spread the word to other people to get them on my side, not to understand her problem so I can try to manipulate her into changing into someone I'm comfortable with, but as a way of understanding where the triggers are in me, what the mirror is reflecting to me, so the story can be looser around them in the future. Because I'm really tired of feeling this way.

It feels like yesterday's conflict brought me closer to both the ino and the tanto and brought me closer to understanding these reactions in myself. We had class last night and the example of karma in action was of a guy who pissed other people off, and by the end of class at least I was able to say to the other woman that I was sorry I'd upset her by my behavior, and to go through the ensuing exchange of words without anger. But to me the window into the karmic formations in myself that cause that behavior was much more important than any progress in learning to get along with my fellow monks. Please forgive me if all of that was incomprehensible. Better monks and better writers than I have tried to deal with this stuff and failed. But I found its arising interesting.

Before I had personal conflict to talk about, I was going to talk about the various doan jobs and what they're like. So let's go forward with that. Tenken is the hardest of the jobs for me, because this is the one who starts the whole wheel of getting-to-the-zendo in motion. Doans (doan is the name of one specific job I'll talk about, but also the general name for people who do all of these jobs) always have to be on our seats five minutes earlier than everyone else, but the tenken has to be in the zendo 16 minutes before that. At 4 a.m., those 16 minutes can feel like a lot, and throughout a day all of those 16 minutes add up. So first the tenken lights the altar (the first illumination in an empty dark zendo — nice!) then goes back out on the engawa (porch) and starts hitting the han (wooden block hanging from a rope with a gatha written on it about how precious life is and how we shouldn't waste it) in a particular pattern to call the monks to the zendo. At the end of that pattern, the abbess enters and officially starts zazen. When all that's settled down, the tenken silently takes roll and sometimes goes and knocks on absent people's doors to see if they're okay. There's a tenken pad hanging at the back of the zendo, and people who are going to be absent are supposed to write their excuse there. It's some of the most entertaining reading in the monastery. One night I read: sleepy," "too tired," "exhausted," and "narcoleptic."

The tenken signals the end of the final period of zazen by slipping out of the zendo and beating a pattern on the big taiko drum and then on the han, and that's a lot of fun. Boom boom boom! Wake up and go to bed!

Doan is the cool job of sounding various bells (from 4 inches to 3 feet in diameter) and clackers to signal the start and end of zazen, and the start and end of the chants we do during service. The challenge here is to make those bells sound both loud and beautiful. It's usually a choice between the two. I thought I was already slick with the bells when I got here. I was wrong. I'm working on it.

Each job has some little extra thing that I usually forget. With doan, it's lighting the small altars outside the zendo before the first period of zazen. The Abbess will go to these altars and present incense before she makes her entrance. A couple of times when I've been doan, she's gone to cold dark altars. Bad doan! On the other hand, I was sitting on the floor by the bell during zazen being doan the other night when both back doors swung open and a raccoon walked into the zendo, so I jumped up and scared him away, protecting all my fellow monks. Good brave doan!

Soku is the fun social job of heading up a crew of people who serve the meals. Remember that we eat our meals in the zendo, and there's a whole big deal about the way the food is served to us. So I work with five other people to get the monks their tofu and turnips. There can be great conflict on serving crews, but mine is lovely and we're having a lot of fun.

Kokyo is the scariest job because in this one the instrument isn't a drum or a bell, it's my voice. This is the person who announces the chants in services and then does the dedications. I can rehearse and rehearse, and my voice can sound fine, and then when I'm in a zendo full of people and the bells just clonked and the drums just bopped and it's time for me to open my mouth and make a sound, I clench up and this tight noise comes out. Morning service is about half an hour long, and I can gradually hear myself relax during that time, but it's tough.

We did nenju yesterday, the weekly ceremony of gratitude, and I must say that I was able to belt it out and have fun with it. At the end of the ceremony the kokyo goes behind the altar and makes a big circle with her hands while she announces *Ho-San!* (literally no dokusan tomorrow, meaning *day off!*) and I raised the roof. It was like an out of body experience with no mental crap about my performance, just pleasure.

The cold that we were all getting early in the practice period has run its course, but there are a few people sick with other things. One of them is a woman from Italy who I've become friends with who was down with, of all things, hemorrhoids. I happened to be the day off doan when she needed someone to take her to the doctor, and I happened to have the opinion that she should have been taken to the doctor many days before that, so I offered to drive her and was allowed to. There was another sick person, a guy who'd been in Borneo who'd come down with a constant low-level fever, who came along too. This meant three of us driving over the 14-mile dirt road (which is really awful at this time of year) and then on from Jamesburg to Carmel

Village, about a two-hour ride. It was So Much Fun. We listened to music! We ate pizza and Haagen Dazs! We bought junk food to bring back! We were somewhere else! The whole adventure took seven hours and we were all good and tired at the end, but it was a really nice break for me. Oh and the medical results were excellent for both of the sick people. Yeah, that too.

Now my friend and neighbor's popped her head in the door to see about taking a walk, so it's time to go out and enjoy the day.

March 24, 2003

I love the way the monastery feels on the day before sesshin. For the next seven days, we're going to have very short breaks and no days off, so everything that needs to get done has to get done today. It feels like preparing for a storm. The cloths that wrap our eating bowls are washed and ironed, our heads are shaved, we have a sufficient supply of underwear to last us, and many of us do a thorough room cleaning. I do. It's irritating as hell to lie on my bed in a zazen-induced haze and become fixated on the dust on the windowsills.

I have tons and tons of tchotchkes that were given to me as ordination gifts that have been on display, and they're all put away. I have lots of coffee in my room and have secreted some hard-boiled eggs in one of the refrigerators (we're asked only to eat the food that's served in the zendo, but very few people can or will do that). A few letters that I've been writing in my mind actually got committed to paper and put in the mail. It's a go!

The doans had a formal tea with the Abbess yesterday morning. She mentioned that she was thinking about having the wakeup bell rung an hour earlier during sesshin so we could sit three rather than two periods before breakfast. All the wimpy little doans said nothing. I alone spoke up (wanting to scream, That's the craziest idea I've ever heard!) by telling her that I wouldn't be able to do it, reminding her that I already had permission to sleep an extra hour halfway through the sesshin, and telling her that my sense of the sangha was that we were all tired. I don't know whether my protest made any difference, but the wakeup bell is ringing at the regular time. 3:40 a.m., after getting to bed at 9:15, is intense enough.

I remember at the end of the practice period in the kitchen, I saw that the way we cooked was the way we were. Well, I saw that about everyone else but couldn't see it in myself. So this practice period I see that we, the doans, approach the instruments in very particular ways. Some have remained timid throughout a whole 90 days. This time I see and hear myself quite clearly. Only one other person hits the han (hanging wooden block that announces that its time for zazen) as hard as I do, and that's a 26-year-old guy. And my time-keeping on the mokugyo (wooden drum in the zendo) is known for its speed. So. Me: loud and fast. Oh I dislike a wimpy bell! Speaking of the han, it's nearly time to get started. Have a lovely week; we'll be sitting for and with you, whatever you're doing.

The Path

Work Period/Summer 2003

April 25, 2003

It's nearly the end of the work period — one more day to go, and then the guests arrive. Practice period has been over and we've been in student housing since April 7th. I got a very good room in the lower barn (good = my own door to the outside so it won't be so much like a dorm, and cave-like so it won't be so awfully hot later in the summer). But when I moved to this student room, I left behind the wood stove in the guest cabin where I spent the winter, and the weather immediately got cold and stayed that way. What a rainy spring. During the last sesshin of the practice period, about a month ago, it was up to 80 degrees and we were sweltering in our robes. Where is that heat now! My unheated summer room is cold and clammy.

Tonight I came back from zazen and got ready for bed before I went to the shared bathroom on the other side of the barn. Now that I'm a priest, I can no longer wear my robes in the bathroom. I walked into a full house wearing: my white flannel long nightgown, ancient chartreuse wool cardigan, gray Polartec socks, black pointy-toed slip-on shoes, and my new black Amelia hat with ear flaps. I was laughing at my appearance with a friend who was brushing her teeth (non-ordained, she was still in her robes) and one of the new girls whispered, You look like my grandmother. I whispered back, I hope you like her and she replied, Oh she's my favorite person in the world. Sweet.

Once I knew I'd gotten my first choice in housing, all of my anxiety settled on my job assignment. I so much wanted to stay in the zendo but I got my second choice, and will be the bathhouse attendant this summer. I didn't take it very well, and didn't handle not taking it very well very gracefully, but that's what transitions are like.

We were a mostly-silent monastery one day, and the next day 80 people swarmed in to help work on the place for a month to prepare for the guest season. Since this is the second time I've been through this change, and since so many of the faces were familiar from last year, I thought I was doing okay, and then I couldn't stop crying for 36 hours. Same old Judy oops I mean Ren.

I changed my name when I received ordination. The name my teacher gave me is Ren Shin Ji Ko, which translates to Lotus Heart Boundless Compassion, so I'm asking people to call me Renshin or Ren. The 55 people I lived with from January through March did pretty well with it, and now there are many more to be taught the new name. I went up to City Center for a few days vacation, and it was strange to hear everyone call me Judy. I knew the change was complete when I called myself Ren once when I was talking to myself.

April 28, 2003

Yesterday morning we had the ceremony of opening the gate at 8:30 in the morning, and the first summer guests came in at noon. The horde of scruffy workers who come to Tassajara year after year are gone, and the people who actually pay money to stay here, and expect something like a vacation resort in return, are with us. Here we go.

I've worked hard for the last few days to get the bathhouse into shape, and felt the pleasure of offering that space to both the students and guests by the end of the day. I also had my first conversation with a guest about the world situation and the importance of monasteries while I was sitting nude by the creek, and throughout had a feeling running of, This is what it's going to be like this year. I'm so enraged by the bogus war and the bogus reporting on it that I've turned away from it entirely, but it's going to come to me anyway.

Someone who I've had a crush on for years and years was down here for the entire month-long work period, giving me a chance once again to look at what's important to me, at what I ultimately want from life. Let it be known: I want it all. And hear this: if I have to choose, my choice will be the life of a celibate monastic. But jeez romance is a strong pull for me.

Turning on the computer this morning, I browsed through My Documents and clicked on an old file of postings in Wonderland. I read my writing from 1999 when I was first getting involved at City Center, and honest to God my struggles and insights were exactly the same as those I go through here at Tassajara four years later. I think of the person I was then, and think I couldn't possibly have known what I was talking about. Which is selling myself short. As I know I've said before, apparently my issues are my issues, and will always be the stuff I'm working on.

In the old postings, I was talking about being given responsibility at Zen Center and dealing with that. Day before yesterday, I was filling in as ino (head of the meditation hall) and as I was rushing up to the zendo, I thought, again, I didn't think it would be like this. I thought that when I was *ino* at *Tassajara*, I'd be some fabulously wise Zen person, someone who got the nature of reality and felt the nectar of forgiveness flowing through her veins. Instead it was just me, bustling along trying to get there on time, trying to remember the assignment, trying not to make too many mistakes. Is this what it's like for everyone?

After doing the ino stuff during morning zazen, I reverted to being the bathhouse attendant all morning. The girl who was helping me deep clean the bathhouse needed meditation instruction, so she and I went to the zendo at the end of the morning. Noon service during work period is a very small affair, maybe two or three people, but still necessary. So I found myself being doshi (the priest performing the ceremony in the zendo) for the first time in jeans that were wet from cleaning the plunge, rushing through the service because the bell-ringer was late. First time as doshi sounded like full robes and preparation and ceremony, but for me this is what it looked like. And the ceremony was done, and the communal life at Tassajara continued peacefully.

The Ventana Wilderness

Fall 2003
6th Tassajara
Practice Period

September 27, 2003

Five months gone, nearly to the day, since I last wrote anything. I'm amazed to find such old stuff in this file (I show it starting March 24th) and wonder whether I didn't send it to Sweeney for posting and forget, but I'll send it along now just in case.

Another way in which this second summer was easier than the first was that my lack of interest in writing, or doing anything else mildly creative or energetic, didn't scare me. Honey, when it's 106 to 110 degrees for two weeks straight, even lying on the bed takes more energy than I want to spend. But as soon as practice period started, I began looking for time to turn the computer on and rev it up again.

Remember, last year we did a rough calculation at the end of summer and figured that something like 8000 people came through this place from April to September. Since more than half of those are women, I figure I interacted with about 5000 people at the baths this year. Many, it seemed, were glad to have access to a resident, and dealing with their stored up questions was a part of my job. A nice part. Sometimes I think about those strip joints on Broadway with signs that say "Talk to a real live nude girl!" But this joint's sign said "Talk to a real live monk!" So, they did. I also remembered Leslie's

191

saying that "People are going to think they love you when what they love is Tassajara," as I received the gratitude of many people for the place we provide here.

Today was probably my last day at the baths. Without the guests around, I pootled about through some of my favorite parts of the job: I arranged flowers; checked to see that the water in the outdoor plunge was staying free of the hated sulfur bacteria; disinfected the shower and filled the soap bottles; and sprayed water on the wooden walkway in front to clean it. The smell of water on hot wood and rocks is one I can store away for the coming cold time. Something that occurred to me over and over is that during the winter I think about what summer's like here, but during summer I don't yearn for the winter. Now that it's here — not the cold weather, but the beginning of practice period — there are lots of smiles and displays of affection among those of us who are carrying over from the summer. Of course, this week of tangaryo is one of the best of the year for continuing students. The guests (God love 'em) are gone and we have the place to ourselves again, and we're on a very relaxed schedule while the new students sit from sun up to sun down for five days. All the rest of us are doing is moving into our new housing, easing into our new jobs, and waiting for our new friends to finish their initiation and join us.

September 28, 2003

The job I wanted at the start of the summer is called head doan. It's the person who works directly under the ino, who's the head of the zendo. It involves scheduling and training doans and generally being second in command in that particularly sacred place. It's a great training job. I didn't get it. The person who got the job is someone who I've had difficulty with before when she was my boss in the kitchen, making the loss even harder to take. At the end of the summer, the slot did indeed open up, but only because she was promoted to ino. So if I got the job I wanted, it would mean working for her again.

On the night I found this out, I went to zazen with a head full of jealousy and anger. I sat on my cushion in my beautiful black robes and my priest's okesa stewing over what a twit she was. I even told myself that if they offered me the job I wouldn't take it because I couldn't bear the thought of working with her. When I went to bed, the disappointment was still raging. Damn her! How much better my life here would be without her! And when I woke the next morning, these words came into my head full blown: I was the one who was causing this suffering, and if I wanted it to end there was a solution: I had to love her.

Reaching that place, the job was once again desirable. So I phoned Blanche and talked with her about the whole thing. Should I campaign for the job I wanted, or should I just wait and see what got offered me. She said, of course, that the latter course represented the more rigorous form of practice, and so that's what I chose to do. Unsuccessfully.

When Charlie, the director, asked to speak with me about jobs soon after my conversation with Blanche, I just smiled and said, Oh anything, I'll be grateful no matter what job you give me. This must have been a relief for him, since the last time he told me what my job was, at the beginning of summer, (when I got my second choice of bathhouse attendant instead of my first choice of head doan) I burst into tears and essentially asked him why they all hated me so. Still, brave Charlie persisted. He explained who all the senior staff people would be, and said that I was in a place right under that group and that much thought had been given to what job would be right for me. He said, "Normally you'd be the ideal person for head doan, but your history with the new ino rules that out." Well wait a minute now! My accepting whatever was offered with gratitude flew out the window, and I talked about how valuable that difficult relationship had been and about my belief in the transformative nature of our practice. When he asked me the key question: Can you support her as ino? I was able to look him fully in the eye and answer yes.

I was involved in many conversations about the job in the following week, and it was amazing to watch my relationship with it evolve. I had to give up on trying to sell myself and instead talk honestly about what was best for me, best for her, and best for Tassajara. Before I talked with the ino, I realized that I had to be all right with not getting the job. Leslie, who's been through all of it with the two of us, said that getting to this point of both of us being willing to even consider this possibility was itself success.

Vacations started, time passed, she left, I left, and for about two weeks it remained unsettled. Finally two days ago we had one more conversation. Again I had to try not to sell myself, and to just tell her that I supported her as ino no matter what seat I was sitting on. One thing she mentioned was that there were so many people in line to be doans that she was considering not having a head doan at all in order to make room. That it would be either me or no one.

Yesterday the tanto told me that my job would be to run the kitchen crew during the afternoon work period. She didn't say much more than that. I don't think she even mentioned the head doan job. I worked with the feelings all day as I did my final day at the bathhouse. Finally today the ino and I talked about it. The first thing she said was "It would have worked." That was all I needed. She'll have no head doan, I'll head up a crew in the kitchen, and we'll both see what happens next time.

October 4, 2003

Last night was the first time I've slept with the windows closed since the beginning of summer. Now, at 8:45 in the morning, it's 52 degrees out and I'm wearing a hat inside. Here comes the cold.

My job is pleasant indeed, and I'm also still involved in zendo jobs for a little while. Although I still don't know what "I just have to love her" means, I do know that my feelings of anger toward my old adversary haven't returned. I had a wonderful dream about two sisters who were looking at me as they morphed through different appearances, smiling as if to say, Do you get it yet? Although their appearance changed, they remained connected. Sisters, and this woman with whom I've had such difficulties is definitely a sister, don't have to be dangerous.

I had a conversation this morning with a woman who's here just for the practice period who was crushed when she hadn't been chosen as a doan. I told her, yes, doan is the heartbreaker.

Nature put on quite a show this summer. I saw a gopher snake and a baby king snake in a fight to the death. The gopher snake won, but he would have starved to death with the body of the baby king snake wrapped around his neck if someone hadn't loosened the body of the now-dead baby king snake with a stick. I saw several rattlesnakes, an animal I'd always wanted to see and hear. I saw a blue jay catch a bat on the fly, bash it on a rock and eat it. Another reason to dislike blue jays.

October 27, 2003

Reb Anderson is leading this practice period. He taught right at the start about Bodhidharma's *Mind Like a Wall*: Stop all outside involvements and inside cease the sighing and coughing of the mind. This was interesting to me, in my ongoing swing between training the mind and acceptance of things as it is (even though Myo tells me that those two are the same thing) and so I gave it a try. Interesting. All of these years of practicing zazen and now maybe there's this way of non-thinking available to me.

I thought about writing another post for this topic and thought, No, that's an outside involvement. And there have been periods of zazen where I've sat quietly composing, composing, composing. So I composed a post that told you all that I wouldn't compose any more posts.

The mind like a wall is one reason not to write, and another is that this thing is increasingly impinging on my monastic life. Last summer, people came here who recognized my name and said they'd read my stuff on *Slow Trains* (a literary website that kindly paid me for my writing). This summer a guy was here who'd not only read it but had printed it out and brought it with him. He would quote me to me at the dinner table. I haven't read the old stuff for a long time, but I don't really remember it as anything that I want quoted back to me. So: no more.

And then Sweeney writes and says people on the Well are wondering what's become of me. And I get a postcard from Debbie saying Hey. And Kathy sends me a bag of books full of memoirs and spiritual writing. In Sweeney's letter there's a list of questions, and so I think, okay, maybe just a little more. But maybe just for the eyes of the Well, maybe not for the unknown world at large any more. So here I am.

Reb is quite a guy. He was one of Suzuki Roshi's original students, and he's the one who became Abbot after Richard Baker left in the early 80s. He's been studying this stuff and teaching it for a long time now, and he's good. There are two main streams at Zen Center: Reb and his students, and Mel Weitsman and his students. My teachers have been Mel's students. I did sesshins at Green Gulch with Reb in the mid-90s, so I've had a relationship with him, but nothing's like Reb at Tassajara. He's a showman and a scholar, intimate and distracted, picky and forgiving.

It's sesshin now, and I'm in my room writing on my laptop because I'm working in the kitchen. For one of the three sesshins during a practice period, volunteers do the cooking so the regular crew can sit.

And Sweeney, there's one of your answers: there are two circles at Tassajara during a practice period, the big group of people in the zendo, and a crew of about six who do nothing but cook all day every day. Some stay in the kitchen for more than one practice period, especially those in management, but most just rotate through and out. This experience of the kitchen is so unlike my time on kitchen crew two years ago. My body's holding up without pain and I and all the other crew members are quite happy. There are small challenges that arise in my regular afternoon job of kitchen management, but that was the point to giving me the job in the first place, to get me started on learning how to

December 29, 2003 - Interim

We'll never know what I was supposed to be learning back there in October, because that's where my computer pooped out. Many many thanks to <sforslev> for the new old ThinkPad that she sent. As usual, the Well community comes through for me.

Now it's 7:25 in the morning on a rainy day. It's interim, the lull between practice periods, so zazen was voluntary this morning. I sat anyway. Yesterday the raccoons had left the door open when they went in the zendo on their nightly patrol, and it was freezing in there — well, 42 degrees, which is nearly freezing — and 30 degrees outside. This morning the door was closed and it's 44 degrees outside but alas the zendo was still cold. When I got back from vacation on the 26th there were six of us here; yesterday seven more came in, and three of those sat in the zendo with me this morning. I was so excited about doing some writing that I took some granola and am eating it while I type, foregoing the lovely communal meal.

Reb continued to grab my attention during the last practice period. If I understood his behavior correctly, he goes ahead and does what he wants to, and if his behavior upsets people he's willing to stick with them while they work through their reaction.

Living in community for this long (it's been 2 ½ years now), getting along with others has been the ongoing big issue. I thought it was my job to figure out how to never upset anyone. Now I think it's my job to find the courage to bring forth my ideas and the softness to be willing to have others react and the wisdom to know that whether the reaction's positive or negative, it doesn't have much to do with me. Some of this is about this deal of being a priest. Now that I've been ordained for nearly a year, I still don't know what it means. The outward trappings are simple enough. My head stays shaved, my robes are fancier (and way more expensive) than those that lay people wear, and I can and do perform rituals.

I reread the oral history that was done with Mel Weitsman some years ago, and there he says that the difference between priest and lay practice is that the priest's life is a life of service. Well there I go again, quoting someone else instead of looking at my own experience. Many people here want to ordain, and some of them are denied over and over by their teachers. I think now that we all see it as a natural progression, or even as a kind of blue ribbon for spiritual excellence that our teacher pins on us. We think being a priest is an achievement. So the words I said to my elders when I went around to the abbots and former abbots to get permission (two years ago, before I began sewing my okesa) were something about turning up the fire on my practice and raising the bar. Now I think that's hilarious: as if there were something called my practice, and as if I could control its intensity or lack of it. Suzuki Roshi said, "Never think that you sit zazen! Zazen sits zazen!" and Dogen said "To carry the self forward and experience the 10,000 things is delusion; that the 10,000 things carry themselves forward and experience the self is enlightenment" and this is the flavor of what I'm trying to express here. So for whatever reason I stumbled into this okesa, and now I get to live with the results of that stumble.

The first thing was that both others and I expected more of me. Just as I thought I'd wanted, only it was very unpleasant when it happened. Some of the people who want to ordain and haven't been given permission may even be a little willing to be critical of those who have. I get very caught up in being a good example and then, as we used to say in AA (or at least I think we did) start to choke on my halo. In Zen we teach by example, so I'm not saying I shouldn't concentrate on my bow and even on my behavior, but I have to be careful of going too far and losing real expression. Just between us, this place doesn't need more people who are all about following the rules. Ugh.

Sitting and staring out of the window, I'm thinking that, as in the sense of the phrase from Dogen, instead of making myself into some idea of priest, I can — no, I'd better — do what I want to do, as long as that's guided by the precepts, and let that be what being a priest looks like.

The renunciation part is a puzzle here at Tassajara. By anyone's standards, we're living a life of poverty: $200 a month stipend, hand washing clothes, wood stove for heat and kerosene lamps for light, two radio wave phones for 60 people, and those broken more often than not. But I have a big beautiful room, three meals a day of mostly delicious food handed to me, my health insurance is covered, and I still have credit cards enough to mail order shoes and film and whatever else I think I need on any given day. So this life of renunciation is actually a life of great comfort and ease. I think this is peculiar to San Francisco Zen Center; I hear this is the only monastery where the monks are given a stipend, and that makes all the difference.

At the end of the last practice period, when it was time to deal with the job thing, I was told that once again there wasn't much here for me. The director even said, The ino wants someone younger to be head doan. Someone younger! Stick the knife in and turn it! Blanche was leaving for Spain and we were going into a seven day sesshin here, but there was just time enough to leave her a message telling her that I was very interested in the job of tenzo (exec head of the kitchen) at City Center, a possibility that she'd mentioned some months back. And there was just enough time to say to the ino, "You should have told me yourself."

It's scary to go into sesshin carrying a lot of anger. Too much of my life already has been spent sitting on a zafu raging away silently. I turned to Pema Chodron and within a few pages she said that if you're sitting with anger, drop the story and sit with the energy. Reb had been teaching on the *Samdinirmochana Sutra*, and he'd exhorted us over and over to drop the story. So for the first days of the sesshin, that's what I did, over and over and over. I saw that my anger at the people in charge here was hanging on a hook called priest training and, around day five or so, had to admit that there was no one to be angry at and nothing anyone owed me. In fact, there was no such thing as priest, priest training, or San Francisco Zen Center. Again, there was just me making up a story that resulted in my suffering. And what was available to me in the upcoming practice period was another chance to follow the schedule and hear teachings; anything beyond that was extra, and any idea of training was only in my head.

Of course, on the day after sesshin ended, the ino said "I made a mistake" and offered me the job of head doan. She even repeated the words I'd had banging away in my head, that my working with her and the doans would be best for her, best for me, best for Tassajara and all of Zen Center.

Before all of this, it felt as if this was the only place I could practice. Now it feels as if the spell of Tassajara is broken, and I'm free to either stay or go. When I was in the city last week I had conversations with the seniors about coming up there, and that's what I think will happen at the end of this practice period. It's an idea that arose in anger, but now that the anger's gone — now that I even got what I wanted, delivered in the most perfect terms possible — the idea still seems pretty good. The kitchen job I was interested in won't necessarily be waiting for me, but I'm sure they'll be able to make some use of me

December 31, 2003

Each day brings another car or two full of people returning from vacation, and several days ago we expanded beyond our group of 12 seats around one table. There are people who've lived here in the past who come and visit over interim, and their company is very welcome indeed.

Yesterday I worked for much of the morning with one of these old friends, taking the stovepipe in my room apart and then putting it back together. Smoke was leaking out from the joints and making me sick, so we sealed the joints with furnace cement. This morning I spent a couple of hours pruning the climbing pink rose in the upper garden, the one we gaze at while we're waiting at the back door of the zendo to go back in after running to the bathroom during kinhin. These are pleasant jobs done with friends.

Tonight, New Year's Eve, a visitor will play a concert on her guitar before dinner, then we'll have the ritual ringing of the big densho 108 times during (optional) evening zazen, and finally at midnight we'll walk out to the flats and build a bonfire for burning the pieces of paper from the altar with names of people who've died this year, along with the incense stubs and zendo attendance records. Tomorrow morning we'll process to Suzuki Roshi's ashes site for a toast and then, after breakfast, recite the Lotus Sutra (again optional) straight through from the first word to the last. These celebrations are like a distillation of the big production numbers that are going on at City Center and Green Gulch.

Happy new year to you all. May we all get whatever it is we think we want in the year to come, and may we all be able to deal with having our prayers answered.

Rakusu Washing – the Tassajara Laundry Area

Winter 2004
7th Tassajara
Practice Period

January 10, 2004

I remember that in past years I've had strong feelings about the people sitting tangaryo — such strong feelings that I'd weep. Not this time. This week was more like, Isn't tangaryo over yet?

We have a young dog who's something like a border collie who's pretty difficult. The feeling is that he's a working dog without a job. That's how I felt for the last bit of interim and the first few days of this week: enough leisure already, let's get on with it! And then for the last few days I've begun scheduling all of the zendo jobs, and I need those people to finish their sitting and get off the cushion so we can train them and get them working. Tonight their long sit ended, tomorrow's a personal day, and then finally the real heart of the practice period begins.

Something very unusual about this one is the number of men. Out of 19 tangaryo students (unusual in itself, usually the January practice period has more like seven or eight, and it's the September tangaryo group that's big) 14 are men. Zen Center is a very female heavy outfit, and these numbers are the reverse of what we usually see.

This practice period is being lead by our new (male) Abbot and that may have something to do with it. Or it could be a coincidence.

The Abbot, Paul Haller, has a spectacular chanting voice: very deep and very penetrating. I'm one of the people who gripes about the chanting we do here, which tends to be too fluty for my taste. So already I'm happy, lowering my own voice to join in with this big booming sound.

Another thing about today, in addition to it being the end of tangaryo: it's my 25th AA birthday. Jeez. That is a big number. Its impact is heightened by the recent news that a woman I sobered up with, a woman who, as nearly as I could see from the outside, did all the same things I did, was found dead in a motel room with a needle in her arm. What an ongoing miracle it is that I'm still sober.

January 12, 2004

This morning during soji (half hour of temple cleaning between study hall and mid-morning zazen) my job was to drive a mouse up the road and release it from the have-a-heart trap. You gotta love that. But even better: after I got rubber gloves, got the trap from the zendo, put it in one of the cars, and drove up the road giving the mouse a lecture on mouse behavior, it turned out that the trap was empty.

February 4, 2004

Another month, another sesshin. This one was five days long, and it ended last night. Strangely, unusually, I'm very energized today, ready to sit some more.

There's a lot of busy work in being a doan. Since we rotate through four or five different jobs, and since two of those jobs mean that I have to be up and dressed and at the zendo before anyone else, I often ask myself on awaking, What am I? This is a great Zen question.

I don't think I'm nervous around any of these jobs any more except kokyo, still working with the fear around having the voice that rings out in the stillness of the zendo to announce the chant being the voice that's coming from my own body, but maybe I was more nervous than I thought on the first day of sesshin. I was tenken, the one who stands on the porch and hits the bell to tell the students that it's time to come to the zendo. Horror of horrors, I hit the bell five minutes early. Since there's only six minutes from the first bell to the second, and since students aren't permitted to enter after the second bell, that was a serious error. And yet, after hitting the second bell, letting the doshi in, and then closing the big double doors and sliding quietly in the back doors, I found the zendo full, everyone in their place, an unbroken line of bodies in black robes arranged around the four walls.

Not only was the bell early, but about 20% of the population had been out with a cold during the previous week, and yet here they all were. That, I thought, is Zen.

Speaking of tenkening, one of my favorite tenkening moments happened earlier this practice period when I whooshed to close the front doors behind the doshi for evening service and saw that I'd caught my long sleeve in the door. These doors, ancient old things from some Japanese temple, are just horrible to open and close, so I couldn't sneak the door open again. I gave the sleeve a tug or two to make sure it wasn't caught on any hardware, and then yanked it out and ran around to the back door to let myself in. What I didn't realize was that people on the inside could see the sleeve. Could and did, and told me later how difficult it was for them to keep from bursting into laughter.

I found a great oryoki wrapping cloth at Macy's over Christmas. It's a Calvin Klein table napkin, a good soft cotton in a lovely khaki brown. My friend Licia was with me (in fact, it was only because Licia was looking for a gift for her sister that I was in Macy's at all). Licia was trained at a monastery in Italy, the monastery that Blanche calls "More Japanese than the Japanese," very strict. I was looking at the Calvin Klein napkin and asked her whether she thought I could use it for oryoki. "Oh yes" she said. "In fact, mine's an Armani."

Paul's emphasis in his teachings is on breath and posture as the entryway into the present moment. This is nothing I haven't heard before, God knows, but maybe I haven't heard a teacher hammer away at it so relentlessly before. It's very powerful. I began to notice how I hold my stomach muscles tight to keep my back straight, and then when I relax my stomach muscles my back slumps slightly. This may not seem very exciting to read about, but it was absolutely fascinating for the last two days of sesshin.

I love the young people, and I love being an elder. And yet I'm leaving, the die is cast, the deed is done. I spent the first day of sesshin being mad at the seniors here for not taking better care of me, for in a way wasting the resource that they've developed in me. Well maybe they did and maybe they didn't, but after all Tassajara is much bigger than any human agency. I had an image of the Ventana wilderness as being the giant sleeping maiden, and Tassajara as being the valley formed by her two legs, and then we, all the little buglets, running around and thinking we're in charge of it. She will be fine, just as she was when the Indians lived here, as she was 100 years ago when this place was a haven for hunters and prostitutes, and as she will be when this land is put to whatever use turns up long after we and Zen Center are forgotten. Tassajara just smiles, closes her eyes, and goes back to sleep.

And then, going beyond regrets for whatever happened to my life here, I get excited about returning to the City and take time to ponder the great question: What will I wear!

February 9, 2004

I went down to the bathhouse first thing today to get warm in the plunge and shave my head. Often on personal days, people congregate in the dining room to sew new tips for their setsu sticks, and remain there talking. Some finish breakfast in a hurry and go off for long hikes. Few go to the baths until the afternoon (our usual bathing time) and so I had the place to myself. I could even whistle (La Boheme, since I'm wearing the big fake fur hat that Mimi gave me, thanks for asking). As I was leaving, I heard the shower dripping. Since I already had my socks on, I naturally thought, Oh someone else will be along soon, leave it. Then, moving toward the door, it occurred to me that taking care of that dripping shower was the best way available to me in that moment to express my vow. So I turned back, took off my socks, stepped on to the wet shower floor, and turned the shower all the way off.

The real ino's father died and she went to be with her family for a week, and I'm acting ino. This is, second only to the tanto, the most important zendo job at Tassajara. Holy shit. The first night of my first day in this position, we had a major ceremony — the full moon ceremony, where we gather and renew our vows. The real ino had prepared the person who was doing the chanting and the person who was ringing the bells, and one of the doans is responsible for doing the setup for ceremonies, so all I had to do was oversee everything. Good thing that's all I had to do, because just doing that nearly killed me.

But more than watching out for the bells and chanting and where the candles are placed, I'm now learning that the ino operates as a great anxiety magnet. All day, people — both doans and regular students — are asking me questions about the minutiae of our way of life -- or, they're making comments on my interpretation of these forms. When I was on the doan ryo a year ago and we had meetings and talked about this stuff, I'd be screaming inside my head, Who cares! Now it's my job to care. But I still think that whether we do a bow here or a bow there isn't so much the point; the point, it now strongly appears, is whether there are rules and, if there are, whether those rules give us a place to stand. And I vote no on that.

February 19, 2004

Whoa, this get-rich-quick scheme is working! I just noticed (my paycheck is direct deposited) that my stipend's gone from $200 a month to $300 now that I'm a crew head. Woo hoo!

February 22, 2004

There's a disintegration in my relations with the ino, a chilling, a reversion. I got sick again, and again felt sidelined and uncared-for. It feels like she forgot our deal when she went back east for her father's memorial. It feels — No! Wait! Who gives a damn! Basing my happiness on the behavior of others, trying to figure their behavior out based on what I know of their family background, trying to get them to see why it's better to do it my way, has never ever worked. So here I am, sitting on my zafu, suffering again. But maybe the teachings and training kick in a little sooner. Can I hope for more?

It's true that Tassajara is a terrible place to be sick. It's also true that one of the reasons I'm leaving is because I've been sick here so much. I recently read Karen Armstrong's account of her time as a Catholic nun in England, just before the Vatican II reforms, and this morning was thinking of what it would be like if we had, as her nunnery had, an infirmary and some people whose job it was to take care of us when we needed it. We just don't. It's up to luck whether anyone comes in to do a practice period who has medical training; and then, as I learned a few days ago, there's no guarantee that that person will talk with you about your symptoms. The German psychiatrist who has medical training and therefore stands as our doctor didn't like the way I asked him for help, and refused to talk to me. Refused. Nine bows to him for the great practice opportunity.

I really mean this. Training is what are here for, and working with these difficult emotions is training. All of my teachers assure me that afflictive emotions and karmic tendencies continue to arise, so meditating so much that we're in a perpetual state of tranquility is not the deal here. So what is? Examining the arising of self, over and over and over, until we are able to see the cause of our suffering and get some distance from it.

Yeeps, the han's been going for four minutes! I'm late!

Later the same day

The han goes for 15 minutes from first hit to last. The first roll down is seven minutes after the first hit, and doans are supposed to be on their seats by that time. Most of the student body comes in during the five minutes between the first roll down and the second, and it's thought that finding the doans already in their seats is an encouragement. This is when, last practice period, I'd file by and think, Why the heck did I think I wanted that job.

Anyway, this morning I somehow got my okesa on and was in my seat by the first roll down, not late at all. And then I settled into two periods of zazen and thought more about the things I was writing about here earlier.

One thing I thought was that when I talk about sending gratitude to someone who's acting like a dickhead, you guys must think I've been captured by some bad cult. I don't have time right now to read what I wrote earlier (this is the little break between lunch and work meeting) and can only hope that I was able to catch somehow the flavor of what I was trying to talk about. One teacher said: Zen is an appropriate reaction.

So what would an appropriate reaction look like. What is Zen anyway? Which brings us to another up topic, the forms. One of the things I read while down sick was the current issue of the *Shambhala Sun* that asked about five teachers to talk about American Zen. Sojun Mel Weitsman, one of the greatest of Suzuki Roshi's students (if you ask me) talked about how we mustn't hold the forms too tightly, but that at the same time they're the very thing that held Zen Center together during our crisis in the early 70s. But a couple of non-SF Zen Center teachers in the same piece talk about letting outmoded forms drop away. I get so jealous when I read that. There's a picture of guy who has a rock on his altar instead of a big old statue of someone's dream of a guy who lived in India a long time ago, and my face and brain pucker up like a little baby who's just seen something she wants.

Okay, no bell yet, looked over this day's earlier words, and want to say this: I wouldn't trade this monastery for Karen Armstrong's nunnery for anything. Because, it seemed to me, the same regimentation that led to the creation of an infirmary was also the regimentation that led to superiors wielding power to punish, to a system where, according to Armstrong, obedience trumped creativity. Nope. Not for me. Not for you either, huh.

February 24, 2004

Skit night tonight. Every three months we get together and get crazy for a few hours. People will read poetry and sing songs, but mostly we put on little plays for each other that are centered around monastic life. My favorite of the ones I'm in this time is a part of one called "True Dharma Eye for the Tangaryo Guy" and my part is being the Pretty Priest representative, advising someone who's about to ordain about whether to see a dermatologist to clean up the scalp, hooking her up with the Calvin Klein wrapping cloth for the oryoki bowls, and the racy lingerie for under the robes. The Pretty Priest motto is "Renunciation: Have it your way!" This is all a pretty good joke, and also all true about me and the way I'm doing this. I'm also in a skit with the doans about mice in the zendo, and a skit by former librarians reading book titles and authors' names from cards from the card catalogue to a Stomp beat. Normal Tassajara stuff. Day after tomorrow another sesshin begins.

March 6, 2004

Let it be known: today was the first day that I didn't light a fire in my wood burning stove either morning or evening. Now, at 9:15 at night, its 49 degrees outside and 63 degrees inside. It was also the day where many of us took our lunch (dining room food, since it was a work day) and ate it on the lawn under the flowering plum. It was also the day where I wore my bright green cardigan sweater in public for the first time in over a year; the clothing restriction from my first year of ordination is over. Many momentous events here at the monastery.

It's nice to see the pleasant stuff come around again. I've mostly been concerned with seeing the mid-practice-period post-sesshin exhaustion and irritability reappear. It helps a lot to recognize it as a regular event, but it's still unpleasant on the inside.

The doans have a long meeting on work days. The other people bring up topics like which spoon to use with bananas and buttermilk; I bring up whether it's really Zen to grab the candle from the altar on days when its someone else's (my!) responsibility.

I must admit, I'm looking forward to living somewhere with heat and electricity, ice cream and movies, and where I don't have to process with people all the time. Being on staff at City Center will surely involve some checking in, but it can't possibly be the constant effort that it is here.

March 13, 2004

Some of the doans spent most of work period today cleaning out the summer student housing. Just a couple more weeks, and the practice period is over. The students who are staying will move down into the old barns — and others, like me, will go over the mountain and onto something else.

I've had the talk with the Director of City Center, and what I'll be doing when I move up there in April is called "fukuten." The head of the kitchen is the tenzo; the head of the kitchen crew, who works for the tenzo, is the fukuten. The most important thing about this is the woman who's going to be my boss. She's a great cook, and a rock solid monk too. Definitely one of the ones I have a lot of respect for. So that's what I'll be doing for at least the first six months back there.

Tassajara, in the meantime, is putting on its very best show. I'd forgotten how fast this spring thing happens. If the creek weren't still roaring from the winter rains, I'm sure we'd be able to hear the plants grow.

March 15, 2004

This morning during the serving of breakfast I saw the earnest face of the drummer through the window screen, saw the great effort all the servers were making to "do it right," and thought, There's the kindness. In our trying so hard with all the forms, in this extremely form-centered life we lead, what we're doing is extending kindness to each other. I will sit here without moving to give you support in your practice. I will serve you breakfast impeccably so you may receive it in the same spirit. I will hit the bell with such clarity that your ears will smile. I'll wash this dish for you, wipe this counter for you, pick up this trash for you, so that you can continue with your thinking and your sitting and your breathing. It even came up as an idea that we know how miserably we fail at being kind to each other because of the driving force of our habit energy, and that's why, with the little volition we have, we bend over backwards to help each other.

After breakfast we did a chosan in the zendo for Meiya's 60th birthday, a big effort by a lot of people including me. After it was over and we were again seated in a clean zendo facing a white wall, I began to cry, as hard as I've cried in the zendo for several years. The struggle against our habit energy, these well-meaning people walking into this minefield of feeling and wanting, the depth of our delusion, just floors me. Sometimes it feels like we don't stand a chance. And yet, what can we do but keep trying.

March 17, 2004

This was a sweet Tassajara moment: After dinner, in the back dining room, Luke (a Japanese-American photographer and Yoga instructor) teaching Erin (a former Alvin Ailey dancer) the tango. I was on one side of the room, cutting out the envelope for the rakusu that I've been sewing for Myogen Steve Stücky. First I pushed a table and some chairs out of the way to give them room, then after the basic instruction was accomplished, I sang the Blue Tango for them.

March 22, 2004

It's almost over. It's unbelievable. I keep quoting Ani Palmo, the nun who spent 12 years alone in a cave, saying "The last three years just flew by." So did this practice period. Tomorrow we start a 7 day sesshin, then there are the (lots of) closing ceremonies, and then we're out of here. Or: I'm out of here.

Of course it's too soon to summarize this practice period (it's not over yet!) and of course I already have. There are two big things that happened: first was the Abbot being rude to me during one dokusan and then praising my practice during the next one (for having the courage to return to talk to him again); second was working side by side with a former enemy, and even surviving the inevitable difficulties that arose between us. I could put in there, too, dealing with my feelings over Blanche forgetting that we had a date for phone dokusan more than once. I've evolved from being extremely upset to knowing that she forgot the phone call and not me.

The woman who heads up the guest office here is an artist. We went through my books of photos and she ordered about 300 cards. That's a lot of money, a lot of glory, and also a lot of work. I'm really pleased. And these are the days when I'm taking the pictures that I always told myself I'd take sometime, particularly shots in the zendo. I'm enjoying it so much, it's amazing to think that I was ready to stop photography entirely.

So, time to eat ginger snaps and drink weak green tea and get myself ready for seven days of nothin' but zazen. Bring. It. On.

The incense holder in the Abbot's Cabin at Tassajara

After Tassajara
Spring, 2004

April 8, 2004

It's Thursday. I left Tassajara last Saturday. For four days, I stayed with Kathy in Monterey, eating and reading. I didn't realize how hungry I was, or how much I've missed sinking into anything with words on it. I attribute this to having someone else determine my menu (I never did grow to like eating seaweed) and having the schedule determine how much time I had to eat and read (damn little in both cases).

Kathy had a Buddhist event at her house on Sunday morning that I thought I'd skip (had enough Buddhist events for a little while, thank you!) so I took her car and went out by myself. First stop was Whole Foods, where I ate a sandwich and drank a cup of (bad) green tea and then bought a bag full of food ranging from beautiful asparagus and baby carrots to bulk ginger snaps.

The prices at Whole Foods were quite a shock, so I next went to Trader Joe's where I loaded up on their good snack food. Finally, to my disappointment, I went to the discount stores behind the Monterey Aquarium. I didn't buy anything, but was sorry to again find myself drifting from store to store, looking looking looking for something to create "pleasure."

Sunday afternoon, spending the afternoon with my own copy of the *New York Times* was just about heaven. Eating the food I'd bought, reading as long as I wanted, having nowhere to be and nothing to do: this worked.

I've heard myself telling the story of Tassajara to two close friends, Kathy and Chodron, and worry about talking it out without getting it down here. So now, from a Motel 6 in Pismo Beach, let's see what there is to say.

I've been telling you all along that the experience was about people --but still I was surprised on the last morning to realize that I was leaving people, and not a place. There were a few who I felt incomplete with, and went out of my way to talk with during my final weeks. Of course, when you're leaving you love everybody and everybody loves you, so even the most difficult had something nice to say.

"Tassajara" gave me 90 minutes to pack — after three years. It took a lot longer than that. Here's what I own: three boxes of books, three boxes of photography stuff, three boxes of general household stuff, and two big plastic bins of clothes. Well, I own more than that (there is that 10 x 12 storage unit in Hayward I'm dreading visiting) but that's an inventory of the stuff I use. And while I packed it away, I kept singing Madonna's "Material Girl." I threw the things I didn't want into "free" boxes on my little porch, and that kept a steady stream of visitors coming by. I can't believe no one took the clown wig!

Paul's final sesshin was very strong. I looked for "the body in the body, the breath in the breath, the mind in the mind" for seven days and nights. On the second day, I got the bright idea of taking a road trip to Southern California. I thought how great it would be to go take a look at Colorado Boulevard, 1205 North Garfield, 527 Paloma Drive, and South Pasadena High.

I've been back twice in 40 years. After having this bright idea, I had to exert some discipline to not spend the rest of the sesshin planning and dreaming about it. I heard Joseph Goldstein say a long time ago that if a really great idea came up during meditation, "give it 15 seconds and then go back to non-thinking." Good advice. I watched this brainstorm pass through many times during the succeeding days, but didn't get terribly caught. And now here I am, on the road again.

It's hard to express how tired I am. I think it's just starting to hit. I drove for about four easy hours yesterday and then checked in here and zonked out for the rest of the day, propped up in front of the TV for reruns of series and bits of movies I've missed. When it was time to go out for dinner, I could just find the energy to move. I think I slept eight or nine hours and am ready to face the day, but the circles under my eyes are a shock.

I doubt that it's possible to "catch up on my sleep" when the deprivation is at this level. The choice that exists out here is just too much. It's absurd, and I think it's one of the reasons I'm so tired. For an example, I went to the dentist and she offered me about five different flavors of dental floss to choose from. I want to say "Are you kidding?" This is sure a way for us to fritter away our lives, putting our energy into these meaningless choices.

What I was investigating yesterday while walking around trying to find a place to eat was my reaction to the other people on the street. And there are plenty of them: it's spring break, and the beach towns are swarming. So can I meet others with an open heart and mind, or is it my job to judge everything and everyone I see. Did I learn anything at all in my three years in Tassajara. My Tassajara time now feels like something separate, like going to school or being in an institution for specific training or treatment of a particular problem. It doesn't feel like a Way of Living that I can or should maintain unaltered. This is very hard to put into words. It's like: I thought that if I worked on it hard enough, I'd become this monk person and be this monk person wherever I went. Now I don't think so. Now I think I'm just another person who has had a time in her life of having her mind trained in a particular way.

I hope it's only that I'm still too tired to think that these words are so perfunctory and inadequate to the enormity of the experience I've had.

The courtyard at City Center

2006
City Center

April 3, 2006

I just read back through this topic. Some of the posts take me back to that very moment, sitting on the deck behind Yurt 1 in the bare warmth of the winter sun, or on my bed in the Upper Barn looking out the screen window at the greening trees, trying to write.

I'm so glad I did those Tassajara word poems, talking about Ben reading to us from *Shobogenzo* as we sewed during the break between dinner and evening zazen, or eating lunch on the lawn outside the stone office on one of the first warm days of spring. I could smell the water hitting the wooden walkway to the bathhouse in the summer heat, feel the joy of joining the other black-robed students with umbrellas as we walked through a rain storm to the zendo. Those are such precious memories.

Some of the posts show me how much I hid, how much personal struggle and pain I had going on that I only alluded to. I talked a lot about my difficulties with one person (who's barely a blip on my screen today) but skipped a wild love affair that ended badly, major surgery, and a long awful period of feeling separate from my teacher.

What I couldn't see in the early posts but finally saw clearly when I was tenzo here at City Center was how much anger I carry. I puffed around about the difficulty of the schedule and living with no distractions to hide us from our own feelings, but it took me a long long time to just get so sick and tired of being angry all the time that I had to admit that the anger was mine. I was pretty concerned with dealing with the irritation and pretty incapable of looking at its source.

Finally, last year, after a couple of false starts, I went back into therapy, this time with Steve Stücky, my original Zen teacher. It's pretty interesting. What I see in the posts is that I have all the information I need practically from the start, but I can't put it into action. Reading about those days of tears at Tassajara over something like a job assignment is amazing, and I'm so glad it's not like that any more. These days I'm not as touchy as I used to be, not by a long shot, so it's not as likely that I'll feel ignored or disrespected and go into reaction. But I can still pop off, as I did last week when I saw that Zen Center had once again used one of my photos without asking or giving me a credit, and cause pain for myself and others.

Last fall as I was sitting on a chair just before talking with Steve, taking off my shoes, my mind went "I'll *never* get what I want." Well hey, mind, what would that be? That would be: getting fixed from the outside. By a lover, a teacher, a therapist, whatever. That was a huge piece of information.

One thing that comes through in reading all of my posts through is the exhaustion of the Zen life. Working in the kitchen at City Center for two years really kicked my butt. It's wonderful now that I'm working in the front office to have a little left over energy to spend with friends outside of Zen Center.

I like the posts where I'm trying to convey what it's like at Tassajara, and I don't like the posts where I'm trying on what it's like to teach Zen. There are a couple I remembered where I thought I'd gone too far (talking to Suzuki Roshi up at the ashes site, caring for Blanche during sesshin) that I now don't think are too revealing at all.

Reading about the exhaustion of the Tassajara life causes me a little concern because the current plan is for me to do the fall practice period there, but not enough concern that I won't withdraw my application. I just love that monastic life.

I seem to veer back and forth in the posts between difficulty and gratitude. Well, that just might be the territory. Right now I'm feeling pretty grateful, and that feeling is augmented by reading through these posts. I'd forgotten what a radical thing I've done by taking vows and moving into the monastery, and how fortunate I am that I had the mixture of courage and naiveté to take that step, and this center with its teachers and stipend checks to take it in.

Another thing I'm grateful for is the Well, and for the several people who've read this topic and encouraged me to continue writing in it for all these years. It really is a precious journal. Thanks to all of you who've supported me in its creation.

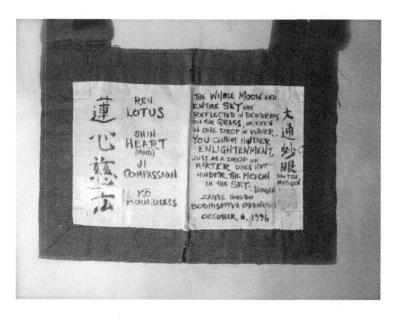

Rakusu with calligraphy by Myogen Steve Stücky, 1996

"In the World"
2009

January 26, 2009

So I wonder: has the monastery been entered? For nearly five months, I've been living alone in an apartment in Oakland. I moved to the East Bay as a condition of a job, entirely willing to leave Zen Center. Now I'm unemployed, sleeping, reading books, and taking walks. I hear that this adjustment, this recovery from being institutionalized, takes about a year.

Here's a summary of the last few years: return to City Center in 2004, work in the kitchen for two years, examine anger, and suffer. Run away to Gampo Abbey for seven weeks in 2006, return, work in the front office, and suffer. Do therapy with Steve Stücky, my original Zen teacher, in an attempt to stop suffering. Separate from Blanche, my ordination teacher, and re-commit to Steve as teacher. Stop working for Zen Center, start training as a hospital chaplain. Go back to Tassajara with Steve as shuso (head student) for my 8th and probably last practice period there. Move out of Zen Center to continue hospital training. Write this post.

Something must be said about separating from Blanche. But what? When I was at Tassajara before ordaining and did three practice periods there with her, we had a dream relationship. There's a picture of the two of us, she looking directly at the camera like a queen, me looking adoringly at her. It changed, either when I ordained or when I returned to City Center, I'm not sure which. We reached a terrible point where we had to separate, to dissolve our teacher-student relationship.

The X factor that I'd never dreamed of was Steve being named Abbot of Zen Center. He hadn't lived there for 25 years and was training to practice pastoral counseling/therapy. But there he was, with his big inclusive hands, ready to catch me as I fell.

Being the head student at Tassajara a year ago with him was a really big deal. The training period is three months long, back in the monastery on the full schedule. Actually, the shuso's schedule is even a little extra full, since s/he rings the wakeup bell and is expected in the zendo for every period of zazen so never gets to cut out to go to bed early. I sat next to Steve in the zendo, shared his seat and had a lot of f2f time with him. I was visible. I gave talks and met with each student in the practice period one on one.

People want someone to love, maybe particularly in that place of great austerity, and shuso is a good target. I was quite loved. There's a ceremony on the 89th day, one of our highest rituals, where the shuso receives and answers a question from everyone in the room. People start teasing you about the shuso ceremony before the practice period even starts. Early on I understood that the practice period would prepare me for the ceremony, and was able to put my anxiety about it (my anxiety about everyone learning that I was inadequate) to the side.

A few days before the ceremony, of course, the anxiety emerged. I demanded of my teacher (in the beautiful intimacy of the Abbot's cabin at Tassajara, the dim light, the resonance through the decades of the student/teacher meetings that have taken place there, the safety of loving and trusting my teacher) "Why do I have to do this ceremony anyway! Is this some kind of test? I hate tests!" Steve thought it over. Steve has never — well, maybe just once or twice — brushed my concerns aside. Steve said, "Instead of thinking of it as a test, think of it as a doorway you're walking through." Okay. That helped.

It also helped that Steve let me, worked with me to, revise the ceremony. At the end of the ceremony the shuso says "With the support of the Abbots, the Practice Leaders, and all of you, I have been shuso. I am grateful for your help, though I'm not worthy of it." Stop!

Is there anyone on the planet who's not worthy of help? Let alone someone who's worked as hard as I just had?? Not to mention an alcoholic who hasn't picked up a drink for 29 years? No! That case was easily made and the phrase was dropped. Later in the statement the shuso says "My mistakes cover heaven and earth" (true -- at Tassajara, there's no escape from seeing them) "and I am ashamed of them." Stop! Ashamed? A lifetime of shame is exactly what I'm facing down and moving beyond here. I am not ashamed. I'm human. Mistakes, yes. Responsibility, yes. Shame: no!

Steve worked with that one for a long time, and then came up with Humbled. Yes. So I said "My mistakes cover heaven and earth and I am humbled by them." Wonderful. On the day after the ceremony, I again had a meeting with him in the intimacy of the Abbot's cabin. It's true, I told him, "It's like going through a doorway, but the door opens into the room I just came from." Everything's changed, and everything is just the same. It's remained like that.

I mean it. It's remained like that. The first talk the shuso gives is the way seeking mind talk, the story of the arising of the desire to practice in his/her life. I told a story in that talk of myself as a child, standing on the neighbor's lawn to watch the Mickey Mouse Club on their TV through their window, and remaining to watch them, curious about how real people lived, knowing only that the living that was going on in my home couldn't be the real thing. At the end of the shuso ceremony, the teacher/Abbot makes a statement. Steve started his with, "You've come into the house. You can stay here now."

I am very slow to trust. I've been that little girl standing on the neighbor's lawn looking through the window, separated and kept safe by the window, my whole life. Steve is a really big guy, I think about 6'4" tall, and strong. He made his living for 25 years by doing landscaping. I picture him as a big mountain. I can lean against him, hit him, adore him, and he remains the same. I had thought that this imperturbability, this patience beyond patience, was just his nature. He was born that way, so what did he know about working with temper. A benefit of living so closely with him at Tassajara was the chance to see the flicker of impatience or irritation cross his face, and see it pass. It's great to know that this quality that could be called serenity is something he's learned, not something that fell on him unearned. Then I believe him when he talks about what's possible for me.

There are a few things I can say about my relationship with Steve. First, he accepts me just as I am and has repeatedly, for the 15 years I've been working with him, asked me to accept myself. His message is always, Don't turn away, Don't turn away, Include, Include. I had, if you recall, hoped that draping an okesa/priest robe over my broken self would heal my flaws magically, and experienced great disappointment when I found that here, again, I'd taken a trip to a better place and found that I'd brought my self along. Steve has taught me deeply that this is what there is to work with, this one right here, not that one over there.

Now that he's the big Abbot I don't see him so much. But I don't need to. I like to, but I don't need to. Because I always know what he would say to me: Include it, Ren, don't turn away, include.

Being shuso, concluding that shuso event, gave me the strength to leave Zen Center when it was time. For several months after returning from Tassajara I worked for Zen Center again, and then I returned to my chaplaincy training at a San Francisco hospital where I worked with seniors. Finally I moved out to pursue a second year residency with a famous Buddhist chaplain who took a leave of absence and never returned. So last December I left that hospital residency to find actual chaplain work. Not so easy to do, but also not impossible.

An interesting part of my situation is that, as soon as I left the hospital I began to receive requests to give dharma talks and lead groups here and there. That's a slight source of income, and also of self confidence. Steve was at the old Dharma Eye Monday night group last week, and I went over to hear him. He talked about how the Tassajara students, two weeks into the practice period, are all unhappy over losing their identity — "I used to be a this, now I'm neither a this nor a that, what am I!" and I thought, that could explain some of how it is to be me right now. I'm not a Zen monk, or even monkish. I have an apartment and a car and a DSL line and even have hair and sometimes wear makeup. I'm not a chaplain, haven't walked up to a sick person and asked them how they were doing for a month. I thought I'd find a bunch of old hippies to live with when I agreed to move to the East Bay, but never did and instead found myself living alone, with my stuff unpacked from the storage unit after seven years, in an apartment very like the one I was living in before I moved into Zen Center. And I wonder, What's changed? What part of me and my life was created by the demands of Zen Center, and will therefore fall away, and what was transformed at the base.

The biggest disappointment is that I still don't have the ability to sit zazen alone for long periods. That hasn't changed. So I've joined Berkeley Zen Center, which is about 10 minutes from where I live, and go up there to sit with others and receive their silent encouragement to stay on the cushion. Because I surely do still believe in the power of zazen.

It's not a surprise is that I go to bed later and rise later. I never, not once, found it natural to start getting ready for bed at 9:30 at night. And that 4:45 wakeup bell in the city? Forget it!

The effects of a life of renunciation are a wonderful surprise. I'm not nearly as gripped by stuff as I used to be. I think I could say that I'm interested in stuff (have an iPod, want an iPhone; have a digital SLR, want another one) but not quite so defined by it. When I moved to Tassajara I unloaded thousands and thousands of dollars worth of clothes, and now am very happy with a uniform of either robes or jeans.

In my shuso ceremony, several people mentioned how I'd changed and wanted to know what that was about. I thought at the time, and agree now, that somewhere I learned to trust the dharma.

Remember, Suzuki Roshi, when asked to summarize Buddhism, thought for a minute and then responded "Everything changes." I came to meditation (as so many do) to be fixed. Once and for all. Now it seems that being fixed means surrendering to the fact that nothing stays the same. That nothing needs to be fixed, that this, this life and this person is unbroken, sufficient just as it is. Learning to trust that, looking at the moon of that rather than the finger pointing to it, lessens that need to make my life and my self look a certain way, and nurtures a spirit of curiosity and gratitude. Yeah. That's about the best way I can say it.

The other big thing that's changed is that I'm connected. I think it's that standing on the lawn looking through glass thing that's gone. I have friends. I can go into quite a few local Zen Centers and be known, be greeted by people who are glad I'm there. People who know me well, for good and ill. I don't have to do it alone any more. I never did, but I didn't know that. Now I do.

Afterword

After Steve died, on December 31, 2013, the Shambhala Sun asked me to write about him. Here is what I said:

My teacher Myogen was only 67 when he received his diagnosis of stage four pancreatic cancer, and had just agreed to serve an additional three years – beyond the initial seven which he was completing – as Central Abbot of San Francisco Zen Center.

Two days after he learned that he only had months to live, he gave the regular Wednesday night talk at Green Gulch Farm. The talk he gave is titled "Gratitude." Listening to him, I was of course reminded of the way he taught us to meet the fire that threatened to destroy Tassajara, our monastery in the Ventana Wilderness, in 2008: he didn't talk about dominating it or fighting it, he talked about meeting it and investigating it and even learning from it. He faced death in the same way that he faced life.

I heard repeatedly that no one expected him to be the first of his generation to die. He was so big and strong and dependable. Six weeks after we received the shocking news, I had a chance to ask him "What shall I tell students in the future when they ask me about your dharma?" He was by this time quite sick and taking many drugs, but he, as always, took a moment to think about my question, and then gave me a straight answer. He said, "Endless inquiry. Not turning away from reality, and when you do turn away from reality -- stop, and resume endless inquiry."

He was humble, and his trust in Buddha Nature, and his love in talking about the dharma, was unstoppable. Steve was never one of those guys who had to prove his point or get the last word. In our 20 years of relationship, he usually stood back and gave me enough rope to hang myself and then, when I asked, stepped in to help me make sense of my experience. He never tried to control me, he never criticized, and rarely even told me what to do. He just watched, and loved.

He was a safe place. He knew how to take care of the secret and tender parts. When I had his attention, I had it completely. He wasn't a Pollyanna or a goody goody and never pretended to be one; he was a whole person, but one who had learned to control his mind. He was able to see the good in everyone because he could see the Buddha Nature in everyone.

We went through a number of ceremonies at his home in the weeks following his diagnosis, ceremonies that became urgent as the disease progressed. When he gave transmission to my dharma sister Koshin Christine Palmer, he handed his ritual implements over to her and spoke of his impending death. Because of the way he trained me, I could sincerely tell him that I now understood that there is no death, and that he will continue to live in the heart/minds of his students long after his body is gone.

Made in the USA
Las Vegas, NV
21 November 2024

12325753R00142